Peace Politics of Nepal
AN OPINION FROM WITHIN

Peace Politics of Nepal
AN OPINION FROM WITHIN

Kanak Mani Dixit

© Kanak Mani Dixit, 2011

First edition, April 2011

ISBN 978 9937 8421 2 9

Cover design: Norbo Lama

Layout: Chiran Ghimire

Himal Books
Himal Kitab Pvt. Ltd.
Regd. office:
Tridevi Marg, Thamel, Kathmandu
Sales outlet:
PO Box 166, Patan Dhoka, Lalitpur, Nepal
Tel: +977-1-5542544/2120321 • Fax: +977-1-5541196
info@himalbooks.com • www.himalbooks.com

Printed in Nepal by Jagadamba Press, Hattiban, Lalitpur   Rs 480/-

Contents

	Preface	xi
1.	The Year of the Citizen	1
2.	History and the Panchayat	4
3.	Insurgency	10
4.	Violence and Society	15
5.	Locating the Maoist Mandate	20
6.	Rebels in Government	25
7.	'People's War'	30
8.	Pushpa Kamal Dahal	36
9.	Animalistic Farm	42
10.	The Democrat-Politician	50
11.	The Process of Peace	54
12.	Cantonments and Barracks	57
13.	Uncivil Mission	64
14.	Birds of Passage	71
15.	The Imperial Progressives	80
16.	Wonderful Liberal Democracy	85
17.	Age of the Politician	92
18.	Gracious Demography	103
19.	Being Bahun	115
20.	The People's Movement	122
21.	Madhes, Arise!	130
22.	Republican Nepal	137
23.	April 2006 – April 2011 Review	145
24.	Kingdom of Conspiracy	176
25.	Civilising Society	182
26.	Community Power, Local Government	189

27.	The Evolving Political Spectrum	198
28.	'The Democratic Maoist'	204
29.	Victims and Justice	215
30.	The Right Federalism	228
31.	India, Nepal	250
32.	China, Nepal	274
33.	Hail, the New Constitution!	282
34.	*Loktantra Jindabad!*	297
	Suggested readings	299

*This work is dedicated to
Shanta,
who sets me to important tasks*

Acknowledgements

I am indebted to Nilamber Acharya, Sushil Pyakurel, Kul Chandra Gautam and Hari Sharma for discussions that have helped shape my political worldview in recent years. Thanks also to Perry Keil Thapa for reading the manuscript as it has metamorphosed since the summer of 2010 and to Shamik Mishra for the fact-checking, as well as to my colleagues at *Himal Southasian* and *Himal Khabarpatrika* magazines for tolerating my absences. Deepak Thapa, the editor of Himal Books, was kind to consider this submission.

Preface

The road to peace and pluralism
As we enter the year 2068 Bikram Era, in the spring of 2011 CE, there is heightened disquiet in this country of 29 million, the 40th largest in the world by population. Political disarray has continued for too long, and the people of Nepal yearn for peace, stability, reconstruction and economic growth. The fact that the intelligentsia is compromised and unable to provide perspective amidst the many variables in a society in transition adds to the prevailing anxiety. There is a need to set the record straight, so to speak, as the peace process stalls, the constitution-writing flounders, and democracy is endangered. On 28 May 2010, the term of the Constituent Assembly was extended for a year as a matter of expediency, once again without agreement on the foundational principles to guide the drafting of the constitution. One political party among the more than two dozen in the House retains its combatant force five years after the peace process began, the ex-combatants maintained by the national exchequer as they receive ideological training in the cantonments. Will the savvy public accept a constitution drafted under the shadow of the gun? Will the force that seeks a 'people's republic' allow the drafting of a democratic constitution?

Obvious answers and straight logic are at a premium amidst the ambiguous public discourse, and those without the facility to follow the Nepali-language debates are at a further disadvantage. With so little material available in English, many students, scholars, diplomats and development partners develop a uni-dimensional understanding of the political landscape: Nepal in caricature is all many tend to see. Incorrect, inadequate and even prejudiced analyses mark the writings available internationally; many have been prepared by individuals and organisations that prefer to disregard the universal values of pluralism and non-violence when it comes to Nepal. In these 'outsider analyses', one finds a neglect of history, a romancing of insurgency, a belittling of our democratic experience, and ignorance of the complex, home-grown peace process. Many an outside observer is convinced that the Maoist agenda of transformation is proper; just their means of violence is a little off. There is a willing belief that the demands for political inclusion, community rights and social justice will be addressed in a societal vacuum; hence, the reluctance to speak up for democracy and non-violence and a willingness to allow the matter of 'identity' to smother that of 'class' in the debate. On the whole, most writers who describe Nepal's ongoing transition to the outside world seem agreeable to leaving us half a democracy, half at peace.

You could ask why there is not a home-grown response to such inadequate analyses. Mainly, it is because the national political class functions outside the English language and is unaware of what is being written about it. Amidst the day-to-day excitement, our politicians and activists lack the wherewithal and incentive to react and remonstrate. It is against this backdrop that I felt the urgency to write a monograph to provide a snapshot of the peace process and related political concerns.

As a writer, I became 'political' only in the late 1990s, as I took up Nepali-language journalism and came face-to-face with issues of democracy and pluralism against the backdrop of the Maoist insurgency. The creeping coup that King Gyanendra initiated in 2002 made it imperative to immerse deeper into civil rights. In translating the late-life memoir of B.P. Koirala, *Atmabrittanta*, I became all the more convinced that the social democratic path is the best means of providing economic growth and equity for the people of Nepal, and that it was political liberty alone which would get us there. This much had been proven by the open society achieved in 1990 with the fall of the Panchayat: only an active, forever self-correcting liberal democracy can work for the people, protecting community rights without threatening the rights of the individual citizen, encouraging the private sector, strengthening regulatory authority, and fulfilling state obligations in public health, agriculture, education, transport and other sectors.

Nepalis have by now experienced the gamut of systems, including the so-called benevolent dictatorship under a 'non-party' system, absolute monarchy backed by the military, and even a period of adventurist

Maoist rule. However, it was in the era of absolute democracy, 1990-2002, that society took long strides and the citizens began to build hope. But the Maoists and, later, Gyanendra, rose to halt the advance. While the 'people's war' is over and the king is now a commoner, the future shape and structure of the Nepali polity is still up in the air. But we have to revert to untrammelled liberal democracy, as nothing but open society can deliver growth and development to make up for our history of marginalisations.

I started out writing a brief, brash monograph in question-answer format to try and explain contemporary politics of Nepal. Over a few months of writing, I ended with a full-length work that has become a kind of rumination on the peace process, but delving into associtied areas from geopolitics to identity politics, economics and transitional justice. In large part, the reader will find my finger pointed at the UCPN (Maoist), which has for some years been the main driver of the polity, the other players reduced to reacting to the agenda set by the Maoist leaders. The Maoist record must be held up for scrutiny, judged against the values of *ahimsa* and *loktantra* (non-violence and democracy), even though some Kathmandu commentators, lost in the fog of demagoguery and repeated misrepresentation, believe that these terms and the values they represent are simplistic and passé. Sooner or later, the Maoists must abandon violence through a public declaration and settle down to long-term politics as a civilian party. There will even come a time, I believe, when the Maoist leaders will come forward to express remorse for having started the 'people's war' in 1996. Beyond the smoke and mirrors, the discerning citizen knows that the UCPN (Maoist) agenda has been to foment chaos, destroy all institutions and due process, and be there to reap the fallout. The citizens recognise that the Maoists have been engaged in a 15-year campaign to annihilate employment prospects in this country of the marginalised, forcing the impoverished peasantry into deeper poverty and accelerated migration for survival.

There are other immediate challenges beyond converting the Maoists into a democratic party, and these include: the cross-border 'militant criminality' in the eastern Tarai, the possibility of caste-ethnic tensions and inter-community clashes of various kinds, and the likely rise of a nasty rightist flank promoted by ex-royals willing to exploit religion. The increasingly skewed distribution of income, the conspicuous consumption of Kathmandu, the flight of educated young adults, the stalled ambitions of youth in a society where there is no employment growth, the failure to convert natural bounty into material wealth – all these are issues that will dog our society and challenge the peace, even after the Maoists democratise. The rehabilitation of those victimised by the decade-long conflict and prosecution of the perpetrators of atrocities must be a priority, without which real peace will never return.

There is gloom, but there is also cause for optimism in the resilience of the public and the ability of our leaders to snatch victory from disaster, to move from suffocation to innovation, to refuse to submit to the prognosis of a failed state. A public that can conduct a people's movement like which transpired in April 2006 cannot be regarded as without agency. It is the spirit of the masses that will keep our society open, bring insurgents to heel and create conditions where sovereignty, good-neighbourliness and a democratic peace will deliver material prosperity denied us for so long.

To confess, this work is not informed by social science scholarship. On the socio-political issues of Nepal, as a neophyte writer, I rely on the analyses and observations of scholars and activists who have battled for decades to build a responsive democracy in Nepal. It is on the basis of this friendly backup that I recently came out with the book *Dekheko Muluk (The Country Witnessed)*. The present work is, in a way, an addendum to and an update of that Nepali-language work. If I am seen to be critical of whole categories of people – Kathmandu scholars, civil society stalwarts, development-wallahs, donor representatives and diplomats – there are many individuals in each group who have the empathy and commitment that will help this society move towards political stability, pluralism, peace and prosperity.

It is always an exercise fraught with difficulty to prognosticate publicly at a time when society is undergoing such upheaval and transition, when the variables are so many. Whether talking about the conclusion of the peace process, the future shape of federalism, the evolution of the political spectrum, or regional geopolitics, there are just too many 'unknowables'. But one must try out opinions, even at the cost of making a mistake, as was proven with my prediction of a third placement for the Maoist party in the Constituent Assembly elections. I have something more to say about that inside. In societies with a more alert civil society looking out for the interest of the citizenry, there is better ability to chart events, but in Nepal one is left to rely mostly on the good sense of the masses and the turning of the wheel of time. There is some risk in writing this book, therefore, but it certainly does not do to be *dai-chiuray*, making believe one is expressing an opinion when actually straddling the fence.

It is with some trepidation that we enter the year 2068 BS. Past the monsoon, autumn and deep winter, spring is the season of discontent in Nepal, the traditional time of upheaval. Before we enter the coming monsoon, Nepal must successfully conclude the peace process so that one party is no longer able to frighten the citizenry with its private army. By then, hopefully, we will be well on our way towards a new constitution whose democratic values provide the basis for inclusive growth and an end to marginalisation. Blocking the radical left is also the way to stop a surge of the reactionary right, to allow effervescent, albeit untidy multiparty democracy to take root in the organic soil of Nepal. The political forces, civil society and the international community, who have to work together for the sake of our people, must be alert to the snares that lie ahead on the trail to peace and pluralism.

Kanak Mani Dixit
15 April 2011
Patan Dhoka, Lalitpur

1

The Year of the Citizen

Bikram Sambat 2068 (2011-12 CE)
The time has not yet come to be proud of Nepali citizenship though the wait has been long. Even though the country has all the natural and human resource potential it needs to provide a fine material quality of life to its people, this has not háppened. And national unification was achieved two and a half centuries ago! National sovereignty and economies of scale give Nepal an advantage over the other countries and provinces of Southasia, creating for it an enviable opportunity to provide social and economic well-being. There is evidence to suggest that once Nepal is politically stable as a democracy, it will do well for itself and evolve as a beacon for the rest of region. At that point, Nepal will notch up achievements quicker than its neighbours, as has recently been seen in some sectors, such as community forestry, local government, the FM radio revolution, and rural healthcare, all successes achieved amidst a violent internal conflict. In order to build on the promise of these successes, Nepal needs peace, democracy and political stability. To develop, we must stand up for pluralism and open, non-violent, competitive politics – the key to social justice and inclusion.

Nepal is by far the oldest state in Southasia, but we are just at the cusp of nation-building. There has been continuous political disquiet in the modern era since the 1950s, and the people have erupted in a movement every ten years or so. These clockwork upheavals are due to the fact that state-society relationships have not yet been defined and that the aspirations of the populace have been bottled up by a remote and autocratic regime for much of history, right up to 1990, in fact, apart from an all-too-brief opening in the 1950s. Political instability needs to be addressed, first, by protecting the simple principles of liberal democracy, including pluralism, the separation of powers, judicial supremacy, human rights and fundamental freedoms. In addition, nation-builders must be mindful of the crying need for social justice and the recognition of community rights. Providing new definitions for state-society relations is the job of the Constituent Assembly, but it could hardly get any substantive work done either in the first two years of its existence or in the one-year extension that will take it to 28 May 2011. Hopefully, the Assembly will get around to its task once the peace process is concluded and define liberal democracy in such a way as to address the historical marginalisation of communities in the hills and plains. At that point, political stability in peace and democracy will trigger economic growth and there will be conditions to make us proud to be born in a country of achievements. Till such time, we will have to make do with the brandishing of national icons and emblems which have little to do with our present-day prowess and achievements – the birth of Siddhartha Gautam, the presence of Sagarmatha/Chomolongma, the historical figure of Arniko, the long-deflated imperial ambitions, the double-triangled national flag, and so on.

Challenges facing people and state

When it comes to writing a constitution, many societies have faced grave challenges, but perhaps none so intense, multiple and simultaneous as those Nepal confronts as we celebrate the Bikram Era (BE) year 2068. Hopefully the upcoming year will see the polity finally overcoming these challenges so that 2068 becomes the Year of the Citizen.

The challenge of re-democratisation. After the decade of insurgency which began in 1996 and the takeover by King Gyanendra which started in 2005, the country now seeks to revert to being a representative democracy at both the local and the national levels. The election held in April 2008 for the Constituent Assembly was a flawed exercise in democracy that nevertheless took the country part way back to being a representational polity and saw the radical left become part of open society. Today, there is an urgent need to revive elected local government and to promulgate a new constitution so that we can proceed with elections to the national and provincial legislatures.

The challenge of post-conflict rehabilitation. The victims of conflict, including the injured and the traumatised as well as the families of the killed and disappeared, have seen the matter of reparations recede further into the background. The truth and reconciliation process is stalled, and the judicial system is unable to pursue human rights abusers. The trauma faced by the population at large has been ignored, and there has been no concerted effort to rebuild the infrastructure destroyed during the conflict and make up for the lost economic opportunities of more than a decade.

The challenge of inter-community rapprochement. In addition to resentment against what is perceived to be the Bahun-Chhetri national establishment, there are multiple fractures along various planes in Nepali society today: hill caste-ethnic (Parbate-Janajati); hill-plain (Pahade-Madhesi); 'high caste'-Dalit; Hindu-non-Hindu; and so on. The hoped-for liberal democratic constitution, chaperoned by a capable leadership, would ensure that these inter-community fissures do not develop into chasms.

The challenge of constitution-writing. The constitution is being written at a time when no party has the required two-third majority in the Constituent Assembly; when many new parties, especially the Maoists and Madhesi groups, are still at the stage of populist posturing; when there is great political polarisation within each of the political parties, including the Maoists. Most critically, constitution-drafting is proceeding piecemeal in the absence of agreement on foundational principles.

The challenge of delivering social justice. One requirement which has been pending throughout Nepal's modern era, which started in 1950-51, is social justice, including a sense of ownership of the state by marginalised communities built on a platform of rapid and equitable economic growth. Of course, a sense of inclusion will not develop in the absence of an accountable, democratic state. At the very least, Nepal must strive to rise from the roster of least developed countries to join the line-up of developing countries.

Well into 2011, and at the start of 2068 BE, all these challenges are coming to a head. Our inability to conclude the peace, write a democratic constitution, ensure equitable growth, and support those victimised by the conflict will lead to a loss of hope. Correcting our course requires the ability to understand and analyse trends rather than giving in to the tsunami of populism and demagoguery.

2

History and the Panchayat

Accountability to the past
Nepal is the oldest country in Southasia, its continuous history dating back to the time when European countries themselves were evolving as nation-states. The abbots of Pashupatinath come from Karnataka, Kathmandu Valley hired mercenaries from Telangana, ancient Nepal developed Vajrayan Buddhism in tandem with ancient Tibet, the myth of the god Bungdeo (also known as Machhendranath, Karunamaya, Avalokiteshwar) has origins in Kamrup (Assam), the Charya texts bind the Valley with ancient Bengal – wherever one looks one finds a deep engagement of old Nepal with the rest of the Subcontinent and the Tibetan plateau. These ancient linkages add value to the continuous history of the state of Nepal, a shared past that provides the population with a certain bedrock of unity that presently goes unremarked. At the same time, the marginalisation of communities by the Kathmandu-centric state continued apace. The heterogeneous population and the rich natural resources of Nepal have the capacity to generate prosperity, but the people at large have been cheated throughout history because of expensive expansionist wars fuelled by imperial Gorkhali ambitions, a century-long rule by the hereditary Rana oligarchs, and constant political instability in the Kathmandu court. A laundry list of historical wrongs that goes back centuries serves little purpose, however, because the histories of most countries can be considered unfair. Nepal entered the modern era in 1951 with the fall of the Ranas, and the cause for the sorry state of today's state and society is mostly to be found in the acts of omission and commission of the last 60 years – most significantly those during the Panchayat years.

Prithvi Narayan Shah was the great unifier of Nepal, an astute strategist who consolidated Nepal as a nation-state even as the East India Company was spreading its tentacles across the Subcontinent. Because of the efforts of Prithvi Narayan, Nepal remains the only naturally evolved country in a region that was colonised for two centuries before the simultaneous events of Independence and Partition transpired in the middle of the 20th century. In the contemporary discourse in Kathmandu, one hears a continuous harping on about the injustices of 240 years of feudal rule, but it is an open question how Nepal would have evolved in the absence of Prithvi Narayan – which clan, language, religion or region would have been ascendant. Perhaps the warring principalities of the central Himalaya, weakened by division, would have been swallowed up by East India Company. Or, instead of the warlord of tiny Gorkha, one of the Kathmandu Valley kings would have fanned out to bring together the principalities as Prithvi Narayan did. Newa Bhay (Newar), Maithili, Hindi or English might have evolved as the lingua franca, and Himalayan or Newari Buddhism might have been privileged instead of Hinduism. These are the counterfactuals of history, but it does not do to blame history when we do not know which way it might have gone. The fact is that we have not been able to take advantage of the country bequeathed to us by our founding king. The citizenry of the central Himalayan region has till today not been able to take advantage of being part of a good-sized, richly-endowed sovereign country in the middle of Southasia. The blame for this failure rests firstly with the Rana era, those 104 years before the fall of the oligarchy in 1951. While the great impoverishment of the Nepali peasantry preceded their arrival, the waves of out-migration began on the Ranas' watch. However, in the modern era, the blame is to be shared among the Kathmandu intelligentsia, administrators, rulers and politicians. While many other countries have advanced in the last six decades, we have not, and are left seeking satisfaction with our progress in the most basic of human development indicators. The bright side of the picture is that the future beckons – if we are able to take advantage of history rather than blame it and learn to make use of our natural resources, geographical placement and diverse demography.

The Panchayat

The present-day public discussion in Kathmandu, in the media and among academics, tends to be somewhat devoid of reference to the Panchayat era, though the root of the problems of today lies in that 30-year period of absolute monarchy. In much of the discourse, all the faults of governance, economy, development and social transformation are placed at the doorstep of the multiparty democracy which started in 1990 with the demise of the Panchayat. Hardly anyone talks of the earlier three decades, and many activist-scholars take a huge leap backwards to place blame on the king who unified Nepal nearly two and a half centuries ago. This focus clearly helps the Maoists, who, in fact, have proactively set the discussion agenda of the last few years. The Maoists find it convenient to demonise the democratic political system and the players of the post-1990 period because that it what they fought to bring down.

The Panchayat era started when King Mahendra conducted a coup against the democratically elected Nepali Congress government of B.P. Koirala and quickly established an undemocratic, unrepresentative political structure from the village to the national legislature. While there were fleeting moments of liberalisation in this system, the Panchayat era was marked by an oppressed society in which the king ruled actively as a dictator. The growth of a culture of subservience to authority, the loss of experience in democratic functioning, the rise of crony capitalism, and dependence on foreign assistance agencies – the ills which we battle today – were the result of three decades of a closed society which lacked self-correcting mechanisms. The initial dynamism of King Mahendra's Panchayat was eroded after the first few years of rule by King Birendra, who ascended the throne in 1972.

In the absence of democracy and representative government, the people, historically marginalised, found themselves stranded in the modern era. The public lost confidence in itself, development failed to be participatory, and the economy became the playground of rent-seekers rather than producers. The People's Movement of 1990 was the outpouring of the democratic desire the public had nurtured since the 1940s but had only been able to experience for 18 months in 1959-60, under B.P. Koirala's government. This People's Movement led to the fall of King Birendra's autocracy, and Nepal's transformation into a constitutional monarchy through the Constitution promulgated in November 1990.

The good Constitution of 1990
The main problem with the Constitution of 1990 lay not, as is now widely claimed, in its content, but in its implementation. It was a demo-

cratic constitution which, for the first time, confirmed that sovereignty lay in the people. Nepal became a free society, and the building blocks of long-term democracy were rapidly put into place, with the growth of the private media, the spread of local government, and the rise of civil society activism. Even as the Constitution of 1990 ushered Nepal into the modern era, the neophyte political parties showed their all-too-obvious weaknesses in terms of mal-governance, corruption and inter-party bickering. Notwithstanding the weaknesses of the parties, the pluralism introduced by the Constitution of 1990 guaranteed the advance of Nepali society in all sectors, from the economy to human development. The Constitution's weaknesses were of the kind that would have been made irrelevant by time, or resolved by amendments and plebiscites. One such weakness was the blatant declaration of the country as a 'Hindu kingdom', when in fact it should have remained silent on the subject of religion—or proclaimed secularism. The constitutional monarchy instituted by the Constitution of 1990 would have evolved as a benign cultural entity had the Maoists not used it to ride to the top and had a king not emerged to run the institution into the ground.

Kathmandu-centrism had long been the reality of national life, but the 1990 Constitution chipped away at it by providing for representative democracy and the convergence of representatives elected in the districts on the capital in order to run the country. The guarantee of fundamental freedoms ensured that the heretofore silent masses in the far corners of the country could raise their voices in protest and challenge authority, from the village elder to the chief district officer. All said and done, with the burden of history already extant and the Maoist insurgency serving as an additional challenge, the political parties were unable to adequately address the identity-led demands of the Dalit, Janajati and Madhesi. This was not the problem of the Constitution, which allowed the Maoists to rise and the marginalised to challenge the status quo. Developing circumstances required the abolition of the monarchy, the declaration of a republic and federalism, and the announcement of Constituent Assembly elections, but none of these advances takes away from the fact that it was the Constitution of 1990 which ushered in an open society and made all subsequent advances possible.

The Constituent Assembly is a means to improve on the Constitution of 1990, but it would be wrong to claim that the earlier document was somehow deficient in the critical aspects of human rights, pluralism and the separation of powers. On the contrary and the populist rhetoric of recent years notwithstanding, it has to be said that the Constituent Assembly was announced not because of the weakness of the Constitution of 1990 but because of the need to make space for the Maoists to 'land safely' as they abandoned their 'people's war'. The challenge to the members of the Constituent Assembly is to produce a new constitution that preserves the democratic advances of the last one but in addition institutes a republican, federal state structure that is stable and benefits grassroots empowerment and social justice. None of these requirements necessitates a denigrating of the Constitution of 1990.

Hindu kingdom no more

Traditionally, the average Nepali citizen, regardless of his or her background, did not think of *dharma* as 'religion', with its Western connotations, but rather as a set of cultural prescriptions for righteous living. However, in the evolving world of plural politics, as communities sought to assert their identities, it was natural that the formal identification of Nepal as a Hindu kingdom in the Constitution of 1990 would rankle. The appellation was simply not logical, and, fortunately, was done away with in the Interim Constitution of 2007. According to the last census, conducted in 2001, 80.6% of citizens identified themselves as Hindu, and this percentage is expected to drop somewhat in the upcoming census of 2011. Even using the 80.6% figure, it is clear that nearly 20% of all Nepali citizens are non-Hindu. A majority of that minority are Buddhists of different sects; others are Muslim, Kirati, Christian, animists, shamanists, and so on. Clearly, a state which has such a large proportion and variety of non-Hindus cannot be declared Hindu. The constitutions of 1951 and 1959 made no reference to a state religion; it was only the Panchayat Constitution of 1962 which included a declaration of the Hindu identity of the state. This reference was unfortunately retained in the democratic Constitution of 1990, much to the chagrin of many activists and community leaders, who saw in it an attempt to continue the subjugation of the rest of the population by the Bahun-Chhetri establishment.

Simple logic should rule the matter – first, there is no need for the Nepali state to be identified with any religion; second, there can be no identification by one faith when there are people of other faiths in significant numbers within the population. The state's identification with specific faiths, through support for festivals and rituals, should be wound down, while being careful to distinguish between what is a cultural up-welling of society and what is hard-and-fast 'religious'. Over time, beyond the secularism certain to be guaranteed by the upcoming constitution, the state apparatus must abandon cultural practices that are identified with religion, such as the President's role in certain public rituals inherited from the kingship or the national army's identification with certain deities.

3

Insurgency

A war against the people
Many believe – mistakenly – that the Communist Party of Nepal (Maoist) began its insurgency against the monarchy. In actual fact, the Maoists went underground and ignited their 'people's war' in February 1996 with the avowed aim of bringing down the parliamentary system of government introduced by the Constitution of 1990. At that time, Sher Bahadur Deuba was prime minister and King Birendra, the constitutional king. Nepal was a democracy based on the king-in-parliament Westminster model. Nepal's was hardly a perfect democracy in the early 1990s, with political parties accustomed to the role of underground opposition to the Panchayat regime struggling to learn the ropes of representative governance. Parliamentary democracy was a work in progress and no one – least of all the Nepali people – expected a rapid advance to a democratic utopia.

The CPN (Maoist) – the Unified CPN (Maoist) since 2009 – participated in the first general elections of 1991 as part of an extreme left grouping, and, with its nine seats, was the third largest party in Parliament. This was not good enough, and a party leadership hungry for quick-and-easy power opted for armed insurgency rather than social revolution. The Narayanhiti royal palace was not displeased when the Maoists took up arms and went underground because that step had the potential to (and later actually did) weaken the other political parties and the democratic process itself. While King Birendra is remembered for being a lenient king – a memory embellished by the horrific royal palace massacre of 2001 – the fact is that he ruled for nearly two decades as an autocrat. In the democratic era after 1990, after first acceding to constitutional monarchy, he and the palace secretariat sought to constantly access power at the cost of successive elected governments. The palace, with its hold on the Royal Nepal Army, blocked the civilian government's attempts to deploy the army against the rebels. The links between the Maoists and King Birendra were confirmed when Baburam Bhattarai wrote in an eulogy after the palace massacre that there had been *karyagat ekata* – a working unity – between the underground rebels and the slain monarch. As circumstantial evidence, one can also point to the fact that it was local-level leaders belonging to the UML and Congress parties rather than those with royalist leanings were more often hounded and killed by the Maoists than royal supporters, and that the army was not deployed against the insurgents until five years into the 'people's war'.

Birendra's successor, Gyanendra, is widely believed to have been planning a joint putsch with the Maoists against the parliamentary parties, until he betrayed them with the royal takeover of February 2005. It was only then that the Maoists agreed to work with the parties against Gyanendra's autocracy, a collaboration that culminated in the People's Movement of April 2006. When the Maoists came above ground, some diehard royalists joined the party as advisors, while others went on to grace the Constituent Assembly as nominated members of the UCPN (Maoist) party. In open society, the Maoists seemed to drift towards the right, assisted by the magnetic pull of anti-India ultra-nationalism. The coded terms used by the Maoist leadership to refer to their fellow-travellers among the royalists is *rastrabadi shakti* or *desbhakta*, words which translate roughly as 'nationalist force' and 'patriot'.

It is a gross error to believe that the Maoists picked up the gun against the royal palace when, in fact, it was the parliamentary system at which the gun was squarely trained. The 40-point demand placed by Baburam Bhattarai before the government of Prime Minister Sher Bahadur Deuba, the demand on the basis of which the Maoists went underground, does not demand an end to the monarchy, merely a doing away with the 'special privileges of the king and royal family'. The Maoist-royalist collaboration very much in evidence at the time of this writing is something that is rooted in the party's historical ambivalence towards the monarchy.

Comparisons: Maoist, Congress and UML
Many profess to see all the political parties of Nepal, including the UCPN (Maoist), as similar in their use of violence and unprincipled competi-

tion for power. However, there is, in fact, a significant difference in terms of history, scale and intention. Some early members of the predecessor organisation of the present Communist Party of Nepal (UML) did, following the lead of the Naxalite movement of India, engage in the targeted killings in the far-eastern Tarai in the early 1970s. Altogether 18 individuals – 'capitalist landowners' – were killed in what is known as the Jhapa Andolan. This Nepali Naxalite adventure was built on the premises of class war, but it never got big enough to challenge the state. Besides, the majority of today's CPN (UML) leaders were not even part of the proto-UML organisation which carried out the Jhapa Andolan. In contrast, the violence wrought by the Maoist 'people's war' left more than 13,000 citizens dead and many others maimed, wounded, orphaned and displaced. The entire population was traumatised. The devastating economic impact of the extended Maoist conflict makes the impact associated with the short-lived Naxalite uprising pale in comparison.

The Nepali Congress party came into existence in the 1940s as part of the campaign to rid the country of the Rana oligarchy, which had run the country as a private fiefdom for almost a century. The armed uprising led by the Nepali Congress was an attempt at regime change, a protest against an extractive feudal system; the uprising ran parallel to and was comparable to the Indian independence movement. The Maoist 'people's war,' in contrast, was a move against a democratic, parliamentary system at a time when there was no obstacle to starting a social movement for political transformation. In 1996, there was ample political space for the Maoists to try to transform society through open politics, space the Nepali Congress did not have during its protest against either the Ranas or the Panchayat. The anti-Rana Nepali Congress insurgents fought against government's troops and did not engage in the targeted killings of individuals, whereas the Maoists conducted their fight against both government forces as well as the citizenry at large, especially against those citizens in the districts perceived as blocking their spread.

Not revolutionary a party
The CPN (Maoist) used revolutionary rhetoric to excite young adults and prepare them for war, proclaiming the idea of social justice but using the tools of violence. It is impossible to concede that the proper conditions for a people's war existed in Nepal in 1996, barely five

years after the advent of democracy and when an elected representative government was in place. The diversity of Nepal's demography, the absence of large landlords in the country except in parts of the Tarai, the movement towards a pluralistic state under the 1990 Constitution – these and many other factors lead to the inescapable conclusion that the Maoists had more or less closed their eyes to the demographic diversity, economy and political evolution of Nepali society when they declared 'people's war'. Had it truly been a visionary, revolutionary party, the CPN (Maoist) would not have contested the first elections of 1991 and joined Parliament. What happened was that the Maoist leaders realised that theirs would remain a party perpetually in the shadow of the mainstream CPN (UML) if they did not adopt a drastic plan of action. One cannot accept the Maoist proposition that conditions were ripe for revolution in Nepal in 1996 but must recognise their skill at utilising violence and the geographical terrain to build a base and their ability to change tack, jumping into open society to emerge as the largest party in the Constituent Assembly in 2008.

The organisation of a guerilla war

Starting and sustaining an armed insurgency in Nepal was not as difficult as it might seem at first glance. The country's hinterland was marked by the absence of government administrators and the weak road transport network prevented the security forces from covering the ground rapidly to stamp out the incipient insurgency before it took off. The mid-hills are ideal terrain for insurgents, characterised as they are by what can be described as a fusion of Afghanistan's ravines and Vietnam's undergrowth. Their physiography made it easy for the guerilla force to fight clandestinely, cowing the citizenry of scattered hamlets with the threat of violence. A gun in hand, a willingness to kill, and the public demonstration of torture or a brutal killing – these three factors allowed the insurgents, in the absence of state forces, to control large swathes of the country. The locals were easily brought low, especially when an example was made through the murder or maiming of a community leader, political activist, teacher, development worker or journalist.

The Maoist expansion happened at a time when the royal palace was restricting the civilian government's use of the national army, political parties were bickering, and civil society was unmindful of the devastation a 'people's war' could bring. The rebel organisation was able to expand even more rapidly after 2002, when the representative local government which had been functioning at the village and district levels was allowed to lapse. One must hold the Maoist fighters and cadre of the initial years in high regard, for many went into battle for a cause they truly believed in. The same forbearance cannot be extended to the rebel leadership, however, for it introduced physical, political aggression rather than taking the much harder road of advocacy, mobilisation and social revolution.

Support and subjugation

The oft-repeated Maoist invocation is that they 'speak for the people'. But why should we take them at their word? How we can we believe the leaders of a party which targets civilian opponents to empty the villages of political competition and whose supreme leader proudly admits on the radio the Maoist policy of *safaya* (elimination)? The Maoists had the run of the Nepali countryside, utilising every geographic, demographic and political possibility available, but they never had a base area or a compact zone, and their 'people's government' was nothing more than ornamentation to befuddle the starry-eyed outsider. The fact that, throughout the decade-long conflict, police and army outposts continued to remain in the remote corners of the country and that state security forces were able to go wherever they were assigned indicates that the Maoists never had control of a territory as, for example, the Tamil Tigers did over the Jaffna Peninsula in Sri Lanka. All 75 districts continued to be manned by government administrators, though under great duress. All the Maoists managed to do was to disrupt the provision of all manner of government services, from agricultural extension to health services, to the public. As to whether or not they had the support of the people, in some areas the Maoists certainly did, but in most parts 'support' was merely acquiescence achieved through terror.

4

Violence and Society

Public, physical, political violence
As is the case the world over, Nepal's recorded history is replete with incidents of political violence. However, much of the violence in our history, from pre-unification days till modern times, was concentrated in the court amidst the nobility. A variegated society can never be subsumed under one description, but one could say that the villages of Nepal were generally peaceful, only occasionally facing physical violence from the direction of the state. Government administrators were largely absent from villages, and community leaders and clan elders exercised customary control and maintained order. The powerful certainly did pressure the hapless peasantry in many parts of the country, and coercion existed from the national to the village level, but the quantum of physical violence was low. Historian Ludwig Stiller, in his book *The Silent Cry*, makes a convincing argument that the villages of Nepal were exploited and marginalised, but that, in contrast with the feuding aristocrats, were relatively conflict-free.

Over the last two and a half centuries, Nepal's demography became increasingly marked by the mixing of population groups down to the village level, even though communities still tended to live in discrete clusters. *Melas* (fairs) brought people of different communities together in a secular setting, where commerce, entertainment and the rituals of faith helped establish inter-community empathy. The advent of modernity began to loosen the control of traditional community organisations, and there was a need for society to evolve beyond centuries-old structures of order by incorporating suitably adapted institutions of state. Unobstructed, democratic evolution would have yielded certain Nepal-specific innovations, such as those in community forestry, local government or media, more quickly and made them more sustainable. It was just when society was on the cusp of a period of great innovation that the Maoists introduced public, physical and political violence of an intensity and scale never before experienced by rural Nepal. Force and the threat of force introduced fear and panic among villagers, and the employment of counter-violence by the state security forces only deepened their distress.

The introduction of public, physical and political violence changed the face of society across the lines of class, community, region, ethnicity, caste and faith. Taken to scale by the Maoists, the reliance on violence and threat has since spread to other groups. Getting what you want through the use of the firearm, the fist or the vehement tongue has become the order of the day, and abductions, targeted killings, and all manner of violent acts are now common. Breakaway Maoist factions have taken the culture of violence further afield and spawned criminal outfits, particularly in the mid-eastern Tarai and the eastern hills. The culture of violence has spread beyond the realm of politics and entered the social psyche. During the conflict years, children learnt to distinguish between a .303 rifle and 'SLR' (self-loading rifle) and 'GPMG' (general purpose machine gun), between the 'socket bomb' and the 'pressure-cooker bomb'. They began to draw guns, helicopters and barbed wire instead of rhododendrons, village dwellings and mountain peaks. Highway closures for the smallest excuse are but a further extension of the predilection to predatory culture, and a terrible highway accident is often characterised by onlookers rushing to beat up the driver rather than to take victims to hospital. While the increased presence of violence in our lives and minds is a part and parcel of the transformation to modernity, the Maoists helped to spur violence to a drastic level.

For a period in the early 2000s, Nepal was one of the most politically violent countries in the world, with the appalling average of more than seven killings a day. The number of dead stopped mattering as massacred policemen were stacked unceremoniously in helicopter holds for transport and dead Maoist fighters were left to the animals in jungles and riverbeds. There was a time, not too long ago, when the country came to a standstill when a ricochet from a police firing killed an innocent bystander. Within a decade, we became inured to the daily death count, untouched even as the cremation *ghats* at Pashupati overflowed, closing our ears to the sobs rising from the villages. We became so used to violence that the scores of people who perished in an army-Maoist skirmish were forgotten the following day. This dulling of the senses has stayed on as a legacy of the years of conflict: the meek acceptance by the media and public alike of the high numbers of highway fatalities that reflects our desensitisation to death. To fight this painful legacy of the conflict years, society leaders must work to roll back the culture of violence that has overtaken the land so that children go back to sketching mountains rather than automatic rifles, so that the villager one meets on the trail will strike up a conversation rather than look away in fear and suspicion.

Structural violence
Structural violence exists, deep and unrelenting, in the mountains, hills and plains. The marginalisation of whole communities on the basis of ethnicity, caste, faith or region is a distressing facet of Nepali history, some of it enforced by a caste-heavy state struggling to maintain itself over two and a half centuries. The subjugation of women in large parts, most excruciatingly visible in the *chhaupadi* system of seclusion in the western hills during menstruation and childbirth, is also the result of patriarchal mores that continue to command society. The policies of the Kathmandu-centred state impoverished the villages, building an underclass in all communities. Whether through usurious taxation to fund imperial ambitions or to maintain the Rana oligarchy in Occidental splendour, it was the people who were made poorer despite the nation's wealth of resources.

The structural violence promoted by the state down through history is something that has been recognised throughout Nepal's modern era. The entire national agenda of socio-economic development of the last six decades has been aimed at addressing a wide range of structural inequalities which discriminate on the basis of gender, caste, faith, language, ethnicity and region. Development efforts became more participatory, and hence more effective, after the arrival of open society in 1990, as individuals and communities discovered their voice as citizens and began to make demands. The assertion of identity by ethnic activists since the early 1990s, with the added impetus of the Madhes Movement of 2007, helped society at large to understand structural violence as it was applied against communities.

Reference to structural violence should not, as is sometimes intended, downplay the physical, public and political violence that has overtaken society, impacting individuals and families of all communities and instilling bodily and mental harm on a scale never seen before. This violence and threat of violence has resulted in psychological scarring so deep it saps the national energy. We should not allow genuine concerns regarding structural violence to diminish the physical violence that has us in its grip today. Those who suggest that violence has always existed in Nepali society distort reality; what the Maoist party introduced was horrifically beyond anything that had preceded it.

State accountability

During the feudal and monarchical era, the very real threat of state violence kept the citizenry pliant. The state was capable of great excesses, including killings, disappearances, torture and unlawful confinement. Again and again during the Panchayat era, the government misused its monopoly over the instruments of violence, the heavy hand of the central authority being deployed through the office of the *anchaladhis*, or zonal commissioner, and the chief district officer. Unaccountability and impunity among state officials continued in the democratic period after 1990, but these were no longer part of a motivated, centrally mandated effort to exercise state control as they had been in the past. The continuance of state violence in the democratic era can, by and large, be attributed to the weaknesses of the political leadership in challenging the culture of impunity as well as the inability of an as yet weak civil society to effectively serve as a watchdog against the excesses of the administrators and the police.

In the current democratic era, civil society leaders must accept that the state rightfully needs to retain its monopoly over the use of violence, but this fundamental aspect of democratic governance is not yet fully part of Nepali public discourse. This inability to appreciate violence as a state monopoly was one reason the Maoists were not adequately challenged back in the mid- and late-1990s when they decided to take up arms. This monopoly must be exercised with accountability and under legal prescription, and civil society must guard against misuse. The extra-legal use of violence by governmental authorities must be battled with social mobilisation and activism, watch-dogging, shaming and the use of courts. What the Maoists did was challenge the state and fellow citizens with the gun. The government responded in kind, and brutality spiralled out of control. The need to demand accountability from state institutions is one challenge the civil rights community faces as Nepal heads into the future, putting its memories of war behind.

5

Locating the Maoist Mandate

Electoral mandate
The April 2008 elections to the Constituent Assembly, a body which also serves as the Parliament, made the UCPN (Maoist) the largest party by far in the legislature. Still, the Maoists do not have a majority. The party, itself expecting a poor showing in the direct (first-past-the-post) elections, had insisted on using a proportional election system to elect half the members of the Assembly. As it turned out, the Maoists did rather well in the direct elections, winning exactly 50% of the contested seats. But when the proportional vote was included, they had just over 38% of the members in the 601-seat House.

The UCPN (Maoists) has neither the two-thirds majority required to adopt a constitution unilaterally nor the simple majority needed to form a government on their own. Its leaders, themselves new to parliamentary politics, seem unable to explain to their cadre the need to have more than a 50% plus majority to form a government. Ignoring the 12% shortfall, they constantly refer to a 'mandate' from the people to govern and to promulgate the kind of constitution they envision. Of course, there is no such mandate, which is why the nine-month Maoist government which fell in May 2009 had to be a coalition. After Maoist Prime Minister Dahal resigned from government, the party that professed to have a mandate from the people through the ballot was forced to resort to street action to try to bring down the government which replaced it, that led by Madhav Kumar Nepal of the CPN (UML). Unable to garner the magic number of 301 representatives needed to re-form a Maoist-led government, the Maoists constantly repeated the mantra that they were not into 'the parliamentary game of numbers', though the only way to check if one has a majority is to count!

The last word on elections

The last word on the Constituent Assembly elections has yet to been written. In his election forecast, this writer predicted that the Maoists would come in in third place behind the Nepali Congress and CPN (UML). When the Maoists won the most seats, I was forced to mull over my forecast and determine where I had gone wrong. An unwillingness to countenance violent politics had perhaps made me project my own lack of enthusiasm on the populace at large, forgetting the many variables that go into the decision-making of an electorate. In defense of my poor prediction, I must say that many politicians and observers were also caught off guard and that the Maoists were themselves unsure of victory. (In fact, they were so unsure of success that they used various stratagems to cancel the polls slated for November 2007 and only agreed to the April 2008 date when they felt they had control over enough of the total 75 districts to ensure a win.)

An ex post facto analysis of the Maoist electoral success indicates a) the electorate's desire for change in the face of disenchantment with the old parliamentary parties, which translated into support for the ex-rebels; b) the public's desire to keep the Maoists engaged in the peace process rather than see them return to the jungle, as they openly threatened they would do during the election campaign; c) the lack of a first-hand brush with Maoist violence among a large section of the voters; d) the psychological impact of the Maoist fighting force in the cantonments; f) the Maoists' willingness to use wild populism and irresponsible promises in the election campaign; g) the abandonment of the villages by the other parties, leaving the Maoists as the most proximate 'politicians'; and h) election-day intimidation, violence and rigging, carried out as promised by Chairman Pushpa Kamal Dahal in the Shaktikhor videotape.

The vote for change was given by an electorate which regarded the other political parties as already failed and the Maoists as an untested force in governance. With the weak and inarticulate national intelligentsia doing nothing to provide perspective, many voters were unable to distinguish between the Maoists' rhetoric of social justice and their methodology of violence. The other parties were on the defensive for their past record and unable to present a dynamic ideology and promising programmes. Girija Prasad Koirala, the old warhorse of the Nepali Congress and prime minister at the time, had been weakened by bad health and decided to stay away from the election campaign completely.

This devastated the Congress campaign and left Chairman Dahal as the only personality in the race. Maoist threats had swept the villages clean of local political leaders, and many saw the ex-rebels as having done everyone a favour by abandoning their 'people's war'. A reward, it seemed, was fitting.

The election coffers of the Maoist party were full; they had the ability to buy voters and community leaders and to order up local merry-making as part of their election campaign. The other parties, shrivelled after years out of power and hounded out of the villages, and with no intention or ability to extort funds like the Maoists, could hardly match the Maoist in purse or muscle power. With its command-and-control system having been honed to efficiency during the just-ended conflict, the Maoist party machine was made ready for the elections. To excite youth in remote areas, the Maoists made full use of populist rhetoric, making promises of ethnic federalism and presenting their chairman as the first elected President of Nepal even though that office was not part of the ballot. The loud suggestion by the leadership that it would go back underground if the Maoist did not win was flagrant blackmail. But it worked.

Overall, and in retrospect, the Maoist electoral success may be ascribed to three equally important causes – a vote for change that went to the Maoists; their well-oiled, populist election campaign; and the violence and threats during the campaign coupled with election-day fraud and intimidation. The National Election Commission was not able to react to the violence and threats that marked the campaign and the election itself, nor were national and international observers able to pinpoint lapses as they competed to announce the elections free and fair. There is a need to dispassionately analyse the last election in preparation for the first general elections after the new constitution is promulgated and to understand the weaknesses of the 2008 election observation exercise, including the rush to announce the polls free and fair and to flaunt them as part of a successful peace process and the turning of a blind eye to the unfair practices which made the exercise quite undemocratic.

Looking back, primed with information made available in the meantime, one must say that the elections of April 2008 were marked by fraud and intimidation on a scale that should have been unacceptable. Starting with the days of conflict and leading right up to the day of voting, there were large parts of Nepal which no non-Maoist political party was even allowed to enter much less campaign in. The CPN (Maoist) collected voter data and made efficient use of the voter list to pad out its own voter count. On the day of the election itself, in many areas Maoist cadres screened voters in order to intimidate those who supported the other parties. Those few candidates from other parties who were capable of counter-violence made a good showing in places, as did the few who were in the Maoists' good books. The national army, which had been deployed on election duty in previous general elections, was this time, under the terms of the peace agreement, confined to its barracks. The Maoists, in contrast, made free use of their ex-combatants, especially in the districts which hosted their cantonments. On polling day itself, the National Election Commission – which included a commissioner nominated by the Maoists – was unable to respond to desperate calls for action against unfair practices. Journalists felt they were contributing when FM radio networks flashed news of Maoist violence countrywide, but these reports actually had the effect of intimidating candidates and voters alike. In the absence of state security, greatly weakened by the curiously feeble posture of Home Minister Krishna Prasad Sitaula throughout the time the interim government ruled, the news of Maoist violence only served to frighten voters.

There was such desperation to get back to representative democracy after the anti-democratic interregnum of King Gyanendra that both politicians and civil society activists were willing to support the elections even if the preparations were somewhat flawed. This feeling was what led to the central fault in the election exercise: the inability of the national and international players to insist that the polls be kept pending as long as one party held on to its private army. The United Nations Mission in Nepal (UNMIN) should have known enough to warn the polity of the dangers of elections when one party had its own fighting force but it preferred to remain silent. The Maoist ex-guerrillas may have been sequestered in cantonments but they were perceived as a force that could still be mobilised by the party, and everyone seemed to have underestimated the psychological impact that perception had on the electorate.

It is legitimate to ask why if the elections were so flawed responsible people did not speak up. One critical reason was that that the Maoist momentum at the time was such that those in the districts who stood up to challenge Maoist excesses or the vote count could be, and often were, thrashed in short order. Another reason was that the polls were perceived to be a part of the peace process, and even though many politicians believed that the elections had been stolen, the overwhelming push for reconciliation with the CPN (Maoist) at the national and international level saw them maintain a sullen silence. No proper evaluation of the April 2008 election and its links to the peace process can be carried out until that process is complete. However, it is important that a review be conducted long before the next general elections so that we learn from the last exercise, which was so wanting in democratic values. Once the dust has settled – and it has not yet, three full years after the elections – national and international election observers must go back over their notes and, resisting the pull of populism, re-evaluate their perspective on the Constituent Assembly elections of 2008. They will need to consider where they may have gone wrong in terms of both monitoring the run-up campaign and handling election-day challenges. Future elections must never be held under circumstances in which there is such a high level of intimidation in the villages, the Maoist or any other party retains a combatant force, the National Election Commission is compromised, and the national army cannot be deployed for election duty.

6

Rebels in Government

Adventurists in Singha Durbar
The Maoists engaged in continuous adventurism during their nine months in government, displaying a lack of maturity in dealing with the hopes and fears of the people. The party's leaders did not seem to understand the need to responsibly exercise the great power they, with all the major ministries at their command, held, nor did they have the fortitude required to achieve their long-term agenda and interests while in government. As a member of a cabinet which seemed to move from one crisis to the next, Baburam Bhattarai, as finance minister, was generally lauded for raising revenue and not shuffling government bureaucrats. However, the other Maoist ministers, including Prime Minister Dahal, clearly had a lot to learn during the transition from being an underground force to members of an open society in which a free media was present to report on excesses. The Maoist inability to understand diplomatic protocol and geopolitics soon became obvious, as three ministers made a 'secret' visit to Tibet, apparently as guests of the Chinese People's Liberation Army. A heavy hand was used on matters of faith, including an ultra-nationalist campaign to dislodge the three-century-old tradition of the Pashupatinath temple of employing priests from Karnataka in present-day India. There was country-wide intimidation of the bureaucracy and the police, but when it came to delivering justice and security, the Maoists just did not have the credibility needed to be effective.

The peace process stalled during the Maoists' time in government despite Prime Minister Dahal's promises from the podium of the Constituent Assembly to immediately address issues related to the return of captured property, the dismantling of the semi-military structure of the Young Communist League, and so on. He announced more than once in public as well as before the Constituent Assembly that the cantonments had come under the Special Committee on Supervision, Integration and Rehabilitation of Maoist Combatants as required by the Comprehensive Peace Accord of November 2006. However, the chairman failed to follow through, even as late as January 2011 when a 'handover ceremony' was carried out at the Shaktikhor cantonment in the presence of the national leadership and the international community. To this day, the chain-of-command of the fighting force remains with the UCPN (Maoist). The central task of the peace process was left untouched during the nine months the Maoists were in government. The leadership did little when the Maoist union sought to force its writ on industry and reacted with glee when the various media organisations were attacked or threatened by goons from their own ranks.

Over time, the Maoists would perhaps have gained experience in governance and performed better, but the 'commander-in-chief episode' put paid to that possibility. In 2008 and 2009, Dahal was in an enviable position to push through the peace process and secure his party's future: he was lauded both on the international scene and, more importantly, in New Delhi; the Nepali people were giving him full benefit of doubt; and the party was under his total command. Instead of doing what a true statesman might have under such favourable circumstances, which was to prepare his cadre and ex-fighters for careers in peaceful politics, Prime Minister Dahal engaged in adventurism and tried to short-circuit the Nepal Army's chain-of-command. In the fallout, he was forced to resign from the coalition government over which he had overwhelming control. Having resigned from government in conditions as yet rather unclear, the chairman and his party would realise soon enough how difficult it was to get back in power.

The Maoists' nine months in government was a time when the lay public and the intelligentsia alike were able to judge whether the Maoists had the ability and intention to implement their agenda of social justice. What they realised was that the Maoists lacked the philosophical foundation to see through the long-term task of social transformation and that they did not have the statecraft to run the polity. They were neophytes in geopolitics, dragged into the mud by their own radical rhetoric, obviously meant only to keep the cadre charged. The party leadership emerged as deliberately schizophrenic, promising a 'protracted people's war' to the party rank-and-file while presenting the face of social democracy to Western diplomats. Immediately after the election, the first meeting the Maoist leaders held was with Nepal's business community, to whom they promised to support untrammelled capitalism. The second meeting was with the diplomatic community, where they committed to full democracy. Before long, the Maoist chairman had travelled to New Delhi to attend the Hindustan Times Leadership Summit, where he was feted as a charismatic former rebel and where he, once again, promised capitalism, mega-projects and an enthusiastic welcome to those in the Indian private sector wishing to invest in Nepal. The reality of Maoist evolution, however, has always rested on what the leadership tells the party faithful, and there the talk is all about using the tactic of momentary compromise to fulfil the long-term strategy of achieving a one-party state. There is no way to pooh-pooh this propagandising of the cadre.

The 'commander-in-chief episode'

The Maoist leaders falsely promised their ex-combatant cadre full integration into the national army in disregard of its written agreement with the other parties, which stipulates that integration into the security forces will take place on an individual rather than 'unit' basis and abide by standard norms of recruitment. Those who were not to be integrated in one or all of the three security wings (the Nepal Army, the Armed Police and the civilian Nepal Police) were to be rehabilitated in society with dignity. All of this was to have happened within six months of 25 June 2008 and long before the new constitution was to have been promulgated in May 2010. When the Maoists came to power following the elections of April 2008, holding all the important ministries, including that of defence, they sought to get Chief of Army Staff Rookmangad Katawal to agree to the full integration of the ex-fighters into the national army. General Katawal refused to play ball, but it seems that the army second-in-command, Lieutenant-General Kul Bahadur Khadka, was willing to do the bidding of the Maoists. An apparently reluctant but cornered Prime Minister Dahal, unable to mollify the cadre to whom he had made such wayward promises, took action and, on 3 May, sent a letter sacking the army chief, based on a cabinet decision with which only the Maoist members concurred.

The Interim Constitution asks for an all-party consensual decision on matters of a serious nature, as a decision impacting the army chain-of-command surely is. The letter of dismissal was not a recommendation to President Ram Baran Yadav, who, as supreme commander-in-chief, should have been addressed, but a note sent directly to General Katawal. In response, the President, deciding that the sacking was *ultra vires* and acting also on the signed request of 18 parties in the Constituent Assembly, directed General Katawal to stay in his post. Having thus faced the humiliation of all parties abandoning him, feeling cheated by UML Chairman Jhala Nath Khanal, who had asked him to proceed with the sacking, and cornered within his own party, Dahal resigned as prime minister.

In retrospect, the Maoists were, of course, unwise to let matters reach such a head that they were forced to go into the opposition, from where they were to spend the following year and a half trying to get back into the government. Trying to retire General Katawal before his time was an attempt to compromise the army as a critical institution of state during time a of transition and to extend the Maoist party's writ over the soldiers. The Maoist leaders perhaps did not understand the unified response their action would unleash among the other political parties, many of whom, in panic and fear, joined the a 22-party coalition led by the CPN (UML) and stayed together despite numerous Maoist efforts to pull them apart. Nor did the Maoists seem to understand the concern their 'activism' would generate in Nepal's all-powerful southern neighbour, India, whose military establishment was keenly following the run of events in Nepal vis-à-vis the Maoists and the Nepal Army. We do not know exactly what forced Prime Minister Dahal's hand, because his resignation was precipitate. Was he pressured by the demands of his ex-combatants to be integrated en masse into the national army, an ambition that he himself had stoked? Or was the whole episode, as well as Dahal's resignation, engineered by those within the party leadership who opposed his growing personality cult and stand-alone leadership?

A desperate craving

The very Maoist commanders who so astutely got their way in underground warfare were caught on the wrong foot in open society and in government. The structuring and mindset of the national army, the proper procedure for getting rid of an incumbent army chief, the extreme geopolitical sensitivity of what was attempted in defying protocol, and the legal and constitutional matters involved – the Maoist leaders failed to consider all these aspects, focussed as they were on internal leadership issues and the need to push for the full integration of their ex-combatants into the national army regardless of the cost. The leaders seem to have realised the folly of Prime Minister Dahal's resignation on 4 May soon after it was submitted and accepted. For an entire year afterward, the Maoist focus was on launching a campaign for 'civilian supremacy' over the national army, casting President Yadav as the enemy, and using every means possible to bring down the Madhav Kumar Nepal government. From a parliamentary closure to street action to an ultra-nationalist campaign and finally to the indefinite nationwide strike following May Day 2010, there was no approach they did not try. Each of these efforts ended in a loss of credibility for Chairman Dahal, however, and helped expand the fissures within the party. The rest of 2009 and all of 2010 was marked by Dahal's increasingly desperate attempts to become prime minister again. In this effort he seemed to act alone: no longer did he find the support of the entire UCPN (Maoist) leadership. With Dahal's resignation, the Maoist leadership had given up command over the polity, losing control of the major ministries, including finance, defence, local government, general administration, peace and reconstruction, law, labour, transport and tourism in a single stroke. They also lost the all-important Home Ministry portfolio, which had a Maoist-leaning leader of the CPN (UML) as in-charge. The obvious anxiety of the UCPN (Maoist) to get back to leading the government clearly had to do, first, with its late realisation of the importance of not giving up the government machinery, and second, with its plan to be at the helm during the next elections. Control of the government would help the party to repeat its success of April 2008 in the first general elections after the new constitution was promulgated. In fact, some Maoists harbour the hope of garnering a two-thirds majority at that time, so as to be able to amend the new constitution to their liking. However, these two reasons alone do not explain the Maoists' level of desperation to reclaim the prime minister's seat at Singha Durbar. That has also to do with Chairman Dahal's need to maintain leadership within his party.

7

'People's War'

War in inverted commas
My suggestion is to never leave the term 'people's war' outside quotation marks, because it was a conflict started by one political party, the CPN (Maoist). The claim to represent the will of the people of Nepal is specious. Certainly the party did not ask the people whether they thought a war that required the killing of over 13,000 fellow humans was required at the start of the year 1996, just when parliamentary democracy was finding its feet. The Maoists can call it their war, but they cannot pin the 'people' tag on it. Indeed, there existed no conditions for an armed insurgency in 1996, when the Maoists went underground. There was poverty, a growing income divide, socio-economic marginalisation, and political centralisation, but these conditions did not differentiate Nepal from other parts of Southasia, or the developing and developed world beyond. Democracy had arrived barely six years earlier and had just begun to show results. Even if that had not been the case, the objective conditions for a proletarian revolution simply did not exist.

The 'people's war' was an opportunistic game by what was then one small party, to get to centre-stage, utilising violence and populist rhetoric to bring young cadre and supporters to its side. The rebel leaders must be held responsible for introducing political violence into the people's lives. They pushed the economy into a devastating 15-year downturn that continues today, creating conditions for ever-deeper poverty and added frustrations. In the five years they have been above ground, the party leaders have not shown the courage to confront their cadre to tell them that the revolution has been called off, a reluctance that suggests to many that above-ground landing was simply a tactic on the road to state capture. Of course, there could have been some ancillary advantages related to the Maoist shakeup of society, but, overall, the 'revolution' has spelt doom. Talk of social justice does not translate into work for social justice.

The Maoist doublespeak was ideally captured in one setting where, after coming above ground, Chairman Dahal was giving an interview to an international channel in a room full of women party workers. Turning towards the camera, he was the suave, democratically minded ex-rebel. Once the interview was over, he swivelled towards the cadre and reverted to his real self, selling revolt and revolution. Vice-Chairman Baburam Bhattarai promotes the social democratic face of the UCPN (Maoist) to the Western diplomatic community but indicates in website interviews that the 'protracted people's war' remains very much the Maoist agenda, and that the entry into open politics was but a temporary adjustment made to address national and international realities. It cannot be that Dahal and Bhattarai do not understand national politics or geopolitical realities, but they do seem to have come to the conclusion that a cadre groomed to revolt will never understand the ways of open politics. Still reluctant to let go of the cantonments even four long years after the peace process began, the Maoist leaders have found it increasingly hard to be everything to everyone. One option would be to drop all pretence and go for state capture by trying to control the government machinery even as the various party organs move to establish a lockhold on society.

Cost-benefit of conflict years

There is a need to evaluate the conflict years, especially the start and conduct of the 'people's war', in order to give the Maoists credit or hold them to account. Like so many other urgent matters that are stalled because the peace process has not been concluded, a cost-benefit analysis of the 'people's war', too, will have to wait for the denouement. Even the political competition prefers not to conduct the exercise at present, because cornering or humiliating the Maoist leadership may create difficulties on the road to ex-combatant demobilisation. However, a cost-benefit analysis of the 'people's war' has to happen sooner rather than later, and it will expose a gaping negative in terms of stalled development, destroyed infrastructure, lost economic opportunities and greater poverty for the poorest.

Nepal's economy was growing at six percent annually in 1994-95, but went downhill with the start of the insurgency in 1996. The tourism sector was hit, factories packed up in the Tarai, foreign investors fled, there was flight of capital and the educated young, and opportunities for employment growth were decimated for a dozen years and more. The arrival of Indian multinationals in the Tarai, positioned to serve the massive population of the Ganga plains, slowed to a trickle, then there were departures. The companies that remained were those that serviced the captive Nepali consumer market – the people had to have their instant noodles, soaps, sodas and cigarettes. The standstill in employment will be marked as the most devastating feature of the conflict, leading as it did to a mass labour out-migration that sent proud subsistence farmers to work in the most menial jobs available in India, Malaysia, the Persian Gulf and farther afield. There is no counting how many millions of extra citizens have joined the migration tide because of the conflict-induced downturn in Nepal. The poorest left for India, for *chowkidar* duty, agricultural labour, domestic work and restaurant help, and their incomes have been reduced due to the over-supply. Some estimates put the number of Nepali citizens working in India at six million, and their vulnerability has been increased by the anti-Indianism championed by the Maoists over 2009 and 2010.

For more than a dozen years now, national GDP growth has remained below three percent, placing Nepal far behind its neighbours China and India, which consistently report rates between 9% and 11%. Given its neighbours' economic expansion, it is likely that Nepal would have maintained its six percent growth of the early 1990s up to the present. But for the 'people's war', we would likely have left the LDC category behind to become a 'developing country'. The opportunity cost of the conflict years when it comes to lost tourism, hydropower development, exports, skill training, planned development (in urbanisation, agriculture, pollution control, road infrastructure, and so on) can only be imagined. Overall, the disadvantages of the 'people's war' far outweigh any auxiliary advantage that may have accrued, as economists, political scientists and sociologists will be telling us once the dust settles, the 'conflict consultancies' dry up, and true scholarship begins.

The insurgency and social advance

There were social advances that can in part be credited to the insurgency, for example, in bringing women to the forefront of public activities, enabling ethnic communities to assert their identities, mitigating discrimination against Dalits. On the political front, the UCPN (Maoist) can take satisfaction in and credit for having, in large part, ensured the representation of communities in the Constituent Assembly by insisting on a formula which included proportional representation. However, one can hardly credit the Maoists exclusively for the social advance that Nepal has achieved since 1990, as is the tendency among many in the intelligentsia. That advance, while certainly far from complete, has been decades in the making.

The work of the development agencies, local and international non-governmental organisations, community and social groups, and progressive individuals have all contributed to the transformation of society, as have market forces and the expanded media sector. Only the most obtuse would ignore the activities of the United Nations agencies, the bilateral aid agencies, development experts, international non-profits, and the veritable army of grassroots development workers, all of whom contributed to improvements made in Nepal's social landscape over the last two decades. The work of feminists in pushing back patriarchy, the work of ethnic community leaders in fighting the 'Brahminical' mentality, the intense engagement of agricultural extension workers and female health volunteers – who can deny these efforts for social progress? Awareness and transformation comes from long-term work to build foundations; short-term explosions provide spurts that immediately lose momentum.

The most lasting transformations occur with social movements built on the base of awareness and willing participation. The Maoists were relentless only in combat, their social campaigns invariably ran out of steam. The gender equality in the UCPN (Maoist) ranks is generally lauded, but can teaching women to use guns in the battlefield be regarded as social advance or exploitation, especially when women fail to break into the echelons of political power in the districts and centre? What could be the social commitment of a party which blithely uses child soldiers in the frontlines of combat? In large parts of western Nepal where sale and use of alcohol was punishable under Maoist diktat during the insurgency, it was back to business as usual before long, even during the conflict years. The underground Maoists were known for their anti-gambling campaigns, but no sooner had they come out into the open then their unions under the command of trade union leader

Salik Ram Jamarkattel moved in to control the operations of the half dozen Kathmandu casinos. In 2010, the Maoists even actively lobbied against the law which bars Nepali citizens from playing at casinos in order to generate more business for the proprietors – and for themselves.

The unfinished peace process

Perhaps because the peace process is still incomplete, most political parties have been reluctant to mount an all-out political challenge against the UCPN (Maoist). This is a key reason why the deeper truths of the 'people's war', the Constituent Assembly elections, and the delay in the demobilisation of ex-combatants have not been fully exposed. While there may have been some appeasement and romanticisation, or fear in the hearts of some, and the poor organisation of the UML, Congress and other parties stymie action, the main reason for the weak challenge of the Maoists is the unfinished peace process. The democrat-politicians who reached out to bring the Maoists to a safe landing from the jungle were reluctant to challenge the Maoists so sharply that the latter would feel humiliated. Many began to see this leniency as a mistake, because the UCPN (Maoist) took advantage of all the goodwill while reneging on its own numerous public commitments. Just as it was important to challenge King Gyanendra when he sought to destroy democracy, there is a growing conviction at the start of 2011 that the democratically minded must speak out openly against the Maoists and, if necessary, organise. Given the country-wide spread of the party, and its command-and-control systems, this fight for democracy will require much more intellectual investment and daring than was required against Gyanendra's autocracy.

The democrat-politicians in the seven parliamentary parties agreed to work with the Maoists under the 12-Point Agreement of 2005 not because they had come around to accepting the latter's violent ideology, but because of the urgent need to stop the killing and violence. It is once again a concern for the people that has these democrat-politicians unwilling to present the Maoists with a sufficiently stern challenge despite their prevarications on so many fronts. This is why the pre-election intimidation and election-time fraud of April 2008, as well as the subsequent election results, were accepted in silence. Over time, the UML and Congress in particular, succumbed to ennui and did not do what was required of them with regard to raising issues and creating public opinion as the Maoists began to cheat blatantly on the peace process. Thus, the parliamentary parties were willing to accept UNMIN's verification of 19,000-plus Maoist combatants when it was well known that this figure tripled the actual number of hardcore fighters. The exposé of the Maoists plans as blatantly on show in the Shaktikhor videotape was not used to the extent it might have been to expose Maoist designs; Krishna Bahadur Mahara, who was caught red-handed negotiating for Rs 50 crore to buy elections was allowed to be elevated to Deputy Prime Minister in the Khanal cabinet in March 2011 without protest; and no one – least of all the democrat-politicians – is asking for a cost-benefit analysis of the decade of insurgency and the Maoist-instituted instability since.

But perhaps one should not fall for the easy explanation, labelling the unwillingness to take on the Maoists as a lack of guts or an appeasement by pushover politicians taken in by the fast-talking ex-rebels. That may be true for some, but what is in fact the case is that seasoned and wily democrat-politicians are working gingerly with a violent party that espouses terrible values. The democrat-politicians know what they are doing, which is why the Nepali peace process was still a success at the start of 2011, even though it has gone on for too long for those victims who have to suffer the delays. The careful attitude of the parliamentary parties comes from the same sophisticated sense of compromise that got the peace process started in the first place with the signing of the 12-Point Agreement in the late autumn of 2005. Their current forbearance will transform into staunch opposition as and when it finally becomes clear that the Maoist leadership will not or cannot conclude the peace process. In this context, the seven point secret deal between the UML and Maoist chairmen is a clear notice to reject the peace process, and creates a challenge for peace and democracy. Any attempt by Chairman Dahal to force his and his party's agenda on the populace will lead towards one more people's movement, but it will not be as easy or as clean as the movement against the king.

8

Pushpa Kamal Dahal

The Shaktikhor videotape
In January 2008, Chairman Pushpa Kamal Dahal addressed a gathering of ex-combatants at Shaktikhor in Chitwan District, the largest of the 28 Maoist cantonments. His hour plus-long speech was professionally videotaped with good sound and light, apparently to serve as a training tract for distribution to other cantonments. Unlike what some diplomats believe, this was not a film taped clandestinely by Maoists opponents but was the Maoists' very own production. There were questions about how the tape got leaked to the public, but this was a videotape generally available within the Maoist party and some disgruntled member probably gave it out in spite. The speech was obviously meant to be a motivational oration to galvanise the cadre, but it also contained seminal elements of the Maoist strategy after they came above ground. To an appreciative audience that laughs knowingly in all the right places, Dahal talks about how UNMIN was fooled into verifying the existence of 19,000 fighters when the actual number of Maoist combatants was no more than seven or eight thousand; about how the elections would be won even if it required breaking the legs of opponent candidates; about how a third of the stipend given by the government for the upkeep of the ex-combatants would be used to buy truckloads of guns for revolt; about how all the combatants would be integrated into the national army once the party had won the elections; and about how the Nepal Army would then be made *'maobaadi-maya'* (moulded according to the Maoist image) to complete the party's control of the state.

Some national and international observers suggest to their Nepali colleagues that the Shaktikhor videotape ought to be seen 'in perspective', that it was just an election-time motivational speech designed to raise the spirit of the cadre. This is the kind of advice given by foreigners who are on short-term assignments and who do not have to live with the fallout of their great sagacity. The videotape is actually an accurate representation of the plans and designs of the Maoist leadership, as became clear later in the 'commander-in-chief episode'. These plans and designs, as shared with the Shaktikhor residents by Chairman Dahal, are to push for the full integration of the ex-combatant into the national army. While the importance of the videotape was underplayed by most international observers and analysts, including UNMIN, it stands as an archival audio-visual document to inform scholars and historians about how the Maoists planned their above-ground trajectory. The episode also show how contemporary observers and analysts were unable to grasp evidence placed before them on a platter, in this instance a videotape that left nothing to the imagination.

Chairman Dahal's accountability
The primary responsibility for the problems that have arisen with the peace process and constitution-writing lies with Chairman Dahal. It is only since 2006, when the Maoist party came above ground, that one has been able to clearly follow their professed goals versus their programmes, their inner workings, the depth of their ideology and commitment, and the strengths and weaknesses of their leaders. Until before he arrived in a helicopter directly from the 'jungle' to a crowded press conference at the Baluwatar residence of Prime Minister Girija Prasad Koirala on 16 June 2006, not even photographs of the elusive 'Prachanda' were easily available. His looks were a matter of conjecture, best left to illustrators. Above ground, Dahal came across as a passionate, quick-witted leader who could ingratiate himself with different constituencies, from cadres to diplomats; his affability and apparent candidness also stood out. However, when placed before the microphone in front of a mass gathering, Dahal tends to take the low road to incitement. Above ground, Dahal has found himself having to juggle different constituencies – the Nepali political class, the diplomatic community, and the Maoist faithful. However, because he failed to come clean with the political class representing the non-Maoist public, all his nimbleness with the diplomats and cadres has not been enough to earn him security in open politics.

As challenges to his leadership arose within his own party and as the media exposed Dahal's numerous shenanigans, the chairman found it increasingly difficult to control an outfit he had easily managed to command while it was underground. Dahal became insular in his approach to politics, and the divide-and-rule tactics he tried to use to co-opt the so-called radicals and pragmatists within the party grew increasingly ineffective in the media glare. His increasing desperation, visible in 2009 after his resignation in May and throughout 2010, was based on the fact that the loss of the top position in a less-than-democratic radical party tends to mean oblivion. For all its people-centric rhetoric, the UCPN (Maoist) has always placed the party above the nation, and now its chairman began to place his career above the party.

Chairman Dahal is more responsible for the crisis in the peace process and constitution-writing than any other leader in his own party or any democrat-politician. He is a master at moving goalposts, making public commitments, breaking the promises and issuing public apologies. His critical weakness has been his inability and/or unwillingness to wean the cadres away from their guerilla mindset and help them adjust to the demands of an open society. Dahal has continued to use the same rhetoric of state capture through revolt as he did before the peace accord was signed, perhaps in the realisation that the cadre simply would not understand the reversal of course.

Dahal's exhortations to his cadre can be contrasted with those of the late Madan Bhandari, the leader of the CPN (UML), who led what was then strongest communist force into multiparty politics in the 1991 elections. After a good showing at the polls, which saw the Marxist-Leninists become a major force in national politics, Madan Bhandari publicly urged his more radical followers to abandon their 'militarist mentality' (*yuddhako dhangdhangi*). In terms of his control of the Parliament and having a welcoming geopolitical environment, Chairman Dahal was in a much better position in 2006 than was Madan Bhandari in 1991, but he failed to use the opportunity to transform his party to suit the demands of long-term national politics and what a careful reading of regional geopolitics would have revealed. Among those Chairman Dahal has let down are the many old-world communists in India and overseas who, in their ignorance of the reality of Nepali soil, projected their own hopes for a socialist utopia on the activities of the Maoists of the central Himalaya.

The Maoist party groomed its fighters for revolt and revolution.

Later, confronted with his inability to shift their mindset and to regain the Singha Durbar seat and all its possibilities of patronage, Chairman Dahal decided to use the radical wing within the party to prop up his support base. He decided that if the prime minister's seat was out of reach, he would consolidate his hold over the party using other, more devious means. And so, at a mass meeting in Naya Baneswor in December 2009, Dahal went public with his ultra-nationalist, anti-India campaign, which was clearly an attempt to bolster his personal hold over his cadre even at the cost of his party. When, under pressure from within and outside, Dahal showed himself to be incapable of temperate speech, claiming among other ludicrous things that his deputy Baburam Bhattarai was an Indian stooge, that the Maoists were willing to swim in the blood of a million citizens to get back to power, and that India was a *prabhu* (deity, master) and the parliamentary parties the *nokar* (supplicants, servants). Geopolitically, he put his party in the crosshairs of the New Delhi establishment with his continued anti-Indianism, which saw one brainwashed cadre hurl a shoe at Indian Ambassador Rakesh Sood in October 2010 and numerous others wave black flags in the districts he visited over 2010 and 2011. Dahal's suggestion during a trip to Shanghai and Beijing in October 2010 that India and China jointly declare a strategy for Nepal served to further weaken the regional weight of the country in a manner that no other national leader has ever adopted in the modern era.

Having resigned from the government under what seems, at least partially, to have been pressure from party colleagues wanting to cut him down to size, Dahal led a year-long campaign after May 2009 to get back to Singha Durbar. This campaign had the advantage of keeping him in the headlines, but it was also one with diminishing returns as it severely weakened the UCPN (Maoist) and its revolutionary image. A party with nearly 40% of the seats in Parliament was concentrating on street action all because its chairman sought to retain his position as top dog. He did grave harm to the Nepali sense of nationalism when he proposed that the Madhav Kumar Nepal government was something put in place by India though it is abundantly clear that the Nepali people and polity are more than capable not just of forming a government under their own steam but also of bringing about regime change, for that was what the People's Movement of 2006 did.

Dahal did everything he could to keep himself at the helm of his party and reassume the post of prime minister: first he prostrated himself before New Delhi, and, when that did not do the trick, he launched an anti-India campaign. In addition, he would not allow the UCPN (Maoist) to stake a claim to lead the government unless it was he who would be the prime ministerial candidate. If he could not be prime minister, he would be willing to support UML Chairman Khanal – anything so long as it was not his own deputy, Baburam Bhattarai, who became prime minister. So focussed was Dahal on his personal agenda that the peace process and the writing of a democratic constitution were all reduced to mere tools to be manipulated to secure his overriding objective: remaining boss.

As an energetic Machiavelli of Nepali politics, Dahal uses his disarming doublespeak to waylay diplomats, donor organisation representatives and political opponents alike. He is a political chameleon who uses make-believe earnestness to confuse one and all. Characteristically, Dahal, in swift succession promised the first presidency of the Republic of Nepal to both Girija Prasad Koirala and Madhav Kumar Nepal, only to nominate the long-time militant Ram Raja Prasad Singh. After he left government in May 2009, he used the disconsolation of Koirala and the UML Chairman Khanal, both beleaguered leaders, to set up a 'high-level mechanism' to direct the affairs of state in competition with both the parliament and the government. It order to create a rift within the Nepali Congress when Ram Chandra Poudel was put forth as the party's official candidate in the autumn of 2010, Dahal offered Sher Bahadur Deuba the Singha Durbar seat.

Dahal's antics did not end there. To prepare for the long-delayed sixth party plenum scheduled for November 2010, he convinced other party leaders to set up a working group outside the Constituent Assembly, with himself as coordinator, to address outstanding constitutional issues. He convinced them to organise a 'secret' conclave at Hattiban Resort on Kathmandu Valley's southern rim, supposedly also to find a way to share power. His machinations constituted a master stroke for a leader who, for many reasons, including the 'Maharagate' vote-buying scandal, had, in the autumn of 2010, come under a cloud. By organising the meeting, he was able to convey the impression that he had command and influence over the polity. To the diplomatic community he presented the meeting as the initiative of a man doing all he could to reach compromise on the peace process; whereas to the party faithful he projected it as evidence that he had stood up against the demobilisation of the party's fighting force.

Not even the chairman of the UCPN (Maoist) gets all that he wants, however, and it is the law of diminishing returns at play as he is 'found out' that has raised a sense of alarm in him. Even as his unabashed left radicalism helps foster the rise of a right-wing movement, and as he raises geopolitical concerns with his adventurism, Dahal creates conditions under which not one single cadre from the cantonments may see integration as provided for under the Comprehensive Peace Accord. Given that his cadre do read the newspapers and do know that all is not right, it is best that the chairman give up his ambition to be a 'great helmsman' in perpetuity. 'Prachandapath', the ideology of the Maoists of Nepal, has already been discredited and Dahal's grievous loss of image between 2009 and 2010 is not something perhaps even his worst enemies would have wished on him. The only way forward for the party is demobilisation and democratisation. To accomplish these ends will be a challenge for Chairman Dahal, but at least if he tries he will not be accused of dragging down the party with him.

9

Animalistic Farm

Credit where due
The question may arise whether this writer credits the UCPN (Maoist) with anything at all. To respond, I must say that I firmly believe that it is not a party of transformation and that the implementation of its ideology has impeded society's advancement. I thank them for abandoning the 'people's war' once they concluded that pursuing the fiction of revolution and continuing to fight would have decimated the party. The Maoist leadership raised the demand for securing social justice and gender equality and for putting an end to marginalisation and regional disparity, mainly to garner easy support. These are noble goals, but five years above ground has shown that not even social advancement or prosperity of the people will come between the UCPN (Maoist) and state control. The Maoists' lack of staying power on many of the social agenda they have espoused makes me question their sincerity. For the other parties, whose founding and continuing philosophy has been social democracy, the goals of social justice were a given even when, on occasion, they were diverted by the economic liberalisation agenda of multilateral financial institutions. The Maoists spoke loudly of social justice, as if they had discovered something new, something that other parties had overlooked, and they may even have believed in the social justice agenda more than this writer gives them credit for, but they cannot be forgiven for resorting to the language of the gun to achieve the goals, however great.

The question is whether the professed Maoist goals of promoting social inclusion and ending marginalisation were built on ideological commitment or whether they were simply part of an opportunistic agenda to attain power. By now, the reader knows where I stand. The use of violence, including extreme brutality against political opponents at the village level and the choice of armed insurgency rather than social revolution, leaves no doubt that the main goal of the three leaders, Pushpa Kamal Dahal, Baburam Bhattarai and Mohan Vaidya, was to take the party to the seat of power. The rhetoric of social transformation was to be used to get there, and then to create a one-party 'people's republic', or something as close to it as possible.

The Maoist 'revolution' was built on a weak or non-existent philosophical foundation. That the leaders sought to capture state power rather than pursue social transformation was made clear when the Maoists gave up their 'people's war' and joined parliamentary practice as soon as their military advance was halted and they saw the possibility of state capture through open politics instead. The fact that they were willing to return to the very system of representative government that they had raised arms against in 1996 begs the question of why a decade of devastation was required.

Anti-violence or anti-Maoist

Those, like me, who challenge the Maoist agenda of revolt are derided in some quarters for having been fooled by the Maoists' bluster and rhetoric. The only answer to this misplaced derision is that it is wise not to take any risk which would result in our being saddled with a People's Republic of Nepal. To challenge the Maoists at a time when they have not given up recourse to the gun is not to be anti-Maoist but to be anti-violence. For those who believe, as I do, that Nepal's villages used to be largely free of physical political violence and that there was no justification for a 'people's war', it is a duty to exhort the Maoists to give up violence. One cannot surrender to a *fait accompli*, one cannot fail to challenge the Maoists about their use of force and their threat to use of force simply because they have a countrywide base and considerable power. One cannot simply ignore the reality of what the Maoists have been training their cadre in since coming above ground – revolt, state capture, extortion, doublespeak – and any other means required to subdue opponents and keep people insecure.

I am not convinced that an armed insurrection was required in 1996, when the Maoists, disheartened by their third-place placement and resultant ineffectiveness in Parliament, went underground. Five years after it abandoned its 'people's war', the UCPN (Maoist) still has not given up its policy of violent politics. Even so, for the sake of peace, the polity has accepted them and given them a safe landing. Realistically, it will take more time before the ex-rebels are able to make a public declaration that they have abandoned violence, and it will take even longer for, as I hope it would, the Maoist leadership to actually apologise for starting the 'people's war'. For now, in the spring of 2011, my hopes are more modest – I simply wish that the Maoists detach themselves from their military and paramilitary forces, return captured land and property, abandon talk of state capture, and move the peace process towards a civilised, successful end.

The Maoists have been the central actor of the last decade: they have defined the political stage and made everyone else react to them. It is obvious, then, that any analysis of contemporary politics must focus on the Maoist party. Indeed, it is only a vehement and hard-hitting critique that can help bring them into mainstream politics. The party must evolve into a democratic, civilian party so that the sacrifices of so many of its own members are not wasted. My criticism is directed not at the rank-and-file, who fought for what they were made to believe, but at the leaders who made them believe it. These leaders were opportunistic, manipulative and feudal.

The feudal Maobaadi
It is appropriate to call the Maoist leadership *samanti* (feudal), especially in comparison with the democrat-politicians of the parliamentary parties. The Maoists are feudal because they propose to usher in transformation not through the long toil of social revolution but by foisting on the people a fast-track, armed insurgency approach to change. If a feudal, as I believe, is defined as a person or group which uses violence or the threat of violence to get what he or it desires, whether material or political, then the Maoists are just that. A feudal political party amasses wealth through unfair means and uses it to buy power, votes and fealty. The feudal shuns class conflict as the defining feature of human society, and adopts whatever strategy will give him or it status, wealth and power – including non-Marxist identity politics, doublespeak, and nationalism so extreme it puts Marxist internationalism to shame. The feudal will even go as far as making the economy and population of one's own country vulnerable vis-à-vis neighbouring countries.

There is a great divide between what the Maoist leaders are, what they actually want, and what they say. There can be no doubt, now that we are able to study them in above ground politics, that their goal is unadulterated capture of the state. They are willing to make any compromise necessary to achieve it, whether it is reviving the monarchy, buying members of Parliament, or abandoning the Constituent Assembly. During the years of conflict, the cadre was groomed to use physical threat and intimidation to extort food, lodging and other services from rural householders simply for the asking. Only the rarest of the rare would have welcomed a band of Maoist fighters at the doorstep with their hands open. Easy access to food, shelter and pocket money created a swaggering, *goonda*-like mentality among the cadre, who have continued to use the threat of force to gain profit and services in peacetime. For sure, the leaders did not teach their followers about the dignity of labour. Maoist leaders reject suggestions for the dignified rehabilitation of former fighters, decrying public health, agriculture extension or micro-enterprise training as being too demeaning for their ex-fighters. Cantonment residents have been taught to shun *eelum*, or diligent labour, and to disdain skill training geared towards taking up a vocation or starting a small enterprise.

The Maoist leaders reveal their covert feudalism in their use of language: on the one hand, they decry Sanskrit as a regressive language, and, in a violent display of their hostility, torched the Sanskrit University in Dang District in May 2002; on the other hand, the leaders exhibit a propensity for complex Sanskritic constructions in their orations. Mid-level Maoist leaders, particularly the Bahuns among them, also use the deferential honorific *hajur* more than democrat-politicians do. In their education-related agitation, one problem Maoist 'revolutionary student leaders' have with private school proprietors seems to be that – according to one of them – 'those who came in with sandals to Kathmandu have now built mansions'. Another leader went so far as to claim in a television programme that it was acceptable if such a mansion had been inherited from privileged ancestors but not if it had been earned through hard work. In March 2011, when one of the Maoist mouthpieces, *Lal Rakshak*, carried a cover feature portraying me as a 'modern day Shakuni' (equivalent to Machiavelli), I was identified as the descendant of a *bhanche*, nothing more than a supposedly lowly Bahun cook. Such disparagements suggest the Maoist leadership has little respect for the dignity of labour. For it, unionising is nothing more than a clever way to build the party's base and its extractive power; it has nothing to do with supporting the rights of the labourer.

At a May 2010 mass rally in Kathmandu, Chairman Dahal, in a bid to ingratiate himself with the local Kathmandu population, railed against 'those who came from outside the Valley, and have been able to just about build a house'. In a speech delivered the previous winter, he had called India the lord and master of Nepali politics, served by servants who were none other than the members of our parliamentary parties. Both references indicate the deep-seated arrogance of a member of the aristocratic class and no doubt sting the millions of Nepali citizens forced to work as 'servants' within the country and outside it. Hidden within much of the Maoist rhetoric is the prejudice of the upper classes against the working class. While such condescension failed to surface when the rebels were underground, once they joined open society the leaders began to slip.

A whiff of the farm
There is more than a whiff of *Animal Farm* in how the Maoist leaders have evolved in open society. There was no staying power in the party: the majority of its captains and cadres, it turns out, are not committed to its high-minded ideology. This was a party whose supreme commander stayed safe in hideaways in India while his committed cadre, sold on the idea of revolution he presented, suffered and died. In their initial days in the hills of the mid-west, the Maoists organised communes and set up parallel 'people's governments' and 'people's courts'. This step may have contributed to some social upliftment if it had lasted, but, ironically, it was all show for a leadership which exhorts everyone else to distinguish between *roop* (form) and *saar* (content). As the Maoists spread rapidly from their core areas in the mid-western districts of Rolpa, Rukum and Jajarkot, their 'revolutionary' spirit waned rapidly and the number of local ruffians recruited to build the organisation nationally grew proportionally.

Above ground, the ex-rebel leadership leads a life of leisure in Kathmandu: they have the largest fleet of SUVs, several times the size of that of all the other parties combined. The opulent lifestyle of Dahal may be contrasted with the spartan living of Sushil Koirala, the head of the Nepali Congress. The Maoist party coffers are full of funds from extortion, and it would be foolish to ask for transparency in its accounting. In the districts, the Maoists leave the other parties far behind in utilising muscle power to get what they want, whether it is government contracts or control of high school management committees, monopoly over rackets of contraband smuggling or the freedom to decimate forests, export boulders from the Chure hills, pursue environmentally unsound sand mining or exploit medical and aromatic plants in the name of profit. Maoist leaders at the centre and in the districts have got quickly enmeshed, mafia-style, in the entire gamut of illegal operations, from transport cartels and urban parking to local government fund disbursement, forest encroachment, control of the trade in the purportedly aphrodisiacal parasitic fungus *yarsagumba*, land-sharking and casinos – not to mention extortion of businesses large and small. A party that professed to fight for 'scientific land reform' has its cadre busily engaged as real estate middlemen right across the nation, taking advantage of skyrocketing prices in an economy where – thanks to the Maoists – there are few opportunities for investment other than land.

Proof of what everyone had long suspected about corruption and aggrandisement within the Maoist 'farm' arrived when journalists accessed reports Vice-Chairmen Mohan Vaidya and Baburam Bhattarai had prepared for the long-delayed plenum of the UCPN (Maoist) scheduled for late November 2010. The two leaders accused 'headquarters' (meaning Chairman Dahal) of being non-transparent in financial matters and helping a *nouveau riche* elite within the party rise through contraband trade, smuggling and corruption. Bhattarai accused Dahal of leaving party workers hungry while spending hundreds of thousands buying members of Parliament to become prime minister and claimed that corruption and transgression within the party were undermining its proletarian character. Bhattarai also flayed the chairman for having forgotten the party and the revolution and for 'consorting with the defeated royalist feudals and revisionists'. For his part, Vaidya wrote, 'There are grave problems with the party's income generation and there is no control in place. Transparency, cooperative decision-making and accounting systems seem to have been all but destroyed. The rise of the nouveau riche class has led to the departure of revolutionary cadre.'

The double-speakers
Certainly, no one should privilege Baburam Bhattarai and Mohan Vaidya for openly defying Chairman Dahal. The two vice-chairmen

are part and parcel of the party's introduction of numerous tragedies into the homes and hearths of the citizenry. The gap between what the Maoist leaders profess and what they do became clear once the party joined open politics in 2006. The ability of the Maoists to take women into its fighting force was said to be an example of its progressivism and gender sensitivity, but the party's own topmost hierarchy relegates women to *pro forma* showcase positions. In terms of inclusive politics, many Madhesis felt so left out by the Pahade (hill caste and ethnic) top echelons that they broke ranks under the leadership of Jai Krishna Goit. The Maoists may have many leaders of hill ethnicities in its higher echelons, but the top three slots are controlled by three Bahuns – Dahal, Bhattarai and Vaidya (who is not a Newar as many assume but belongs to the Bahun clan of Pokhrel).

How is it that while they galvanise supporters with harangues about ethnic emancipation, the top three Maoist bosses are Bahuns, each intent on incorporating the cadres into his individual coteries? How is it that they deride the Sanskrit language and burn Sanskrit texts and libraries, yet use Sanskritised Nepali when talking to both their cadre and the public? How is it that they campaigned against religion but now visit charlatan godmen, worship buffaloes, and willingly attend Hindu discourses. When a group of political leaders were taken to Benaras for a seminar by the Indian Government soon after the rebels came above ground it was the Maoist leaders present – irrespective of caste and ethnicity – who were the first to rush down the *ghat* steps to the Ganga River to pay obeisance to the mother goddess. The Maoists killed one of the most prominent Hindu preachers of Nepal in June 2005 but saw nothing, once above ground, of asking his son and successor to lead a Maoist religious fundraiser. The leadership used anti-Indianism to garner support from the ultra-nationalist base of Nepali politics, yet their 'revolution' was nurtured in India and, even today, the leadership would be obsequiously pro-New Delhi if the latter would help them get back into power.

The hypocrisy of Maoist leaders is well recorded, but civil society and the political class have been forgiving because everyone understands that the leadership needs time, space and verbal agility to wean the cadre off its 'revolutionary' agenda. The leaders have taken advantage of this goodwill by misrepresenting their interests and lying with abandon, not only to their cadre but also to the Nepali public at large and to the international community. Their dishonesty is a matter of concern for those who still believe in the Maoists' professed goals and who would like the party to evolve into a democratic entity which promotes social justice. The lifestyle of top Maoist leaders, the play of money and muscle among the district cadre, and the easy recourse to misrepresentation and demagoguery seem to indicate a shaky future for the UCPN (Maoist).

10

The Democrat-Politician

Left and centre

Members of the Kathmandu intelligentsia as well as many diplomats and donor representatives regard the parliamentary parties as no more than a laughingstock. Among the educated classes and opinion makers, few come forward to defend the democrat-politicians that make up these parties. The beleaguered political parties of Nepal have always been asked, in the modern era, to do more penance than the sum total of their sins though, when compared with the political parties of other democracies, Western or Southern, they do not stack up negatively at all.

Our democratic politicians of the left and centre have had to struggle for pluralism more continuously than their present-day counterparts in most countries. Keep in mind that many of the individuals that are pilloried today spent, in the name of democratic ideals, more than a decade behind bars during the dark Panchayat decades; the sacrifices they made should, at least, elicit acknowledgement, however grudging. These politicians and their parties have also shown great flexibility: it was they who compromised when it came to bringing the Maoists above ground. Where many would have succumbed to the sort of ultra-left demagoguery that can only give birth to a right-wing regime in reaction, the democrat-politicians refused to forget the simple prerequisites of a democratic state. There is no need for the democrat-politicians of Nepal to be defensive vis-à-vis the national intelligentsia or the international community: while they may have sometimes failed in governance, they have consistently stood by pluralism and democracy.

My use of the term 'democrat-politician' may perplex some readers. The qualifier is required because, having participated in elections, the Maoist leaders, too, have become 'politicians', but are still far from having accepted the values of competitive politics and pluralism that are required for democracy. 'Politician', therefore, loses specificity in the present context of Nepal and cannot be used in the way we are used to until the Maoist become a democratic party both in word and in deed.

International misconstruction
The parliamentary parties are misconstrued by many international representatives because democrat-politicians do not bother to either explain either themselves or the complex meanderings of Nepali politics to the expatriate donor and diplomat. The main focus of the democrat-politicians is, after all, their constituencies and the national discourse, not providing clarifications and justifications to the outside observer. Democrat-politicians dialogue in Nepali and other national languages, and rarely in English. The absence of English in the discourse is, of course, due to the fact that Nepal was never colonised and is both logical and proper. However, with so little English used in the Nepali political sphere, the production of public information designed to reach out to the rest of world has been severely constrained. To the extent that both the middle-class intelligentsia and civil society communicate with each other through the media in Nepali rather than English, Nepali politics, one might argue, is rather insular. In this sense, Nepal is more like Thailand than those of its Southasian neighbours which use English extensively.

Donors and diplomats do engage formally with democrat-politicians, but almost to the last man and woman, the latter do not have the parlour English needed to converse easily. Not only are Nepali politicians thus ill-equipped but they also tend not to bother to refute the international analyst who shows arrogant ignorance of the Nepali fight for democracy, the causes of the 'people's war', the agenda for social transformation, the peace process and the constitution-writing. To explain or argue in English with a Westerner whose mind seems made up that the Maoists represent the trail-blazers for social justice in Nepal seems pointless to the democrat-politician.

In the aftermath of the People's Movement, most national and international observers have failed to understand the vital role played by the democrat-politicians of the Nepali Congress, the CPN (UML) and the other democratic parties in preventing the Maoist plans for 'state capture'. The constant battling with the Maoist juggernaut by these democrat-politicians is, however, appreciated by some of the Asian ambassadors resident in Kathmandu and by the occasional visitor from an Eastern European democracy who has had first-hand experience of communist one-party rule – they know to recognise the doublespeak.

All of this is not to justify a xenophobic, anti-Western plank that promotes son-of-the-soil 'Asian values' in Nepali governance. Indeed, classical liberal democracy as an import from the West is the only matrix that can work for Nepal, which is why it is so ironic that Western donors and diplomats have put the Maoists on a pedestal after 2006, some even retroactively justifying the insurgency. There is no option but to take this liberal democratic model and to make it deliver on its promise; doing so will require the Maoists to convert and democratise. It has been the mainstream political parties of Nepal which have been the carriers of pluralism, representative governance, human rights and fundamental freedoms though many in the Kathmandu intelligentsia, outside academics, as well as Western representatives, have got carried away in their denigration of the democrat-politician and the elevation of the Maoist leadership.

The absence of close contact with Nepal's democrat-politicians prevents the Western diplomat and donor from following anything more than the broad contours of Nepal's rapidly evolving public sphere. To try and explain Nepal, therefore, they turn to what they know of other societies, which is not very useful. There is little or no institutional memory among these donors and diplomats, and those who were here during the People's Movement of 2006 – not to speak of the People's Movement of 1990 – are long gone, having left no trace of their understanding and involvement. There is no one left to tell the plenipotentiaries who are so prescriptive that their embassies and donor institutions were vehemently anti-Maoist during the rise of the insurgency or that they did not favour the parliamentary parties' reaching out to the Maoists between 2003 and 2005. Nor would they know that naïve Western ambassadors were in favour of accepting Gyanendra's first concessional speech during the People's Movement of 2006, a speech which conceded so little it was rejected outright by the parliamentary parties led by Girija Prasad Koirala.

There are certain categories of people towards whom internationals naturally gravitate in order to understand Nepali politics, neglecting mainstream politicians, the very ones who are the most knowledgeable and who have been the most continuously engaged over decades of despair and triumph. Beyond the staffers in missions and embassies, the main guides to Nepali politics are experts, consultants, heads of development-oriented non-governmental organisations and other recipients of donor largesse, all of whom are be inclined toward reinforcing prejudicial mindsets in the missions, be they about caste-ethnic relations, the peace process, political parties or constitution-writing. Internationals are also influenced by the class they are closest to by demography, the English-savvy Kathmandu gentry, a class that likes to sneer at the democrat-politicians. Having developed a perspective that is based on inadequate and prejudiced knowledge, many diplomats and donor representatives, with the funding at their disposal giving them a high pedestal, prefer to tell the Nepali political class what they think is required rather than to seek to understand them.

While they did generally support the fight for democracy against Gyanendra's autocracy, Western internationals seemed to lose their moorings when it came to countenancing the above-ground Maoists. There was sympathy for the latter as 'the underdogs' even after the Maoists rose to be the largest party in the Constituent Assembly and became part of the Nepali establishment. Assisted by the pusillanimity of the Kathmandu intellectuals, ambassadors and donor representatives have continued to see great weaknesses in the democrat-politicians and to imagine the Maoists to be the masterminds of social transformation. They fail to credit the democrat-politicians for their courageous reaching out to the Maoists, which resulted in the 12-Point Agreement of 2005, a sacrifice for the sake of peace.

11

The Process of Peace

The price of peace
For all the day-to-day frustrations, the Nepali peace process has been exemplary: the ability of the insurgent force to see the reality and join competitive politics and of the democratic forces to understand the need for compromise, even at their own expense, is amazing. The peace process has been essentially home-grown, based as it was on the conviction of the parliamentary parties that the suffering of the people required that they reach out to the rebels. Meanwhile, the Maoist leadership had come to the conclusion that the best they could hope for from insurgent warfare had been achieved. The democrat-politician leaders (Girija Prasad Koirala, Madhav Kumar Nepal, Khadga Prasad Oli and others) met secretly with the Maoists even while the international community was sceptical, and in many cases outright negative, about a peace deal with the insurgents.

Towards 2003, the Maoists began to see it in their interest to come above ground: the law of diminishing returns was beginning to apply to their 'revolution' mainly because the state security forces had begun to push back after their initial shock and inactivity. New Delhi, which had preferred to look the other way during the first half of the conflict, now put its considerable weight behind a peace deal because it saw the Nepali Maobaadi as a threat to its own internal security. In order to help the Maoists save face as they abandoned the insurgency, the Nepali negotiators decided not to mention the term 'disarmament' or 'demobilisation' in the peace discourse; instead, they chose the euphemistic *hatiyaar byabasthapan* (arms management).

The seven parliamentary parties, in negotiation with the CPN (Maoist), agreed to the 12-Point Agreement. The agreement was essential for the Maoist leaders to justify their abandonment of the 'people's war' and something the democrat-politicians felt was required in order to stop the bloodshed in a peace process that would remain in Nepali hands. Once they came above ground with the People's Movement of April 2006, the Maoists utilised their propagandistic skills to set the political agenda. As the price for peace, they got the other parties to declare Nepal a republic, meaning the abolition of the monarchy, constitutional or otherwise. The reason the peace process accelerated so rapidly was mainly the willingness of the parliamentary parties to make compromises with the Maoists, even when they could have got international backing to go after the insurgents, whose defeat in the battlefield was certain. The Maoists deserve credit for being practical and even opportunistic, for capitulating when the chips were down was better than being 'revolutionary' and fighting to the last man, leading to huge loss of innocent lives in the process. It is a different matter altogether that the Maoists dragged their feet when it came to fulfilling their part of the bargain with the seven parliamentary parties and keeping the promises they made to the people and the international community. What has happened in the five years since the end of the conflict and the People's Movement of 2006 is that a) the other parties have been unable to hold the Maoists to their word; b) a large section of the influential international community has not challenged the Maoists because they do not comprehend the latter's double-dealing; and, c) elements within the Maoists with the ability to force their will upon the larger party have decided to reject all prior agreements, holding both the peace process and constitution-writing hostage to demands for power-sharing.

Loss of momentum
For the most part, the Nepal Army has followed the terms of the Comprehensive Peace Accord of 2006, but the UCPN (Maoist) has not. It seems that ex-rebel leaders were unwilling or unable to inform their followers about the changed political context and their jettisoning of plans for armed revolt and the capture of state power. The reluctance of the Maoist leadership to speak with honesty has delayed cantonment management nearly three years beyond the initial six-month deadline. In essence, the polity has been kept hostage by the Maoists, who were emboldened to resist by their success in the elections of April 2008. That success clearly led to a shifting of goalposts, and those who rejected the

agreed peace process emerged powerful from a party conclave held at Kharipati in the Kathmandu Valley in November 2008.

There is a deadlock in Nepali politics in the spring of 2011, and, besides the peace process, the Maoists have the writing of the constitution in their grip. This deadlock has at its core the matter of cantonment management, and the Maoists' unwillingness to demobilise is the greatest sticking point. Throughout 2009 and 2010, day-to-day politics had the average observer frustrated at what seemed to be a mad scramble to lead the government. Two matters of principle were at the core of the tussle: the successful conclusion of the peace process and the writing of a democratic constitution.

Without disbanding the cantonments according to the agreed-upon formula of integration for some and rehabilitation for the rest, there can be no credible constitution-writing. How can the matter of writing the basic law proceed, after all, when one party – the largest in the Constituent Assembly – retains its own private army? If the matter sits unresolved for too long, the peace process will end of its own accord, and in a manner that may not be to the liking of the Maoists, that is, there may be a forced resolution which denies the ex-combatants all possibility of integration or rehabilitation. To have a disgruntled population of young ex-combatants outside the camps would be dangerous, but state and society would survive. There is a fear among some that the Maoists will go back underground in such an event, but it is clear that only a small number would do so –life above ground has been too comfortable and lucrative. If the Maoists insist on reneging on their promises of peace, they will lose status as the Constituent Assembly itself becomes irrelevant. The possibility of a full and unique conversion of a once violent insurgent force into a democratic party will have been foiled by the Maoists themselves, but there will be no return to war.

12

Cantonments and Barracks

Cantonment management scenario
Those who believe Nepal is a country without experience in peace and democracy might think that the Maoist combatant force is close to being the equal of the national army and that, under the peace deal, the state is obliged to integrate most (if not all) of the ex-combatants into the three security wings. Those who respect Nepal as an open society, in contrast, see the fighting force as the violent arm of one political party and will only concede to having a limited number of the ex-combatants joining the security forces, with the rest provided dignified rehabilitation. Wholesale integration would result in the 'ideological contamination' of the Nepal Army. When the need is to reduce the size of the army and make it more professional, the large-scale integration of ex-combatants – largely individuals who do not meet the standard norms of recruitment – would be a move in the wrong direction. In meeting the terms of the Comprehensive Peace Accord to 'democratise' and professionalise the military, one must guard against Maoist plans to make the Nepal Army *maobaadi-maya* in order to make it easier to take control of the state.

Over the last three years, there has been intense discussion between the Maoists and the leaders of the democrat-politicians and parties involved in the earlier peace negotiations to find a formula for integration-rehabilitation. Dialogue has also taken place under the aegis of the Special Committee on Supervision, Integration and Rehabilitation of Maoist Combatants, which is made up of representatives of the main parties, including Madhesi parties, and supported by a technical committee. A peace formula is within reach if the Maoist leadership agrees to hand over command of the 28 cantonments to the Special

Committee and specify the number of ex-fighters to be integrated into the security forces.

For a long time, as long as the decision could be postponed, the Maoist leadership seemed willing to specify a number for integration. In fact, Chairman Dahal actually talked numbers with the late Girija Prasad Koirala and Indian Prime Minister Man Mohan Singh when on a visit to India as prime minister in September in 2008. Against the backdrop of Dahal's having conceded to the negotiators during the peace talks in 2006 that the number of fighters hovered around 6000 (he said in the Shaktikhor videotape that it had been between 7000 and 8000 at the end of the conflict), the other parties acted magnanimously in offering to integrate between 3000 and 5000 ex-combatants. Some suggested a one-gun-one-combatant count, which would have seen the integration of just under 3500 ex-combatants. Thus, even when Chairman Dahal in conversation with Prime Minister Madhav Kumar Nepal in February 2011 had more or less agreed to the number of 6000, he was unable to pull it off because of resistance from within his party. By raising the expectation of full integration, especially after the 2008 elections, the Maoist leadership painted itself into a corner vis-à-vis the cadre. There is another view, that the leaders exaggerated the possibility of resistance from the ranks as an excuse because it had no intention of becoming a 'civilian party'. However, there is no doubt that the cadre in the cantonments would have gone along if the top three leaders – Dahal, Bhattarai and Vaidya – had agreed on an integration figure that the other parties could have accepted.

In early 2011, resolving the cantonment management issue is most crucial for a) ensuring a successful end to the five-year peace process, and b) writing a democratic constitution. Culpability for the delay lies mostly with the Maoist leadership; it is they who must agree on an acceptable number for integration and they who must allow the cantonments to be managed by the Special Committee. This step will take the ex-combatants out of the direct command of the Maoists, something that was agreed on paper and even declared by Chairman Dahal when he was prime minister. Unfortunately, the longer it takes for the leaders to come to an acceptable compromise formula (in what seems to be, essentially, a war of nerves between the so-called radicals and the so-called pragmatists within the Maoist party), the more likely it is that the process will stall. An impasse would be reached if the other parties and the international community came to the conclusion that the UCPN (Maoist) had no intention of proceeding with the peace process. Geopolitically, the growing battle between the Indian Maoists and the Indian state willy-nilly impacts the Nepali peace process even though the process should be seen as independent of the dynamics in the Indian polity. A nervous New Delhi is sure to use its international clout and influence within Nepal to push against any integration that is more than a token gesture. On this issue, there would be a meeting of minds with the non-Maoist politicians of Nepal.

The Maoist side suggests that there be special provisions made for the lateral entry of Maoist fighters and officers into the Nepal Army, and its negotiators have spoken of 'bridging courses' for the ex-combatants and so on. In March 2011, the Nepal Army came out with a paper in which it refused to countenance group entry of Maoists but showed some flexibility in terms of applying its long-standing standards of age, fitness and education of possible recruits from within the ex-combatant ranks. But the Maoist leaders have long insisted that they will not join the army through the standard norms of recruitment, though in the accord they signed they agree to those norms. Their stance seems to reflect a willing diminution of the Maoist fighters by the leadership and at the same time a desire to weaken the national army. The Comprehensive Peace Accord does not specifically speak of integration into the national army, but the other parties have been willing to honour the gentleman's agreement that there will be some integration.

When pro-Maoist commentators suggest that the concessions made by the parliamentary parties are inadequate, they forget that the peace deal already lays out the road map for integration and rehabilitation. They forget that getting a state army to agree to the idea of integrating the fighters of a former enemy is already a great concession, one that speaks volumes about the Nepali peace process. The UCPN (Maoist) leaders have to consider the danger that further prevarication may lead to the collapse of the peace process and the evaporation of the integration and rehabilitation formula altogether. The leaders must lift the barriers if they wish to see at least some integration into the security forces. On a larger plane, agreement and action on integration-rehabilitation would unravel many knots in national politics, including the possibility of a national unity government and movement forward in the writing of a democratic constitution.

Military democratisation

The term 'democratisation' of the Nepal Army appears in the Comprehensive Peace Accord. It was coined with reference to the long-time back-up the erstwhile Royal Nepalese Army had provided to the autocratic monarchy and also to serve as a balance to the need for Maoist demobilisation in the post-conflict period. The job of any army is to protect national sovereignty as well as to maintain internal stability in extreme circumstances, not itself to function 'democratically' in the general meaning of the term. The democratisation of Nepal's national army means that the force should be under civilian rule and professional, non-political, and honest. It should also be inclusive and represent the national demography through a process of voluntary recruitment. The critical need was for the national army to be brought under the control of the elected government and this goal has most definitely been met. An army that used to function largely under the dictates of the royal palace, even under the constitutional monarchy of 1990-2002, was brought within the control of the civilian government after the 2008 elections to such an extent that the former rebel commander, Ram Bahadur Thapa, was made the defence minister in the Maoist-led government. The Nepal Army has no master now other than the civilian politicians.

Downsizing the Nepal Army is a vital matter which must be addressed once the peace process is complete. This step can be considered part of the 'democratisation' agenda. However, downsizing cannot logically proceed until the Maoist combatant force has been demobilised according to the peace formula and there is a modicum of political stability in the land. The army is the tool of last resort for law and order at a time when the police forces are extra-susceptible to politicisation, including that brought about by the Maoists in government. The plan for federalism has brought a new dimension to the matter of security sector reform, and any tinkering with the army must wait till the shape and line of authority of the civilian police and armed police are sorted out. Given the possible emergence and proliferation of provincial warlords, violent renegades, and armed radicals, it is important to professionalise the military even while strengthening civilian control over it.

Once the state restructuring exercise has brought stability and the peace process is completed, it will be important to consider reducing the size of the Nepal Army from its present strength of 96,000 soldiers. A step-by-step schedule to halve the force size would be logical, given that the country now has the Armed Police Force to tackle extreme domestic events. At that time, we should even be able to debate whether Nepal should have a military at all. The need to maintain a large national army at considerable expense could be questioned, especially when the Armed Police Force has been established precisely to respond to in-country disturbances. For the present, however, downsizing the Nepal Army cannot be linked to the matter of Maoist ex-combatant demobilisation, which the UCPN (Maoist) had an obligation to conclude before the end of 2008 without preconditions.

The Nepal Army, right and wrong
The Nepal Army deserves credit for having stayed within the bounds of the Comprehensive Peace Accord even as the country went through great transitions, including the inclusion of the Maoists in government, the transition to a republic and so on. The military submitted to being confined to barracks under various strictures and did not react when the Maoists presented themselves as having won the 'people's war'. It is to the credit of the military leadership that it did not allow the frustration among the cadre to boil over amidst that humiliation. After all, many soldiers died battling the Maoists under the directive of the constitutional, democratic government, but their sacrifice has hardly received any national recognition in the long years since 2006.

The credit due to the army brass for forbearance, however, does not mean that the democrat-politicians and civil society can lower their guard. In all societies, the military needs constant watch-dogging for wayward ambition, and given the recent memories of impunity among the officer class the need for vigilance is even greater in Nepal. While the generals like to say that their force has always been non-political and that they have followed the orders of the government of the day, whether democratic or autocratic, the bias was towards the latter. Already, in the few years since 2006, the Nepal Army has started taking undue advantage of the fear of Maoists among the other parties to flex its muscles and publicly snub civilian authority. To cite one egregious example, the Nepal Army has blatantly refused to abide by a Supreme Court directive that an officer sought for questioning with regard to the killing of Maina Sunar at the Panchkhal barracks during the conflict be produced before the Kavre district court. The government of Madhav Kumar Nepal saw fit to remain silent about that episode, and the weakness of the human rights community became apparent when it was unable to raise public awareness and pressure on the matter.

The continued inability of the government to hold accountable Nepal Army soldiers accused of excesses during the conflict will make it impossible to demand the prosecution of those Maoists who are similarly accused. Indeed, its ineffectiveness will kill the entire process of justice sought for the sake of the victims and society. The standard army officers' complaint against human rights defenders during and after the conflict is that the Maoists are being treated with kid gloves while the military is targeted; this complaint shows the willingness of the national army to be judged on the same plane as rebels who reject the constitution and the rule of law.

Before the Maoist conflict emerged, the national army's major deployments were long-ago imperial wars and some skirmishes with the Chinese-Tibetan army a century and a half ago. The most recent operation was the action launched against the Tibetan Khampa rebels in the early 1970s to stop their incursions north of the border. In the modern era, the army remained an in-country ceremonial force concentrated on international peacekeeping work for the United Nations. Even long after the 'people's war' started in 1996, the Royal Nepal Army was kept out of the battle while the untrained, inadequately armed, and poorly-led civil police force was asked to take on the insurgents. When the army had no choice but to deploy after the Maoists attacked its barracks in Dang in November 2001, the soldiers found they had some very quick learning to do, and in the process, the army reacted to Maoist brutality with its own excesses. The military's greater firepower meant that the soldiers killed and wounded many more combatants and civilians than the rebels did. There were terrible instances of atrocities, such as the massacre of unarmed Maoist cadre in Doramba, Ramechhap District, the killings of innocent peasantry in Bardiya District, and the disappearance of dozens of Maoist activists from the Bhairabnath battalion in downtown Kathmandu. Lacking the skills to fight a guerrilla force and stymied by a subdued populace unwilling to provide information and intelligence, the army was unable to show great prowess in fighting and, as if to compensate, resorted to an extraordinary scale of human rights abuses. As the slow wheels of transitional justice begin to turn, it is important to try to locate command responsibility in relation to the army's excesses: how much of it rested in the army headquarters in

Bhadrakali and how much in the Narayanhiti royal palace during the times of Gyanendra?

To its credit, with the support of the Nepal Police and the Armed Police Force, the army did not lose command over territory even as it suffered great losses. Though they were taken by surprise and showing clear lack of military savvy at the outset, the soldiers learned at least to defend themselves even if they could not conduct proactive operations. Their ability to hold remote outposts with nothing more than occasional helicopter support was crucial, for it led the Maoist commanders to conclude that they would never win the 'people's war'. Ironically, the soldiers were unable to take credit for their slow but steady pushing back of the Maoists because King Gyanendra chose to use the army for his putsch against civilian parties in February 2005. After this coup, when the Maoist suggestion that the 'people's war' had been started against the king and 'his' army gained ground, the army's role in the conflict – as well as the contribution and sacrifice of individual soldiers – was erased from public imagination. The democratic forces which began fighting Gyanendra's creeping autocracy in 2002 and then his full-fledged coup of 2005 saw the army as the tool of the royal palace, which had used the excuse of the insurgency to entrench itself in power.

Because the army's reputation was sullied by its links with the royal palace, the heroics of the soldiers in the conflict were forgotten. Similarly, the restraint showed by soldiers in the penultimate moments of the People's Movement and the role of the army generals in forcing Gyanendra to bow down before the People's Movement have gone unremarked. As scholars begin to study conflict-era Nepal with the advantage of time and the populism that leads much analysis astray at this juncture has weakened, a true picture of that period will emerge. What the Nepal Army commanders do to win back the public's trust and confidence will depend on their willingness to abide by the principles of civilian supremacy and to allow the prosecution of Nepal Army personnel accused of abuse and excess.

13

Uncivil Mission

Expectations of UNMIN
At the very outset, we must distinguish between the United Nations as a whole and the United Nations Mission in Nepal (UNMIN). The UN has been in Nepal working on development projects since the advent of the modern era in 1950-51, while UNMIN was a new kind of UN presence in the area of peace-building. Many UN agencies, including UNDP, FAO, WFP, WHO, UNICEF, UNESCO and UNIFEM (now UN Women) have supported the country's attempt at modernisation over the decades; their efforts generated considerable recognition of and goodwill towards the world organisation among the public.

The deployment of UNMIN was seen by Nepali actors as necessary for the peace process mainly to keep former enemy forces separate and build the confidence of the Maoist leadership. Nepali democrat-politicians and civil society stalwarts successfully established UNMIN in January 2007 over the strong initial reservations of India, which perceived the presence of a UN peace mission in Nepal with distaste because of the implications it had for its own internal conflicts. The deployment of UNMIN was important for the Maoist leaders because they could use its presence to assert the parity of their party with the state and to ease its cadre into the post-conflict era. The three-point mandate of the mission was to provide assistance during the Constituent Assembly elections, verify and register ex-combatants, and monitor the seven main and 21 satellite cantonments housing them. The latter job also required monitoring the rebel arms stored in containers. The army was also to be brought partially under the purview of UNMIN, both to provide the Maoists with a sense of equal status in the initial days and to keep the military out of mischief during the Constituent Assembly elections.

Unfortunately, UNMIN did little to serve the peace process of Nepal. In fact, it helped delay the process, and, ultimately, it had to leave ignominiously before a resolution was reached. Its leadership developed a technocratic, self-serving view of its mandate, one happy with a quick-and-easy, half-democratic peace. Its defined its mandate alternatively as restrictive or extensive, according to what served its interests or according to the accusations it faced. The main concern of the 'missionaries' was to avoid controversies with the UCPN (Maoist), whose tendency was to react with blind rage to the mildest criticism. The parliamentary parties of democrat-politicians, in contrast were soft targets. UNMIN's challenges to the Maoists when they got out of line were subdued and cautionary, whereas those made to opponents of the Maoists were strident and critical.

While it is an understandable tendency to perceive above-ground insurgents as underdogs, only a grave misinterpretation of reality would see the Maoists as anything but the victors. After coming above ground, the UCPN (Maoist) secured the districts by fear-mongering and by capitalising on the disarray of the other parties after having spent years away from the villages. At the level of the state, they were part of the Nepali establishment: they had contested in an election and done well. However, UNMIN continued to perceive the Maoists as the underdog. It was them as a party representing the transformation agenda, and the other parties as representing the old-world status quo. The mission leadership failed to challenge the Maoists adequately even though they constantly shifted the goalposts of the peace process. Though otherwise very quick with press releases, UNMIN did not make public the need for the Maoist party to let go of its fighting force for the sake of peace and constitution-writing.

UNMIN's acts and omissions on the ground and how it nuanced its periodic reports to the Security Council generally provided cover and justification for Maoist prevarications. The mission identified somewhat more than 19,000 Maoists as former combatants though it was clear that the actual numbers were considerably less than half that. Maoist Chairman Dahal himself, in the Shaktikhor videotape, claimed gleefully that the mission had been taken for a ride. He revealed that the real number had been no more than seven or eight thousand fighters at the close of the conflict. When there were killings and torture within cantonments or when the cantonment residents exited with their

UNMIN-registered guns in hand, the mission was silent. In one case in Kapilvastu District, UNMIN staff intervened when the police apprehended ex-combatants outside the camps with UNMIN-registered guns, wresting the Maoists' guns from the police and handing them back to the ex-combatants. The mission's report to the Security Council presented its action as a heroic rescue of the peace process. In an excessively literal reading of its mandate, one which relentlessly steered clear of challenging the Maoist for flouting the letter and the spirit of the peace agreement, the mission failed to meet the expectations of the Nepali people. Ironically, much of the Western diplomatic community considered the mission's position to be fair and balanced.

As far as the April 2008 Constituent Assembly elections were concerned, UNMIN, with its 'international experience', should have warned the enthusiastic Nepali politician-democrats and civil society about the danger of holding an election when one party still has its own fighting force. To its lasting discredit, the UNMIN leadership did nothing of the sort. As for the elections, in retrospect one could say that they were hardly free and fair, marred by extensive intimidation and violence on the part of the Maoists. Despite its many monitors on the ground, the mission did not confirm this reality, at the time or afterwards. Together with others who have refused to acknowledge the rampant malfeasance during the polls, UNMIN, too, continued to regard it as a fine exercise in representational governance, and even representational constitution-making.

When challenged, UNMIN officers took refuge in its limited mandate, which accorded it no more than the power to 'supervise'. It also offered the defence of limited personnel. Given the great expectations from the peace process and the high hopes of the Nepali people, if the mission leadership had felt short-staffed it should have openly lobbied for more. Despite the excuses, overtly or covertly, the leadership spent much time trying to expand its mandate, seeking to play the role of a moderator in a process that was always in the hands of capable Nepali political interlocutors. UNMIN did injustice to the peace process by not demanding that Maoists immediately attend to their responsibility to disband the cantonments and by not challenging the actions of ex-rebels as much as it did those of the national army and the (non-Maoist) government. Actually, the mission did injustice to the UCPN (Maoist) itself, because injecting a sense of urgency into the peace process and publicly highlighting Maoist obligations could have helped nudge the latter towards integration and rehabilitation, steps which would also have aided the party's democratisation. UNMIN's laxity has meant that the Maoists have remained a party that spouts radicalism.

The fundamental problem with UNMIN was that, based on its misreading of Nepali history and society and its misinterpretation of what the 'people's war' had meant, it saw a parity between the Maoist ex-combatant force and the national army. What had been suggested as a make-believe equivalence to help the Maoist leaders with their cadre was read by the Special Representative of the Secretary General who led the mission as genuine parity, which is why the leadership, in its public information material ill-advisedly referred to the Maoist combatant force as an 'army'. UNMIN failed to consider that the national army ought not to be sequestered indefinitely, especially during a dangerous time of transition with many elements which could rapidly turn radical. The expectation of the signatories of the Comprehensive Peace Accord was that the Maoist cantonments would be disbanded in the six months after the Constituent Assembly elections, during which time the army would be confined to barracks. This confinement was thought appropriate because of the possibility of conflict with the Maoist force and because the military command could have created trouble for the fledgling republic or influenced the polling. In reality, the absence of the army from election duty proved a bonanza for the UCPN (Maoist). The fact that the Maoists had failed to move towards disbanding the cantonments, an issue of critical interest to the host population, never became a central one for UNMIN. It fact, it never even found emphasis in the reports to the Security Council. In its interpretation of the peace accord as well as its mandate, UNMIN's leadership continued to wear blinders, failing to recognise the adoption of the Interim Constitution, the holding of elections, and Maoist non-compliance, right up to the very day it departed in January 2011. The mission's narrow reading of its mandate robbed the peace process of life and soul.

UNMIN's top brass seemed to believe that the Maoists had emerged in the mid-1990s as a philosophically committed 'revolution' addressing societal injustice and marginalisation. One cannot discount the ambitions of those in the UMMIN leadership: notching up what looked like a success for the United Nations, even if short-lived, would be good for further assignments and career progression. UNMIN's attitude towards

Nepal's democratically-minded civil society and political parties was apparent in the words used by UN Under-Secretary General B. Lynn Pascoe, who, in a speech in Kathmandu that transgressed diplomatic etiquette and was clearly prepared by UNMIN staffers, termed criticism of UNMIN 'absurd' and 'boring'. A willingness to reflect on its weaknesses and mistakes was not one of UNMIN's strengths.

The ability of UNMIN to ignore the universal values of human rights, non-violence, pluralism and democracy in its day-to-day conduct should be a lesson for the planners at the UN Secretariat in New York. With UNMIN disbanded on 15 January 2011, the Department of Political Affairs under which it functioned will hopefully conduct a 'lessons-learnt' exercise. This exercise must be carried out independently, without the 'guidance' of the erstwhile, self-congratulatory UNMIN leadership in New York and in Kathmandu, whose past evaluations have shown a proclivity for self-serving argumentation. Hopefully, the evaluators will learn from the Nepal experience the need for mission staff to be more sceptical of populist discourse and to seek a deep understanding of the society in which they are deployed. Fortunately, given that the direction of the peace process was out of its hands – secure as it was in the hands of the Nepalis themselves – UNMIN could not do much damage, other than to give the UCPN (Maoist) a false sense of security which, unfortunately, extended the peace process and increased disquiet in the population.

Peace politics

UNMIN can be thanked for having helped create a space between the Maoist ex-combatants and the Nepal Army and for providing Maoists leaders with credibility vis-à-vis their cadre and fighters. It need not be thanked for having pampered the UCPN (Maoist) so much that the peace process was delayed and the party's own long-term interests were undermined. On the whole, it was better for UNMIN to have been deployed than not, but it could have done so much more with a more sensitive leadership. Even UN missions are human, after all, and the quality of personnel deputed and their ability to empathise with the local society matter.

By its own failings, UNMIN became a player on the sidelines of the Nepali peace process. By showing its bias towards the UCPN (Maoists), perhaps even inadvertently, the UNMIN hierarchy in Kathmandu and its handlers at the UN Secretariat in New York took it out of the semi-political realm where it might have actually played an effective role as a peace facilitator. A proper interpretation of its mandate would have allowed for this evolution, but UNMIN's evident partiality for the Maoists destroyed trust for it among the parliamentary parties. UNMIN reduced itself to a loud and ineffective entity, whose self-congratulatory reports to the Security Council consistently misrepresented the positioning and desire for peace among the parliamentary parties. The overall impression UNMIN left behind was of an entity that strutted across the stage in its white SUVs fitted with bulky radio masts, collecting a veritable archive of information on a society in transition with its army of staff. The job of the staff went beyond peace-making to include socio-political and cultural matters, but UNMIN ended up doing next to nothing with the information it collected. Down the road, Nepal's government and civil society must demand access to this information and data, to be put to use for the sake of long-term peace and stability.

The peace process has, of course, continued after UNMIN's departure as there is little possibility that the UCPN (Maoist) will return to war. Even though the Maoists initially hesitated in handing over the management of the cantonments to the Special Committee, that actually happened soon after UNMIN's exit. At present, the worst-case scenario will be the disbandment of the cantonments without the integration and rehabilitation of the ex-combatants. Were that to happen, it will be ascribed mainly to the obduracy of the UCPN (Maoist) leaders, who are helping to create a mindset nationally, regionally and internationally that goes against their own interests.

UNMIN's almost wilful misreading of Nepal's peace politics extended to its last days, when it seemed incapable of linking Maoist prevarications with the collapse of the peace process. What was clearly a fundamental issue for democratically minded Nepalis – the Maoists' refusal to comply – was clearly not so for the mission leadership. UNMIN's reports to the Security Council continued to carry an edge of prejudice against the parliamentary parties, as when in late 2010 it proposed waiting for a 'duly elected government' to proceed with the peace process – as if the Madhav Kumar Nepal government was illegitimate. The Representative of the Secretary General, in her last report to the Council in January 2011, suggested that Nepal faces three dangers

– a Maoist revolt, an army coup or a Presidential takeover. The first was hardly insightful, as the UCPN (Maoists) publicly declared this at its November 2010 plenum, and the latter two were conjectures that could hardly be placed on the same plank.

UNMIN served a purpose, to be sure, and so its contribution to the peace need not be seen as unrequited failure. However, it is a distressing irony that it was UNMIN's departure that was actually required for the successful conclusion of the peace process. The Maoists leaders were manipulating and using UNMIN's leadership, and the mission's very presence, to prevaricate about the disbandment of the cantonments. UNMIN's leadership played along with the Maoists, mainly because of its perfunctory understanding of Nepali politics and its prejudice against the mainstream parties. The mission's romanticism with regard to the UCPN (Maoist) was so deep that it was blind to the mischief which was obvious to Nepali players. The Department of Political Affairs at the UN Secretariat, if it seeks more involvement in peace-building efforts in other parts of the world, will have to mull over why it was that by 2010 a good part of Nepal's civil society had come to believe that the mission's withdrawal was key to the success of the peace process. The lesson for the Department of Political Affairs seems to me to be to keep the ideals of pluralism close to heart, respect the fact that local desires for peace and democracy tend to be intertwined, seek to create a sustainable rather than a faux peace, look beneath the surface of the local political discourse, respect the host society, and guard against the unrestrained ambitions of personnel.

While the United Nations will doubtless conduct its own audit of the UNMIN experience, it would be useful for Nepal's civil society and political players to themselves conduct a review of the mission's record. This would be a learning exercise that would help in concluding the peace process and inform the transition towards political normalcy and a non-violent future.

14

Birds of Passage

The 'diplo-donor'
The insufficient understanding of the politics of their host country among diplomats and donors, particularly those from the West who want to be heard on the basis of their funding support, becomes obvious in times of political crisis. Whether it is King Gyanendra's rising autocracy, his inadequate initial concessions to the People's Movement, or the Maoists' 'people's war' and the ongoing peace process, there has always been a considerable time lapse in the understanding of the 'diplo-donor'. Their poor comprehension can be explained mostly by the fact that the political discourse is conducted in the vernacular and the literary corpus in English is hopelessly inadequate to describe the ever-changing panorama of our politics. The lack of institutional memory within individual embassies and donor missions also contributes. If there were institutional memory, foreign missions would feel forced to assume some responsibility for the continuous political, social and economic crises faced by the Nepali people.

More than has been the case in almost any other developing country, the development community has been part of the process of transformation in Nepal since the very beginning of our modern era in 1950-51. It has observed and been involved in our successes as well as our failures and wrong turns. While Nepal's problems are, of course, mainly the making of our own establishmentarian classes, there should be some sharing of the blame with the development community with regard to, for example, our failure to develop infrastructure, end marginalisation, build an inclusive society, revive agriculture, promote skill-building, improve government education, and eliminate caste exclusivity. After all, overseas experts have been assisting and advising the government on all these fronts for more than six decades. While Kathmandu's ruling classes and intelligentsia are primarily responsible for the non-participatory nature of development in the past, the endless political instability, and the neglect of ethnic and Madhesi aspirations, it is worth asking whether the development agencies and embassies which have been so quick with blame, prescriptions and check book today were sufficiently alert to the crises brewing in Nepal. Were the representatives and ambassadors of yesteryears alert to the Maoist insurgency or to the Madhes Movement before they occurred? If not, then some humility in the present day would be in order even as blame is heaped on the democrat-politicians and the bureaucrats.

The tendency among many expatriates in positions of influence is to follow the dictates of populist discourse. For decades, they willingly worked with the powerful centre under the Panchayat regime. Maoist populism rules at present, so, following the proclivity of Kathmandu's weak intelligentsia, the trend is to blame all ills on the democrat-politicians, the political class that came to power after the fall of the Panchayat in 1990. We are asked to believe that political time began in Nepal in 2046 BE, 1990 CE, and there is little consideration that the autocratic Panchayat decades are the source of most present-day societal ills, including the weakness of the intelligentsia. Diplomats and expatriate development experts, who are so vociferous about Nepal's current problems, tend to forget that their predecessors submitted silently to 30 years of autocratic rule which weakened society on every front. The legacy of these decades of support for the Panchayat regime, the willingness to be part of a regime that never allowed participatory, bottom-up development does not inspire confidence in those who preach high ideals without trying to understand how it was we got where we are. Perhaps the foreign representatives posted in Nepal in 2011 and afterwards will, as the populist tsunami subsides, be able to understand matters that their immediate predecessors were unable to, such as the fact that true participatory development was absent for three decades and more and only began with the advent of multiparty democracy in 1990. In fact, almost all the tools and processes of civil society, from free media to developmental activism, were developed after 1990 in the democratic era, the very period that the ill-informed regard as a failed interregnum.

Many present-day diplomats, earnest in their critique of the Nepali political class, set high thresholds in demanding the latter's commitment to the peace process. However, to look back just a few years, India and the Western foreign offices were initially arrayed against the parliamentary parties for talking to the underground Maoists. During the People's Movement of 2006, these embassies were in favour of the parliamentary politicians' accepting the first concessional speech of Gyanendra, which did not speak about the revival of the dissolved Parliament. In the name of the people, however, the democrat-politicians rejected the bad deal. We have subsequently seen many ambassadors – who have no inkling about even the basics of the People's Movement – trying to give lessons on peace-making to those very politicians who were involved in defining a peace process which is an example before a world so full of the 'war process'. It is not for donors to only take Nepal's Constituent Assembly members to South Africa and Guatemala on study tours but to bring groups here to appreciate what Nepal's indigenous peace process has to offer.

One would have hoped for a little forbearance among the expatriate community, a willingness to understand the monumental, simultaneous challenges facing Nepali society and the attempts by the political class to address them. Being mindful of the danger of falling into the pit of xenophobia, a failing in all societies, one does not deny the role of the expatriate community in providing advice, support, comparative information from other societies, and in watch-dogging. But it is not too much to ask for a sense of humility from the guest, to expect that he or she learn the reality of the host society rather than look at its players as one-dimensional caricatures. The diplomat and donor representative are but birds of passage over our hills and plains whereas the democrat-politicians are tied to this land and its future, which gives them – dare one say it – a deeper commitment to democracy and peace. The diplo-donor keen to show a success during his or her short tenure of three or four years, whether in transitional justice, the peace process or constitution writing, should not expect that Nepalis can somehow be persuaded to compromise on anything less than peace in a full democracy.

The representatives in Western embassies and bilateral and multilateral aid agencies perhaps understand that their inordinate power of the purse immediately puts them in a superior position vis-à-vis their Nepali interlocutors. Indeed, many national scholars, bureaucrats, non-governmental organisation administrators, activists and the co-workers of expatriates are programmed not to challenge the *a priori* convictions of the Westerner. And what are these convictions in terms of the peace politics of Nepal? An informal survey conducted by this writer in the spring and summer of 2010 of the opinions of Western diplomats and donor agency heads revealed, by and large, the following mistaken notions:

- The Maoists took up arms not against parliamentary democracy but against the royal regime in 1996.
- Nepal was not at all a democracy between 1990 and 2002.
- The Maoist insurgents not only represented the people as they say they did during the 'people's war', but by the end they held 80% of the national territory as a 'compact zone'.
- Those who challenge the Maoists about the peace process and democracy are merely acting out of resentment of their fair-and-square win in the Constituent Assembly elections.
- There is no reason why all 19,000-plus ex-combatants in the cantonments cannot be integrated into the national army.
- The Maoists are the true and only real champions of inclusion and social justice in Nepali politics, and the mainstream Nepali Congress and the CPN (UML) represent the status quo.
- Nepali politics functions entirely under the dictates of New Delhi, and issues related to power-sharing, the peace process and constitution-writing are all directed by Indian diplomats.

There is no doubt that all forces, national and international, must join the battle to deliver social justice to the long-suffering and marginalised citizens and communities of Nepal. However, many expatriates, including even anthropologists and political scientists, are guilty of a leap of faith when they profess to believe that an armed insurgency was the only recourse. A dual standard is being applied here, of course: the expatriates prescribe for Nepal a political model they would never propose for their own societies. Nepal is hardly the place for experimentation in ideas not appropriate for other, 'more advanced' countries.

One European representative to Nepal believes that the strings of present-day political society are being pulled by the Ranas and Shahs, indicating the gullibility of someone who has been fed a line that became passé two decades ago. Likewise, many diplomats fall for the ruse of Maoist leaders who present themselves as social democrats. When one starts with a faulty understanding of Nepal's polity, it is easy to believe such falsehoods and to spout specious arguments such as declaring that the infamous Shaktikhor videotape highlighting Chairman Dahal's betrayal of the peace process be seen 'in context' or that the voice on the Maharagate vote-buying scandal audiotape was not really that of Krishna Bahadur Mahara or that Chairman Dahal never did propose the reinstatement of a 'cultural king' to the royalist right. The above are actually the views of the head of one bilateral development agency in Kathmandu, the type that rolls his or her eyes when a Nepali interlocutor earnestly speaks for peace and democracy.

Naiveté is at such a pitch that many diplomats profess to see a right-wing swing among the very politicians who are insisting on going through with the letter and spirit of the peace agreements. The Maoists' labelling of all who oppose them as 'rightist' has many ambassadors and donor agency heads truly believing that these individuals are indeed rightists, even the Marxist leaders of CPN (UML), the social-democrats of the Nepali Congress, and the civil rights activists who helped bring down Gyanendra's autocracy. How mistaken they are: within the Maoist party itself, anyone who is opposed to the radical flank is a rightist, but it does not do to pick up the Maoist usage and apply it to the larger political spectrum. Foreign representatives perhaps need to understand that the Nepali language is still struggling to catch up with the semantics of democracy and that translations of current usage do not necessarily convey the correct picture. There is no term in the local political parlance for 'populism' or 'demagoguery'. *Udaar loktantra* itself is a late construction for 'liberal democracy'. The dangers of faulty translation of imported terminology can have grievous implications, as when 'reconciliation' in the proposed Truth and Reconciliation Commission is translated as *melmilap* (friendship). One translator's mistake left the political class of Nepal with the impression that transitional justice is only about forgive-and-forget.

Demagoguery and empathy

Expatriate representatives are stuck not only because of the dearth of institutional memory within agencies and embassies, but also because there is so little competent writing available in English to guide them towards an understanding of Nepal. Because political discussion is not in English, donors and diplomats have to rely on translated news reports and analyses, through which it is difficult to follow the effervescence or complexity or nuances. In the absence of access to politicians and political literature other than consultant reports that they themselves funded, donors and diplomats try to extrapolate from what they know of other societies. This is why so many believe that poverty was the exclusive cause of the Maoist insurgency and that the dozen years of democracy between 1990 and 2002 was a disastrous interlude. Many representatives fall into the trap of perceiving the Maoists as revolutionaries who took the wrong path, that of political violence, but whose goals of social justice absolve them of much of that failing.

The weakness of the Kathmandu intelligentsia and the inadequacy of its output in English, as well as lionisation by the 'imperial progressives' of India induces diplomats and donors to read more into the Maoist commitment to social justice than is real and to gravely underestimate the values and strength of the mainstream political class. They develop a jaundiced view of the rapidly transforming social landscape, mistakenly believing that there is deep social conservatism among democrat-politicians, whereas, in fact, the socio-political flexibility of this category is the marvel of the Nepali polity and peace process. There is a desperate need in Nepal to eradicate social inequality and to maintain an independent, high standard for what we seek, but those who would critique our political players must reflect on the matter of double standards, both in terms of understanding how their own societies transformed as well as prescribing something for Nepal which they would not support in their own societies. They must give due credit to Nepali democrat-politicians for having adhered closely to their social-democratic values and embraced rapid social transformation.

One reason Western representatives in particular seem to overestimate the Maoists and underestimate the disquiet in the polity among their political opponents and the people themselves is that they have not had the experience of living under a harsh radical left or right regime like Eastern Europe or parts of Asia, Africa and Latin America. They are simply not groomed to detect demagoguery. Another reason is that the diplo-donors take their cue from the Kathmandu intelligentsia, such as it is, which has shown a singular lack of spine in countenancing Maobaadi actions during the 'people's war' and thereafter. Maoist leaders, who see influential and educated members of civil society bending over backwards to see things their way, no doubt regard them as useful idiots. Some members of the expatriate brigade are surely perceived likewise by the Maoists. The only difference is that the donor or diplomat will not be around to be held accountable for socio-political stances that affect the lives and livelihoods of the Nepali people; the intelligentsia will.

Peace-building guide
The foreign media comes to Nepal only in the event of a major crisis, so there is a lack of continuous news coverage. Lay persons interested in Nepal as travelers and tourists are scared off by the travel advisories of their respective foreign offices. The fact that regular news outlets do not cover Nepal with any consistency or depth could be read as a sign that Nepal is not geopolitically significant enough to merit attention or that the political problems here pale in comparison with those in other global hot spots. After all, we have no oil, no Al-Qaeda, and are not located in the Middle East. Those who seek to understand Nepal, particularly overseas academics as well as the headquarters and staff of donor agencies, foreign ministries, and the embassies in Kathmandu and New Delhi, have tended to set their opinions on the basis of UNMIN's regular reports to the Security Council and the output of the International Crisis Group (ICG). As mentioned, UNMIN's reports are replete with selective and self-serving readings of the situation in Nepal that consistently gave the Security Council members and the larger international community a decidedly false picture of the peace process and politics. In UNMIN's acts and omissions political scientists have a treasure trove of ideas about how not to conduct a UN mission. Unfortunately, its reports were influential among Western diplomats resident in Kathmandu, those in Western embassies in New Delhi, and at the UN headquarters in New York City. Even more than the UNMIN reports, however, it was the ICG's prescriptive reports which defined Nepal's peace process and transforming polity to the world beyond the Subcontinent.

The main fault of the ICG reports lies in their blatant contempt for Nepal's parliamentary parties and the democrat-politicians, which itself stems from its foundational belief that the Maoist movement represented a societal need and a lack of sensitivity to the democratic experience of the people. This bias was evident, for example, in the ICG's presentation of the Constituent Assembly elections as free and fair and its unwillingness to reconsider its own first-off reportage as the reality of malfeasance became clear. The ICG, like UNMIN, tended to let the Maoists off the hook when they cheated on the peace process. Of course, there are great weaknesses in the political process in Nepal and its tardiness in tackling social marginalisation has been criminal, but to think that the answer is anything other than making classical, multiparty, plural democracy work is to foist upon Nepal a romantic reading of a revolution that would never be accepted by other societies. The ICG had the hubris to provide bullet-point prescriptions for Nepal's evolution into an inclusive, democratic society though it didn't even understand that the Maoists are most emphatically not progressives, not when they hold guns in their hands, practice demagoguery, and lie through their teeth. Published simultaneously in English and Nepali, the ICG's reports are sleek and sophisticated, but there is no sense of humility in an organisation that charges in from across the seven seas to hand down instruction from the pulpit. Not very subtle bias infuses its reports, which, sadly, have been eagerly digested by many diplomatic and donor missions as the authoritative guide to post-2006 peace-building in Nepal.

The writers and editors of both the UNMIN and the ICG reports failed to look at Nepal as the average Nepali citizen does. These outsiders did not recognise the fundamental desire of the people they judged: to bequeath to their children a safe, peaceful, democratic society in which the provision of fundamental freedoms ensures social justice for individuals and communities. There is no sense of accountability among the report writers and the issuing organisations, which use up funds from donor accounts earmarked to help the people of Nepal. These reports, which have inflicted such damage on the Nepali peace process, are not subjected to peer review and English-savvy Nepali interlocutors themselves have been reluctant to mount a challenge because they, too, have a hand in the till. Enmeshed as they are in a web of inter-relationships with donor agencies, which includes social networking, international travel and lucrative consultancies, they naturally have zero incentive to be critical. If conflict resolution was the industry which sucked up foreign assistance meant for Nepal's development over the years of insurgency, after the signing of the peace agreement the funding has been lavished on peace-building, transitional justice and constitution-writing – with little result. As can be expected, the same lack of commitment that defines the ICG and UNMIN reports also characterises the attitude of the Kathmandu intelligentsia: consultancies and seminars and workshops have replaced activism. 'Disbursement' is the one-word mantra that guides donor agencies, and both the old and the new elites of Kathmandu are happy to be at the receiving end of their largesse.

As is the case with UNMIN reports, there is a need to audit ICG output so that the future publications of this organisation, which has the ability to delay or derail a peace process, are more circumspect. Researchers, authors and editors must come out of the shadows of anonymity and be willing to be challenged – or applauded – as the case may be. There is a great deal of useful information in the ICG reports, certainly, but the underlying seam of prejudice must be questioned, not just for the sake of the repute of the Nepali polity, but for the organisation's headquarters in Brussels to learn from five years of misrepresentation. There must be accountability among those who profess expertise in peace, democracy, inclusion and the rule of law.

15

The Imperial Progressives

Designer glasses on Nepal

There is a category of scholar and journalist, many of whom are based in New Delhi, who maintain a passing interest in Nepal, an interest which they see as giving them the authority to have the last word with regard to the 'people's war' and the peace process. These individuals represent the attitude, inherited, perhaps, from the long-departed British colonialists, that the advantage of placement in a powerful capital gives one the right to speak about other societies without doing one's homework. The analyses that emerge from this imperial arrogance and the associated dearth of knowledge about and empathy for ground-level Nepal have tended to romance the Maoist 'revolution' and scorn the parliamentary parties. The imperial 'progressive' is keen to have his radical leftist experiment tried out beyond his city and province; indeed, he would protest mightily if it were carried out in his own backyard. These individuals, who simply have not grown up, wish their jejune fantasies to be justified by the insurgents of Nepal.

In the immediate context, the imperial progressives are those journalists and academics who argue on behalf of the Nepali Maoists but live in affluent New Delhi neighbourhoods, divorced from the devastation wrought by the insurgency on the Nepali economy and a society of 29 million. Supporting the Maoists cannot be seen as a benign activity, as backing the parliamentary parties would be, because it implies accepting that it was necessary to use violence in politics. Do such dilettantes have the necessary understanding of the anthropology, sociology, history and economy of Nepal to be able to reach that conclusion? Do they not need to be responsible in their taking of a position on a neighbouring society which has the potential to skew its peace process and harm its people?

A true progressive scholar or activist living in, say, Defence Colony in South Delhi, who defends Maoist activism in Nepal must be willing to stand for the right of Indian Naxals to organise an armed insurgency in the shantytowns around the Indian capital itself. Only a member of the New Delhi intelligentsia who is willing to stand up and support rebellion in his own housing colony has the right to pass judgement on Nepali peace process and defend the Nepali Maoist agenda. If he is reluctant to do so, it is better he not try to foist on us experimental ideas which can do long-term damage to millions of our poor. We have already trailed behind for too long and the insurgency merely deepened the ruts in a historical trail of misery and migration.

The intelligentsia's take
Of course, I have no right to demand accountability from international observers, including the venerables of New Delhi's media and academia, if I fail to highlight the weaknesses of the Kathmandu's intelligentsia. The latter's response to the Maoists' rise has been abject, and, in that sense, the privileged Kathmandu intellectuals and civil society stalwarts who supported the 'revolution' as long as it remained outside the Valley rim can also be termed 'imperial progressives'. Those who equivocated cannot be thought highly of either. Nepali scholars, activists and civil society members, particularly those with access to English education, did not live up to their responsibilities in how they responded to and presented the evolution of the Maoist movement.

In a society suffering from a dearth of scholars and intellectuals with 'modern' education to begin with, those few who do have the knowledge and facility to speak out descended to obfuscation or outright silence. To begin with, they did not challenge the birth of the Maoist 'revolution' in the mid-1990s, limiting themselves to the simplistic suggestion that 'poverty led to the revolution', and ignoring the complex sociology of that 'revolution'. The peace process has been similarly weakened by opinion-makers, who failed to insist that the UCPN (Maoist) stand by its promise to be true to democracy and abandon its fighting force according to the Comprehensive Peace Accord, which, in recognition of its value and authority, has been annexed to the Interim Constitution. There should be no doubt that the primary responsibility for the misreading of Nepal's politics and peace process by the world rests not on foreign shoulders but on those of Kathmandu's own intellectual class. It is the weakness of this class that allowed UNMIN and ICG report writers as well as New Delhi's imperial progressives the leeway to emphatically define the Nepali peace process according to their own preferences.

The weakness of Kathmandu's educated classes in countenancing the Maoists has a history, of course. Many colonised societies saw the growth of a middle-class intelligentsia capable of rising to the responsibilities of civil society in democracy once independence was achieved. When Nepal threw off the Rana autocracy in 1951, however, there was no urban middle class to speak of, which meant that the intelligentsia and civil society were correspondingly weak. The historical Kathmandu-centrism of elite society had ensured that those outside the Valley were marginalised and excluded from the discourse, a fact that helped develop the insularity of the Nepali 'imperial progressives'.

The first decade after 1950 under a nominally multiparty system and the three decades of the non-party Panchayat era after that saw the state and society concentrate on producing professionals (engineers and doctors, mainly) under the aegis of a development assistance programme known as the Colombo Plan. Thus, there was a mass diversion into the 'hard' sciences of middle-class youth who may otherwise have evolved as activists, journalists, social scientists, historians, lawyers or bureaucrats. Because of the absence of anything resembling a liberal arts education in the newly established colleges of Nepal, even those aspiring to achieve a higher level of critical thinking had little opportunity to learn to do so. The top-down nature of the undemocratic Panchayat-era society encouraged a power-venerating, non-questioning culture among the middle class, which held Nepal back in the modern era. After the Panchayat system collapsed in 1990, the open society saw a rapid advance in private education but mostly in lucrative areas of instruction such as information technology, medicine and engineering. The relatively easy availability of visas to the West led to an exodus of the very category of Nepalis – educated young adults – most needed to build an intellectual base for society.

Unfortunately, the subservience to authority developed during the Panchayat autocracy is still part of the socialisation of today's decision- and opinion-making generation in government, academia, the media and even civil society. This subservience to raw power explains at least part of the flexibility shown towards the Maoists and their 'revolution' by civil society stalwarts. Moreover, the intelligentsia has also been weakened in its ability to speak truth to power – or to populism – by the flood of foreign funding for everything from conflict study to transitional justice, peace-building to constitution-making. Such 'assistance' has lately converted even Nepal's few studious sociologists and political scientists into timid consultants and salaried advisors. Many scholars and heads of international and national non-governmental organisations have so lost their intellectual moorings that they ascribe to the Maoist party the social awareness and advance which their own writings and own organisations helped usher in with such momentum after 1990.

A remarkable aspect of Kathmandu's learned class is its appetite for conspiracy-seeking, which is the refuge of anti-intellectualism. The search for conspiracy as a way to explain events is also reflected in the willingness of this class to run away from taking the unpopular stands that they, as presumed public intellectuals, should. We see again and again the inability of commentators to stand up and speak inconvenient truths, to allow conspiracy to take the place of analysis. This happened in the intelligentsia's willingness to label the death of CPN (UML) leader Madan Bhandari an assassination rather than what it really was, the result of a tragic car accident. Similarly, the educated urbanites refused to stand up to the rumours that erupted about the royal palace massacre of 2001, instead taking the easy path of suggesting ominously (but not factually) that King Birendra's brother Gyanendra was complicit.

It was this weak-kneed intellectualism which made opinion-makers follow populist opinion rather than lead the discourse when the first bullet of the 'people's war' was fired back in February 1996. Since then and to this very day, professors and development experts have failed to challenge the Maoists' justifications for the 'people's war', and they have not questioned the notion of 'ethnic federalism' loudly enough to be heard. The more 'elite', privileged and English-savvy a person is, it turns out, the less likely he is to speak truth to populism. Members of this category of intelligentsia, if they regard themselves as opinion-builders of any calibre, as public intellectuals of any worth, should try answering the following three questions:

- Was the CPN (Maoist) right in going underground and starting the armed insurgency in 1996?
- Should the Maoists make a public declaration renouncing violence?

- Is it possible to write a constitution without demobilising the ex-combatants of the Maoist fighting force?

The reason for asking these three 'test questions' is because the intelligentsia has, by and large, been able to get away without taking a stand at critical junctures, even as they profess a holier-than-thou attitude towards the democrat-politicians, who tend to have the right answers for all three questions. Incidentally, it is not enough to have the right answers to the three questions; you have to be able to utter them in public – and not in a whisper.

16

Wonderful Liberal Democracy

A people's understanding
Nepali citizens do have experience of democracy and they do understand what it is all about. This point is not appreciated enough, and it is this under-appreciation that has led many of the powerful diplomats and donors to consider a less-than-democratic peace as appropriate for Nepal (if not for themselves) and to believe that the Maoists can be incorporated into the mainstream as they are, rather than as a transformed, democratic, civilian party. The story of pluralism in Nepal goes back to the early 1940s, when the first democratic stirrings began against the Rana oligarchy. This movement was led by sons of commoners who were inspired by the values of liberal democracy and the struggle for independence in the rest of the Subcontinent. It was a movement of the politically aware, a representative group of idealist revolutionaries representing hill castes and ethnicities as well as the people of the Tarai. Most of the activists had been schooled in India and had imbibed the spirit of the Subcontinental independence movement. They came together in exile to organise the Nepali Congress, which led the campaign to oust the Rana regime, as well to form the Communist Party of Nepal. The citizenry, thus, has seven decades of democratic experience and desire, a depth of appreciation not to make light of.

After the fall of the Ranas, the people suffered a period of political anarchy which had at its root a tussle for power between the democrats and the king – first Tribhuvan and then, upon his demise, the ambitious Mahendra. When the latter finally grudgingly allowed the first general elections to be held in 1959, the Nepali Congress won a comfortable majority and formed a government under Prime Minister B.P. Koirala. Seeing the country receding from his grasp, in 1960, Mahendra accused the Congress of bad governance and anti-nationalism and removed it from power in one fell swoop. Nepal's democratic progression was badly affected by this royal coup; in fact, we are still paying for it today. While Mahendra was dynamic as a ruler, his self-centred action steered Nepal off the self-correcting path of representative democracy and periodic elections. He seriously retarded the growth of the polity by pushing Nepal into three decades of rule under the partyless Panchayat system, a period during which democrats were reviled as *arastra tatwa*, literally 'anti-nationals', but with connotations of 'pro-Indian traitors'.

The attempts at development during the Panchayat period were constantly undone by the regime's need to disallow open politics; as a result, three decades that could have been spent constructing a democratic culture, bringing marginalised communities into an inclusive mainstream, developing local government, providing a platform for sustained economic growth, and ensuring the rise of a robust civil society to watchdog the political parties and ensure equity, was wasted. In each of the rare attempts by the regime to open up, which included a referendum held in 1980 presenting a choice between multiparty democracy and a 'suitably reformed Panchayat system' and attempts at decentralisation and educational reform, the royal palace always pulled back when the exercise began to succeed. Whenever the people began to take things into their own hands, the reforms were abandoned.

Despite 30 years of undemocratic Panchayat rule, the people never let go of the pluralist aspirations they developed in the 1940s. Even as Eastern Europe released itself from the grasp of the Soviet Union, the Panchayat regime lost its momentum and a people's movement gathered steam. In 1990, King Birendra readily gave up his hold on power, and, under a new constitution promulgated later that year in November, Nepal became a constitutional monarchy and a functioning multiparty democracy. The Constitution of 1990 confirmed that sovereignty lay in the people and guaranteed all fundamental freedoms. A boisterous democratic exercise began, but the weaknesses exhibited by the political parties soon revealed how different governance was from dissidence. The politicians clearly had a lot to learn, but their record was no worse than the records of parties in other societies with much longer democratic legacies.

Fast forward to 2006 and the second people's movement, which proved once again the strength of the lay public's democratic commitment: their conviction was strong enough to destroy the autocratic ambitions of Gyanendra. The reality of the first and second people's movements is an apt answer to those who ask whether the public of Nepal – the collective of individual citizens – understands democracy. Clearly it does. The fault lies with the educated classes, not the general public.

Dozen-year democracy
Many Kathmandu observers maintain that the democratic era, which ran from the 1990 People's Movement to the start of Gyanendra's royal activism in 2002, was a dreadful failure. This vociferously spouted position has influenced many within and outside the country to regard Nepal's democratic exercise as faulty. However, this understanding defies reality, because it was in those dozen years that democracy dug its roots into a society that, other than during 18 months in 1959 and 1960, had never experienced liberty. It was during those dozen years from 1990 to 2002, exactly half of which were disrupted by the Maoist insurgency, that the people learnt to challenge authority from the village level up. This was made clear when the centralisation of state power in Kathmandu Valley was challenged by elected representatives. For the first time, the districts got attention and power and representation became more than a token game in which feudal overlords appointed by the Kathmandu court maintained order and control. It was because of the free society that Nepal became after 1990 that assertions of ethnic identity built up steam, community forestry succeeded, local self-government was put in place, and genuine entrepreneurship began to take root in a business community long used to crony capitalism and contraband trade.

There were, of course, many problems with how the parties ruled during this democratic interregnum, including corruption, poor governance, administrative failings, the politicisation and misuse of the bureaucracy, in-party autocracy, excessive animosity among parties, and the mangling of the parliamentary process. But each of these flaws was in the process of being corrected as the polity gained experience. In 1990, Nepal did not have a substantive civil society of the type essential to keep watch on political parties and politicians and many of the flaws in the democratic exercise between 1990 and 2002 can be explained by the absence of such public oversight. It required a few years for the country to develop an active civil society, including independent media, groups of activists, trade unions and professional associations, forums of constitutional lawyers, and so on. Even without adequate oversight, however, advances were made. In short, the foundation of Nepal's democratic journey to progress was laid during those dozen years.

Analysts bent on diminishing the importance of those 12 years can be accused of having a selective memory: they point to the obvious faults, such as poor administration and corruption, and ignore advances in critical areas which benefited citizens: participatory development, local government, a free media, including FM radio, improved public health indicators, an increase in forest cover, and a spurt in production and employment in the early years before the insurgency spoilt it all. All of this was achieved despite the fact that the infant democracy was burdened, before it was even six years old, by the deadweight of the 'people's war'.

One characteristic of most Southasian societies is the demonisation of political parties by the urban middle class, which, in turn, forces the public as a whole to question its faith in pluralism. Nepal must not fall into this trap; the public must not lose its trust in the play of politics, which is not any more a 'dirty game' here than it is elsewhere. The goal obviously is to constantly improve on what we have achieved rather than to perpetuate the sort of mass cynicism that leads citizens toward technocracies or dictatorships.

During democracy's dozen years, journalists grew to understand their function better and human rights activists and civil society as a whole found their feet and their calling. This development helped introduce good governance. To take corruption as an example, though politicians went wayward in the beginning, the scourge was later tackled by the institutions of open society. It is true, for example, that, in the mid-1990s, many parliamentarians and high officials abused their privilege of being exempted from paying custom duties on vehicles, but once a free and inquisitive media broke the story of the infamous 'Pajero scandal', few dared to cheat the system in quite that manner ever again. By the end of the decade, as parties matured and their mutual animosities levelled off and as a better sensitised civil society raised the bar on behaviour, the numerous problems with the practice of politics were much more effectively controlled. By the late 1990s, the committee system had begun to gain traction in the Lower House of Parliament and the executive branch was increasingly being brought under parliamentary oversight.

This exercise in parliamentary politics and, indeed, the entire democratic era itself would have been far more successful had the Maoist insurgency not created such a colossal disruption. Relentlessly, the insurgency weakened the state and its representative institutions. Democratic governance was brought to its knees by a party that had gone underground in 1996 with the goal of destroying the parliamentary system itself in the name of 'proletarian revolution'. In large swathes of the country, development programmes were hindered and state services weakened to the point of defunctness. Amidst the chaos, the monarchy was able to develop its nefarious ambitions. In the end, King Gyanendra used the excuse of tackling the Maoists to start his soft coup in 2002 by appointing a series of hand-picked prime ministers. That step put an end to a dozen years of democracy and the people were now burdened not only with the public violence fostered by the rebels but with the autocracy of Gyanendra as well. The denial of their democratic aspirations became complete with his coup of February 2005

The cohabitation of the elite and the intelligentsia

The 1991 elections saw the rule of the people for the first time since the short interlude in 1959 and 1960, and parliamentary democracy brought to the high table popularly elected commoners instead of token representatives selected by the Kathmandu elite. Several categories of individuals have found it in their interest to tar the 12 democratic years as an era of ruin. Obviously, the UCPN (Maoist) would like everyone to believe so. Belittling democratic rule also served the interests of the king and the royalists, who lost the absolute power they had held during Panchayat period. Democracy was also less than welcome to the elites of Kathmandu Valley – the Bahun, Chhetri and Newar nobility – who lost their privileges as courtiers, yes-men or crony capitalists to rank outsiders. The web of Panchayat patronage, which had extended across social categories into the bureaucracy, judiciary, academia and even civil society, was broken. In fact, it was the regressive mindset of the Kathmandu intelligentsia which did more than any other group to debase the democratic inclinations of the people and the democrat-politicians who represented them.

In elite echelons, it turned out, the tenets of classical liberal democracy had been forgotten over the 30 years of Panchayat rule, and few came to the aid of pluralism when it was threatened. The weak academia parroted the mantra of 'failed democracy', quite unaware that it was playing into the hands of the very forces that wanted to wreck democracy, and journalists copied what scholars said and wrote. The weak commitment of the intelligentsia to democratic mores was seen again and again. For example, after the Constituent Assembly elections, they failed to declare that the successful conclusion of the peace process had to be a precondition to the writing of the new constitution and did not vociferously demand that the new constitution be 'democratic' (which it is not at all clear it will be given the distance the Maoists have to travel and the fact that they face a weak challenge from the democrat-politicians and others). With the powerful presence of the as-yet-undemocratic Maoists in the Constituent Assembly and opinion-makers and scholars inexplicably silent on key issues, there is a very real danger that the new constitution will be a regressive one a considerable step back from the commendably democratic Constitution of 1990.

Internationals in the time of democracy
Those innocents within the international community who have served in Kathmandu over the past decade did not realise that, by repeating the chant of 'failed democracy' with reference to the 1990-2002 period, they were serving the interests of the royalists, the unreformed gentry and even the rebels. In their desultory search, they thought perhaps a political Shangri La could be located in Nepal. This unrealistic, heightened expectation debilitated the political parties, and put them on the defensive.

The best example of this anti-parliamentary-party sentiment that has been fashionable for so long among Western diplomats and donor representatives can be seen in the high-decibel anti-corruption harangues that began in the mid-1990s. Few bothered, however, to ask how any such campaign could work without a simultaneous demand for effective party-financing mechanisms. The focus on eliminating corruption without making the necessary legal and constitutional arrangements for covering the running costs of political parties indicated a simplistic level of criticism very low on commitment. Politicians are pilloried all over the world, but pillory is best done by the local population, which has a long-term stake in the system, rather than by bird-of-passage visitors. For too long Nepal has served as a convenient place for international scholars, development-wallahs and diplomats to vent against politicians. Our democrat-politicians should learn to respond and react when they are used as a punching bag by expatriates taking out their accumulated frustrations during their Nepali sojourn.

A genuine, committed study of corruption is even more important today, when the absence of periodic elections at the national, district and village levels has led to the rise of 'all-party mechanisms' that have dirtied the hands of politicians and party workers right from the grand halls of Singha Durbar to the village trails in the hinterland. The fact that neither Kathmandu opinion-makers nor the donor community seems to be in the excessively moved by this disaster which has visited governance from top to bottom indicates a low level of accountability to the people of Nepal.

17

Age of the Politician

Youth and political practice
A mantra has penetrated the media and academia lately – the insistence that young politicians *ipso facto* represent cleaner, more competent politics than old ones do. I choose not to utter such nonsense because there is little evidence that Nepal's current youthful leaders at the national level hold any more elevated values than their elders do. Individual politicians, whether young or old, must be judged against their words and deeds in support of peace and competitive politics and their courage in the face of violent opponents and populist politics. Given the knots that entangle national politics as the peace process hangs in limbo and governance takes a beating, it is perhaps natural for the public at large to be disenchanted with politicians. However, opinion-makers and civil society members do not do anyone any favours by seeking out potential leaders on the basis of their birth dates.

One would hope, of course, that young stalwarts are deeply committed to peace and democracy, but the evidence is lacking among the youth leaders that have come to the forefront. Under the circumstances, I, on the public's behalf, place my bet on those politicians in their forties and above, who have fought long and hard for democracy going back to the Panchayat era, rather than on untested youngsters in their twenties and thirties. Nepal's young leaders have tended to emerge from the youth wings of the various political parties, the mark of their success being the ability to disrupt classes in college. By and large, they made it into the limelight by courting the media in the 1990s and, thereafter, acting as the aggressive front of their respective parties. It is interesting that most youth leaders who have secured national recognition did not challenge Maoist violence when the rebels were conducting their underground insurgency. Youth leaders these days seem more intent on attending workshops and seminars and ingratiating themselves with the donor representatives in Kathmandu than walking the trails, building political networks and organising mass rallies. Many are willing to run down their own parties as a way to get media coverage; they do not seem to value the legacy and values of their very own organisations. Nor are most of the young politicos to be heard defending democratic values out of a deeply felt conviction. The front-rank 'elders', in contrast, at least had the privilege of being groomed by the first generation politicians of Nepal such as B.P. Koirala and have the experience of battling the Panchayat for decades, in jail and in exile. The younger lot may have had better schooling and some may have a stronger grounding in political theory (though that is not at all clear), but the mentors of these glamour boys and girls tend to be not party elders but donor representatives who take them hither and yon on study tours to South Africa, Switzerland, Norway and beyond.

Again and again, we hear Kathmandu opinion-makers, and even newly-arrived ambassadors and donor representatives, exhort Nepal's youth leaders to rise to the occasion and displace those long in the tooth from the forefront of party politics. They forget that the tirade against elderly politicians was essentially a way to target the octogenarian Girija Prasad Koirala in his last decade in power and that with his passing there remains no top leader in the main parties who could be termed 'elderly'. Practically every senior leader of the UCPN (Maoist), the CPN (UML) and the Madhes-based parties today is younger than 60. The Nepali Congress has a larger proportion of older leaders because it has been engaged in democratic politics the longest, but no one would characterise its present leadership as 'elderly' in the sense of being doddering and senile, as is insinuated.

If anything, age seems to be a guarantee of probity, and indicates a politician's involvement since the formative years of democratic politics and a courageous commitment to democracy even during the dark years of the Panchayat. The older politicians in the parties, such as Bhim Bahadur Tamang and the recently deceased Bal Bahadur Rai, both of the Nepali Congress, have shown more lasting commitment to pluralistic politics than the younger lot. Rai was a lifelong party activist who, from his deathbed in July 2010 at the age of 90, spoke out clearly against the ethnicity-based divisions that are being created. He needs to be saluted once again in memoriam for having clarity of vision that is not seen among youth leaders. The septugenarian Tamang knows his French philosophers like no one in the younger lot does; he is a politician who fought shoulder-to-shoulder with B.P. Koirala and has served the hill region east of Kathmandu for six decades. He lives in Kathmandu in a modest room in a friend's house, serves visitors tea he brews himself, and uses public transport.

Krishna Prasad Bhattarai, who oversaw the writing of the Constitution of 1990 and the general elections thereafter, exemplified the old-school politician of Nepal who did not compromise on his beliefs till his last breath. Neither was he the kind who would destroy his own political party by starting a splinter group upon losing a battle for leadership, which in his case Bhattarai lost to Girija Prasad Koirala. Till his death in March 2010 at the age of 87, Bhattarai stuck to his personal conviction that abolishing of the constitutional monarchy was a mistake – he would not kowtow to populist opinion and was placed where the influence of the neighbouring countries, the Western ambassadors and the donors could never reach him.

It is not hidden from anyone that the tirade against 'elderly politicians' was actually aimed by political opponents and partisan analysts at the aging Girija Prasad Koirala, who emerged like a phoenix as the undisputed leader in the run-up to the People's Movement of April 2006. Koirala was the only mainstream political leader who did not succumb to the siren call of Gyanendra to join his regime, who stood like a bulwark for pluralism when all the other leaders of the Nepali Congress and those of the CPN (UML) had fallen like ninepins (and while the Maoists were negotiating a secret deal with the royal palace). It was Koirala who uncompromisingly insisted on the reinstatement of Parliament and it is his stand that led Nepal back to an open society after the autocracy of Gyanendra. It was he who took the plunge to negotiate with the underground Maoists; it was his stature that was required for Nepal's orderly conversion into a republic. If a peaceful transition and jettisoning of a violent insurgency requires older leaders, then let us be grateful that we have them.

One cannot agree with the suggestion that the younger lot of politicians immediately be given the keys to the estate; the best-known youth leaders are prone to navel-gazing and have yet to prove their democratic worth. Almost to the last man and woman, they seem enamoured of the suggestion of the diplomats and donor representatives that it is time for the youth to be at the forefront. But these young leaders have played it safe during times of great turbulence, when courage in street action and clarity of political thought was required. Lately, they have tended to read from the donor script when it comes to the peace process (such as on the disbanding of UNMIN, which many youth leaders thought was a foolish step) and constitution-writing. Preferring seminar halls and overseas tours to mass meetings, they are not to be found when it is time to take up challenge. To take just one example, no prominent youth leader urged Prime Minister Jhala Nath Khanal, in March 2011, not to hand over the Ministry of Home Affairs to the UCPN (Maoist). Youth leaders ought to have acted as a wedge to allow the parliamentary parties to re-enter areas of rural Nepal which were evacuated during the Maoist onslaught, but they are engaged elsewhere.

Some youth leaders are making the mistake of using media coverage to get ahead within their own parties, forgetting that a true democrat should seek to lead the party rather than exploit it for self-advancement. Today's youth leaders must be loyal to their parties and speak substantively on the critical issues of the peace process and democracy rather than try to advance through sound bites and media coverage. If they begin to sound more like politicians and less like civil society seminarians, without doubt, they will have built a following before they spring too many grey hairs.

Girija Prasad Koirala

Girija Prasad Koirala was the most eminent personality in the two decades of politics after 1990. His career started in the mid-1940s, when, as a trade union organiser in Biratnagar, he became a reliable grassroots organiser and administrator of the Nepali Congress party, led by his brother, B.P. Koirala. It was from B.P. that Girija learnt the 'simple convictions' that formed the bedrock of his democratic politics. These two words provided the title of one of two book-length works, featuring speeches Koirala gave around the country during the Gyanendra autocracy.

After 1990, in short order, he outmanoeuvred his two senior colleagues, Ganesh Man Singh and Krishna Prasad Bhattarai, for Congress leadership and gained full control of the party, a position he held for the next two decades till his death in March 2010. As the person who was prime minister for the longest period after 1990, he got credit for proving that the country could indeed stand in the absence of an active monarchy, proving wrong the propaganda of the Panchayat regime and the fears of many. At the same time, Koirala shares the blame for the wrong turns of the dozen years of democracy, for the mal-administration and preoccupation with intra-party skulduggery. To him also goes the fault for being unable to understand well enough or soon enough the demand for inclusive democracy from marginalised communities, ethnic groups and the Madhesis.

For a long time, Koirala nurtured distaste for communists of all shades. They, in turn, returned the revulsion in full measure, and it was the intense rivalry between the CPN (UML) and the Nepali Congress that destabilised the politics of the early 1990s. It was only in the fight against Gyanendra, the royal autocrat, that Koirala conceded the democratic character of the CPN (UML). During his first two terms as prime minister, it was the media-savvy propaganda of the CPN (UML) which helped tar the Congress supremo as a corrupt demagogue. Long accused of corruption during his years in power, Koirala actually lived an austere life and his fundraising was meant almost exclusively for the party. The one weakness he had was for his daughter Sujata, on whose behalf he was willing to bend the rules and doggedly swallow criticism.

Girija Prasad Koirala's convictions made him stand firm against King Gyanendra while most of the national leadership, including the stalwarts of his own party and those of the CPN (UML), fell before the royal pustch. Sher Bahadur Deuba became prime minister as royal appointee, while the UML joined the government with the announcement of Madhav Kumar Nepal that royal misdemeanours had been 'half corrected'. The Maoists, meanwhile, were actually holding secret consultations with the royal palace to conduct a joint takeover. Against all advice and opinion, and even as he was made a laughingstock by the 'pragmatists' in politics and in civil society, Koirala insisted on a rollback of the royal takeover through the reinstatement of the dissolved Parliament. His 'simple convictions', repeated in whistle-stop tours of the country, defended proudly before the masses the values of democracy – judicial review, the rule of law, human rights, press freedom, pluralism and civilian supremacy over the military. During all of Koirala's time in power, there was never any question that the government would attack critics in the media or that peaceful demonstrations on any subject would be disallowed; in this sense, he helped build the foundations of democracy for which posterity will remember him.

Koirala's links to Subcontinental history and the fact that he was a fellow fighter of India's independence generation made him a man respected far beyond Nepal. His personal stature provided both access to and protection for Nepal vis-à-vis the country's neighbours to the south and north. When Koirala visited New Delhi in June 2006 as head of the interim government, Prime Minister Manmohan Singh made the extraordinary gesture of meeting him at the airport, a step that went beyond the demands of protocol and precedence. Singh referred to Koirala as 'Southasia's most eminent statesman', and indeed he was the only remaining leader of the 'independence generation' still at the top of active politics. Amidst the cacophony of day-to-day politics, Nepali commentator and lay public alike tend to forget this aspect of the life of 'G.P.' His firm grasp over the Nepali polity and his international stature provided a strong base level of credibility for the Nepali state in the international arena, including in India, during the years of conflict and transition, just as it had helped the new democracy in the 1990s to strike root.

It was Koirala's sturdy presence that enabled the country to survive the crisis brought on by the royal palace massacre of 2001. It was only Koirala who could have disregarded the international community and reached out to the Maoists as early as 2002. Even though the Maoists insisted on a constituent assembly and later a republic, none of this would have been possible without Koirala's acquiescence. Unwilling at first to be carried away by the republican wave triggered by the Maoists, and wishing to ensure the continuity of the constitutional monarchy after the April 2006 People's Movement, he floated several formulae, including placing a 'baby king' on the throne. Gyanendra, however, was unwilling to go along. It was only when the octogenarian prime minister decided that there was no option but to finally let the kingship go that the country became a republic.

While Koirala was a lifelong democrat as far as the larger polity was concerned, he was an autocrat within his party and did not pay attention to organisation and process. Within the party, he was a loner who preferred loyalists to advisors. His power base rested on his personal contact with thousands of cadres around the country and his ability to recall events and incidents from decades ago, and to synthesise information he received through continuous meetings starting in the pre-dawn hours. He also derived support because of an unique ability to empathise with ordinary people and grassroots political workers. Only in death did a person long presented as a demagogue and an autocrat suddenly emerge in reminiscences and obituaries as humane and sensitive.

Gravely weakened by emphysema in the last two of years of his life, Koirala was forced to lead the country from his bed chamber. As a result, he lost touch with his cadre base and his coterie of loyalists and family members provided inadequate feedback and back-up on numerous critical matters – from the chicanery of Pushpa Kamal Dahal to the possibility of the April 2008 elections being stolen by Maoist malfeasance to the Madhes Movement which erupted in the winter of 2007.

The relationship between Koirala and the Maoist Chairman is something that will have to be studied in depth by scholars. To what extent the Congress leader confronted and subdued the ex-guerilla supremo and to what extent he was forced to concede much more than he wanted to, are matters things that the public needs to know. Powerful enough to dictate terms to others, Koirala did the nation an injustice by freely granting the Maoists the same number of seats – 83 – that the CPN (UML) had squarely won in the elections to the Interim Parliament. He seemed to want to give inordinate strength to the Maoists to weaken the UML, perhaps hoping his own Nepali Congress would benefit during elections to the Constituent Assembly. The interim period till those elections was a critical period of instability, and, despite his declining health, Koirala's presence at the helm did assure the relatively smooth passage of the interim constitution and the onward journey to elections. However, this was also a period during which the Maoists were not challenged about their commitment to peace, a silence which defined the calamitous political decline of the following years.

After the elections and the strong showing by the ex-rebels, Koirala felt cheated that Chairman Dahal did not keep his promise of offering him the post of the first President of the republic. Koirala may have thought that, as President, he would have been able to control the waywardness of the UCPN (Maoist). It is this calculation which may explain his leniency towards the ex-rebels between 2006 and 2008, when they perfected impunity to a fine craft. As things stand, with Koirala gone, it is only his party colleagues and then Home Minister Krishna Prasad

Sitaula who can explain why the interim government was so 'soft' on the Maoists, a stance which weakened state administration and spread lawlessness throughout the land.

After the Maoist government fell in early May 2009 and Madhav Kumar Nepal became prime minister, Koirala, at a two-party meeting at his Maharajganj residence, ordered that his daughter Sujata, a junior with weak standing in the party, lead the party in the cabinet as both foreign minister and deputy prime minister. Everyone present, those in his own party as well as the UML, was aghast. However, no one felt capable of resisting the respected elder. In one stroke, Koirala had ensured that the new government would, at its very inception, be weak at the top. This decision by a leader who, in elections past, had even refused to give his daughter a ticket to contest perhaps indicated the old man's growing isolation, if not his loneliness. Koirala went on to further weaken the government as well as the Constituent Assembly by trying to deal with the Maoists outside the political process. To this end, with Chairman Dahal and CPN (UML) head Jhala Nath Khanal in cahoots, he created a 'high-level political mechanism' to bypass the existing institutions and offices.

After more than six decades in politics, on 20 March, 2010, Girija Prasad Koirala died, still very much at the helm of both his party and the country. He died knowing that the country's democracy was as yet a work in progress, with political stability and economic prosperity still a mirage. Koirala's success was intangible, yet, without him, the country would not have had the relative stability it did amidst the continuous turmoil of the arrival of democracy in 1990, the rise of the Maoist insurgency, the royal palace massacre, the countrywide spread of political violence, and the autocratic ambitions of the newly-crowned monarch, Gyanendra. Girija Prasad Koirala died on the job, with his followers and critics both realising that his strengths more than made up for his failings. He chaperoned Nepal into the democratic era, did all that his elder brother B.P. was not allowed to do, and departed while at the helm of national politics. History will judge 'G.P.' much better than many of his ungenerous contemporaries have.

At home and the world

To the question of whether the politicians of Nepal fare well in comparison to those elsewhere, the answer is a robust affirmative. Our politicians have more experience battling continuous adversity than do the politicians in most other societies. The political class has been battling for pluralism for decades on end, with many of the current crop of Nepali Congress and CPN (UML) leaders having spent between 5 and 12 years in jail during the Panchayat regime; others spent years in exile. They had their properties seized, lived on the run, suffered royalist coups, witnessed the assassinations of colleagues, and endured being branded Indian lackeys. They battled four over-reaching kings, starting with Tribhuvan in the 1950s and moving forward through Mahendra, Birendra and Gyanendra. In addition, they had to tackle the Maoist insurgency, the royal palace massacre, and a repeat of the royal coup of 1960 in 2005. Since the peace process began in 2006, they have had to tackle an unrepentant insurgent force bent on cheating on the process and maintaining its fear-mongering ways in the districts and cities. In the latest instance, democrat-politicians, whether of the hills or plains, have also had to confront the populism of identity politics that has overtaken the discourse. Throughout their battles, Nepal's democrat-politicians have had to do without the steadfast support of the intelligentsia and civil society that may be expected in other societies.

Only mature politicians who have suffered for the people and feel for the grassroots would have had the courage to reach out to a radical insurgency at great cost to their own parties and careers. It is this contribution of the Nepali democrat-politicians which makes the peace process of Nepal so unique and for which they deserve credit, credit that the Kathmandu intelligentsia and the international analysts have been unwilling to grant them. Reaching out to the Maoists was a high-risk endeavour, and, indeed, the Maoists have reneged on both the letter and the spirit of the 12-Point Agreement of 2005, in which they promised to disarm, integrate and rehabilitate their fighters. Those who say that the democrat-politicians appeased the Maoists from the start are incorrect, if not spiteful. While the politicians stuck to their word by holding elections to the Constituent Assembly and made it easy for the Maoist leaders vis-à-vis the cadre by acceding to the republic and federalism, the Maoists shifted goalposts and, as of this writing, continue to block the demobilisation of their fighting force. Nepal's politicians are not 'washed in milk', certainly, but they have suffered more for democracy and fought more continuously for it than most politicians of the modern era.

Village abandonment

It is true that the parliamentary parties abandoned the villages during the conflict years, and, to this day, there are many areas party activists are reluctant to enter because of the threat of Maoist violence. There are many who like to pour scorn on the democrat-politicians for their inability to penetrate the villages, but these are only those who have not felt a wooden staff crashing down on their own kneecap or skull. While the Maoists did come above ground and are to be thanked for that, their infrastructure of violence remained in the villages, as was seen in the election campaign of early 2008. The political parties can be criticised for a lot of things: for not being organised enough, for corruption, for being internally undemocratic. However, those who ridicule the politicians from the safety of their Kathmandu living rooms should heed the Nepali saying – only the *achano* (butcher's block) knows the pain of the blow of the *khukuri*.

Indeed, the main reason that the parliamentary parties have found it difficult to enter the villages is their unwillingness to battle violence with violence. The attempt to create an organised youth cadre to counter the Young Communist League is hardly the answer for mature, responsible political parties. The CPN (UML) has started the Youth Force, while the Nepali Congress has openly avowed not to take up this path of challenge to the Maoists. The only place where the Maoists' presence was weakened after 2006 was in the eastern Tarai, where the Madhesi parties pushed the ex-rebels into the background during the Madhes Movement. The most horrific episode after the end of the 'people's war' occurred in Gaur in March 2007, in the plains directly south of Kathmandu, where carnage was carried out by killers who, with the support of some plains politicians, killed nearly 30 Maoist activists with wooden staves, chasing the victims through the fields.

The Tarai plains became the playing field of the criminal-militant nexus, while elsewhere the Maoists remained in control with the threat of violence at their command. The observer of this scenario has to either suggest that the parliamentary parties fight violence with violence, each starting its own militant wing, or try to understand the reluctance of individual activists to be made mincemeat of by Maoist cadre lurking on trails and in villages. The route to restarting political activity in rural Nepal can only lie in non-violent penetration, which presupposes a strong presence of state administration and security apparatuses at the local level. This penetration of the state is happening slowly, but the Maoist leadership does not help matters by maintaining its violence-first message to its cadre.

Time is the great game-changer, and as the months and years roll by, the parliamentary parties are becoming better organised, even as the more aggressive Maoist cadre have abandoned villages for lucrative activities elsewhere. For now, they can still be redeployed in the districts at lightning speed by the politico-military leadership, but this violent efficiency will erode as the clock turns. A level playing field is a hard thing to reconstruct, but it will happen. The proof that normalcy has returned to the villages will be when the political parties feel confident enough to hold mass rallies with the knowledge that the people will not stay away due to fear and that they themselves will not be attacked.

18

Gracious Demography

Dissent in cohabitation
There is an apparent contradiction in views of contemporary Nepal: it is generally seen as a 'friendly country' yet one with considerable dissension among its communities. While tourism brochures do oversell the image of a place where ethnic and caste communities live together in harmony, the basic inter-community relationships of Nepal are robust. But it is also true that inter-community relations have never been this polarised, particularly between those groups seen as a part of the historical establishment (the Bahun and the Chhetri) and those who have suffered the brunt of historical marginalisation. This rift is a temporary phenomenon, hopefully, and is the natural outcome of the advent of an open society in 1990 which allowed bottled-up frustrations to be released. As the various communities of the hills and plains begin to take advantage of the economic and political possibilities that the egalitarian state offers, there will be a move to rebuild the links that have been weakened.

The assertion of ethnic identity over the course of the 1990s was built on the platform of historical disfranchisement and denial of community rights and was successful in building solidarity across myriad groups, mostly those of the mid-hills. Even as identity assertion was gaining strength, it was exploited by the CPN (Maoist) party, which conflated ethnic marginalisation with class subjugation in order to gain momentum for its countrywide spread. The opportunistic use of identity politics by the insurgents was not challenged adequately by the Kathmandu intelligentsia.

The sociability of Nepali society has to do with the nature of our rural settlements – a multiplicity of discrete hamlets defined by ethnicity, caste, language and faith live in close proximity to each other in each of our village development committees. Over the centuries, the proximity of such diversity has produced a unique syncretism, a mixing of mores, traditions and tongues. Nepalis, because they are separated by identity and yet in constant contact, have a national character defined by inter-community empathy, or what outsiders know as 'Nepali friendliness'. The local-level sociability that comes from understanding the points of view of others has become the leitmotif of our society taken as a whole and is, as much as does the Himalayan landscape, what attracts the tourist to Nepal. No people are innately friendly; it is socio-cultural conditioning that has rendered the people of Nepal to be so affable towards each other, and, by extension, towards the outsider.

Demography of complexity
The diversity of Nepal's demography is the legacy of its geology and climate and the migration of peoples. As it gained height over the eons due to tectonic shifting, the Himalayan chain rose to block the monsoon clouds and the water which flowed down its slopes cut deep river gorges that isolated one region from another from east to west. Over the last two thousand years, groups migrating from the north, east, south and west discovered this agreeable portion of the Central Himalaya and settled down in what was to become Nepal. Because of the topographical separations, these arrivals retained their distinct languages and cultures and evolved separately. While the rivers and river valleys separated communities in the hills and mountains, deep jungles and wide rivers separated those in the Tarai. For ages, the plains have been inhabited by ethnic and caste groups, including the Tharu and Danuwar in forest tracts, Hindu castes in the Mithila region of the mid-eastern plains, and Muslims in the centre and west. The last two centuries in particular saw more intermingling of communities, but the hamlets remained mostly distinct.

The rulers of Nepal knew well the diversity of the population they had consolidated into a unified kingdom. Indeed, the founder of the Rana oligarchy, Jang Bahadur Kunwar, felt the need to impose a legal code based on the hierarchical principles of Hinduism but able to address the caste and ethnic plurality unique to Nepal. He devised the Muluki Ain (Civil Code) of 1854 as a kind of tool in social engineering, dictating the place of each community with respect to the others and based on the interplay of caste determinism, power relationships, and distance from the Kathmandu Valley 'centre'. The Muluki Ain may have been devised by the early Rana regime as a means to bring order amidst the diversity of the caste-ethnic interface that was Nepali society, but it locked communities into straitjackets of disfranchisement for more than a century.

The variety and perceived exoticism of the mid-hill and high-Himalayan communities was what spurred the study of Nepal by ethnographers and anthropologists. Research picked up in the late 1960s, when Nepal had opened up considerably and India, after its war with China in 1962, had became suspicious of foreign researchers traipsing about its Himalayan belt. Over the next two decades, Western scholarship on Nepal's demography concentrated mainly on the study of individual ethnic groups and sub-groups in the hills and mountains. The world was introduced to the exclusive, stand-alone ethnic communities of Nepal and these communities, in turn, became more aware of their own heritages and identities. The study of the unique inter-relationships among the ethnic and caste groups, however, received scant attention though such study could have played an important role in devising a formula of cohabitation for modern times.

Part of the reason it was not possible to devote time and apply the same rigour of scholarship to inter-community relationships and the inter-linking of their interests was the raging insurgency of the late 1990s, which kept away all scholars other than the most intrepid. The ethnic assertion movement which picked up in the early 1990s rightfully took advantage of Western scholarship on individual groups, but society as a whole would have gained much more had there been more study of inter-community linkages. Instead of academic studies, we got consultants' reports on marginalisation and the Kathmandu-centric state. There was little on how communities were to live together under one roof.

The Tarai region was largely unexplored by Western scholars, an exception being the political scientist Frederick Gaige, who showed an extraordinary interest in the plains people in the 1960s. The scholarly neglect of the Tarai had partly to do with the pull of hill diversity and partly with a tendency to regard the people of the Tarai as similar to those of adjoining Bihar and Uttar Pradesh, and hence as the domain of 'non-Himalayan' scholars. The disinterest of the power players in Kathmandu in the modern era left the Madhesi community seething with anger over their exclusion; the scholarly disinterest added salt to the wound. The mid-hill ethnic groups felt excluded, certainly, but at least they were not excluded from ownership of the hill-centric nationalism that had evolved.

Scholarship within
Social science scholarship within Nepal itself is hopelessly inadequate to address the complexities of ethnic politics and identity assertion. For various reasons, fine Nepali scholars such as the economic historian Mahesh Chandra Regmi, the geographer Harka Gurung, and the cultural historian Prayag Raj Sharma are few and far in between. The few remaining scholars and political scientists capable of serious study have been compromised variously by their attachment to the earlier royalist regime, the pull of ethnic populism, the fear of communitarian backlash, attachment to ambitious civil society groups, the lure of consultancies, the absence of liberal-arts colleges, and the weakening of existing academic institutions, especially the departments of economics and political science.

With independent Western university scholars having been diverted by the conflict and the Nepali academia weak or compromised, the job of defining the history of the ethnicity-politics interface in the post-2006 period fell on bilateral donor and UN agencies, Western embassies and the United Nations. Funded by a mission to 'set Nepal right' based on a caricature of Nepal's history and culture, it was natural for rigour to be replaced by timidity and bias. Some scholars of yesteryear turned firebrand activists, while others became soft around the edges through lucrative report-writing contracts.

Energised by a genuine sense of deprivation, many scholar-activists seemed to decide that identity was the 'be all and the end all', and relegated the matter of class to the shadows. This abandonment of class analysis and its replacement by the discourse of community marginalisation should itself be a subject of future scholarship, but we cannot wait because its conclusions are required here and now, while constitution-writing proceeds. The Maoists themselves abandoned all pretensions to Marxist ideology in opportunistically accepting the notion that class deprivation in Nepal is synonymous with ethnic identity – that to belong to an ethnic community is to be poor – and its corollary, that to be a caste member (other than a Dalit) is to be privileged. Hopelessly inadequate and overly simplistic as an analysis of class, such a proposition does not even hold water: it fails to recognise the massive poverty among caste Hindus in the mid-hill and plains, the sector from which a revolt could arise amidst a sense of reverse discrimination. Meanwhile, little thought is being given to how the rise of community identities will adjust to the counter-current of globalisation so evident in Nepal's economy and society, where youngsters have far more complex identities than their immediate elders.

Fortunately, Nepali society has shown itself adaptable and capable of rapid adjustment, and the polity has been alert and responsive to ethnic assertion and community identity issues. Nepal's home-grown community activism, though still inadequate because it misses many communities and as yet unarticulated desires, is powerful for the very fact that it represents a political demand for inclusion. The two grand episodes in the fight against the marginalisation of communities were, of course, identity assertion by the ethnic leadership which started after 1990 and the upward surge of the Madhes Movement in early 2007. Both movements forced the state establishment to open up to the idea of *samabesikaran*, or 'inclusion', a term which has quickly become part of the vernacular.

The remarkable thing about Nepali society taken as a whole is the trip-wire mechanism that prevents inter-community conflagration even when there are deliberate attempts to light the fuse, such as the Maoists' proposal for ethnic federalism and the attempts of the Madhesi and Pahade to provoke community divides in the Tarai. As an example, one can take the Chandrauta tragedy of September 2007, in which the Muslim community and the local hill people of Kapilvastu District came into direct confrontation. This clash did take several lives and had the potential to spread rapidly to other parts of the Tarai, but the sagacity of the district civil society, religious elders and politicians helped douse the fire before more damage could be done. The Kapilvastu experience is just one example of rapid, local-level response to defuse dangerous situations. Though it is true that inter-community animosities in the hills and plains have never been as bad in the modern era, one can have confidence that they will not get worse.

History of poverty

The geography, climate, natural resources and diversity of demography and ecology of Nepal all offer great opportunity for the country to provide the populace with a high quality of life, but historical factors have kept the people continually impoverished. First, the deprivation was due to the wars of imperial ambition conducted in the late 1700s and early 1800s, wars which placed a usurious burden on the peasantry. The migration of peasants for mercenary and menial work in Mughlan (the Indus-Ganga plains) began at this time. Later, turmoil in the Kathmandu court led to a disruption that lasted decades, until the satrap Jang Bahadur Kunwar consolidated power and negotiated a live-and-let-live arrangement with the British in the mid-1800s. The Rana regime he established filled its private coffers while depriving the people of modern-day advances in terms of infrastructure, state bureaucracy, judicial system, and learning, all resources available in some measure to the colonised peoples in other parts of the Subcontinent.

While the state administration was exploiting the populace to the hilt, the land itself grew increasingly unable to provide sustenance to the ever-burgeoning population. Without sufficient means of production, the subsistence farmers of the hills, across ethnicity, caste and region, found it necessary to leave home to perform menial labour in the plains of British India. This tradition of labour migration continued over two centuries, and even today remains a stark reminder of national poverty and the failure of governance.

During the two centuries of Kathmandu-centred rule, power came to be concentrated in three communities, the Chhetri/Thakuri, the Bahun (hill Brahmin) and the Newar, even though the conquest of the Gorkhali state had utilised the services of many ethnicities, particularly those of the Gurung and the Magar of the mid-western hills. The Maithili nobility had had influence in the Kathmandu court in the earlier Malla era but lost out when the Gorkhali arrived. The Newar, by virtue of being the inhabitants of Kathmandu Valley, were able to participate in commerce and influence national administration. On the whole, those ethnic groups which resided outside the centre, even the Tamang, whose region of origin surrounds Kathmandu Valley, were excluded from governance except at the bottom-most rung.

Nepali, which evolved from Khaskura to become the language of the Gorkhali state, also became the language which linked diverse communities as their need for interaction increased in the 19th and 20th centuries. This gave a natural advantage to the Bahun and the Chhetri, however, the hill Dalit, the underclass in the caste hierarchy who also spoke Nepali as their mother tongue, were unable to take advantage of this turn in Nepal's linguistic history.

Future of communal relationships
The Nepali nationalism that developed over the course of two centuries was centred in the mid-hills, which meant that the inhabitants of the high Himalaya, the Bhotiya, and the much-larger Madhesi and other groups of the Tarai, felt discriminated against, economically and culturally. The mid-hill ethnic groups, while they did identify with the state, were nevertheless kept out of the state hierarchy. This is Nepal's grand narrative. And yet there are complexities that have to be considered, for example, the extreme poverty of the Khas caste population of the western hills. The Newar are, of course, ethnic, but they have a caste hierarchy and a Hindu-Buddhist differentiation within themselves. Many Newars do not want to be identified as an ethnic group, while some regard the Newar as too advanced to fit into the ethnicity-equals-poverty prototype. It is worth considering that there are many very small ethnicities which have not yet managed to raise their voice amidst the hubbub of the last few years but will when the time comes for making a decision on critical matters such as defining federalism in the new constitution. At the same time, there are sub-identities within each and every community, most of which have not had the time or the confidence to come to the fore and stake a claim vis- à-vis larger, more vociferous, identities.

What is unique about Nepal's demography is that it is entirely made up of minorities: the two largest communities, the Chhetri and the Bahun, comprise just 16% and 12% of the total population respectively; the Magar and the Tharu are around 7% each; and the Tamang and the Newar just over 5% each Every other community – and there are over 90 – is smaller. In light of this reality, one hopes that after the first flush of identity assertion and resulting empowerment, we will move towards class-based representational politics, and that society will revert to an even keel based on political inclusion and common sense. The attempt to displace class with identity ideology is not something that will take a society forward. It could be that the various identities within the Janajati (ethnic), Madhesi and parbate (hill castes) will coalesce to form three broad representational streams in Nepali politics. However, it is more likely that, in light of the individual freedom achieved in 1990 and the possibility of a level playing field created by community activism after 2006, the future of politics will be defined by each citizen feeling empowered to engage in the public sphere beyond the boundaries of ethnicity or caste.

Among the communities and ethnic groups in the Tarai, experience shows that internal distinctions come to the fore once the first threshold of rights assertion is past. Especially if, as the Maoists have proposed in their plans for ethnic federalism, no more than ten communities are awarded individual provinces, smaller ethnic groups will definitely start feeling left out by larger ones. One must also consider that the High Himalayan communities of Nepal, from Humla in the west to Walung in the east, have not yet spoken up, though they will if it becomes clear that they either will be subsumed under someone else's territory, or relegated to *bantustans* with few economic prospects. To take an example, if one considers the eastern province that some propose calling 'Limbuwan', it is not just the demands of the majority Limbus that need to be considered but those of the Rong (Lepcha), the northern Bhotiya, the Rai, the Koch and all the other ethnic communities as well as of the Dalit and the Bahun-Chhetri who live there that will need to be considered. The fact that, in the fall of 2008, the Tharu felt a need to initiate their own movement against perceived domination by the Madhesi, and that the Tharu members of the UCPN (Maoist) of the far-western Tarai launched their own internal battle against Maoists of hill origin, was a sign there would be more articulations of dissensions in future among Nepal's highly variegated identities. A cursory glance at ethnic politics at the national level gives an inadequate picture in a situation in which the debate is still unformed. For example, the great divides between the agendas of the mid-hill ethnic and the Madhesi activists and between the Tarai and Hill Dalit have not yet come up as an issue, but no doubt will.

While it will, of course, be impossible for everyone to be simultaneously represented in the topmost echelon of national, or even future provincial and district-level politics, what one hopes for is equal opportunity at the topmost levels, not only for representation but for wielding influence. One looks towards the progressive decline of Bahun representation in national politics until their presence coincides with their proportion in the population. At the same time, with representational politics revived at the local and provincial levels, there will be more opportunity for different communities to garner experience in politics and energise a 'new Nepal' from the bottom up. Inclusive politics will become a reality when citizens from any community can succeed not only in the legislature at all levels but also as power brokers at the centre, a role that has been monopolised by the Bahun since 1990, with even the Chhetri relegated to the sidelines.

The Dalit, the Bhotiya, Muslims and women

Without doubt, those among the marginalised communities who have the power of numbers, wealth, education, exposure, and historical proximity to the state, are heard the most. This is seen best in the proposals made by the Maoists and others: full-fledged ethnically-defined provinces are to be reserved only for the Tharu, Gurung, Magar, Rai, Limbu, Tamang and Newar communities, while the scores of other groups which populate the countryside are neglected. In terms of the large communities of Nepal, Muslims, at about five percent, and the hill-plains Dalit, at not less than 12 percent, are among the most marginalised. Despite their size, their voice is weak indeed; in fact, debates about the definition of Nepal's new provinces have more or less completely ignored them.

The Dalit as a whole are subjugated by the caste system and class realities, but conditions differ among Dalit sub-communities. Tarai Dalits are more deprived nationally and locally than hill Dalits, and within both groups there are stratifications between the cobbler, the scavenger, the smith, the tailor and other occupations. In the hills, Dalits of the west are more discriminated against than those in the east, though in both regions the Dalit are excluded not only by the so-called 'upper castes' but also by ethnic groups. It may be because of intra-Dalit hierarchies that the community has yet to rise in a singular movement as have the hill ethnicities, the Madhesi and the Tharu, even though Dalit leaders have regularly expressed their intention to organise such a movement. An additional reason could be that the liberal disbursement of development funds since the early 1990s has diverted many among the Dalit 'elite' away from political activism and towards raising awareness through workshops and seminars. So extreme is this diversion that there has not been a strong protest from the Dalit against the spectre of ethnically-defined federalism, which would surely marginalise Dalits further. The suggestion by proponents of ethnic-federalism that a non-territorial council would be created to address Dalit concerns in the provinces fails to convince. If class exploitation is to be equated with community marginalisation – if identity analysis is indeed to replace class analysis – the interests of the Dalit should come before those of all other communities.

Just as the Madhesi are made up of many groups residing in the southern plains, the northern mountains are inhabited by the '*tsampa* (barley flour)-eaters', the Bhotiya, who speak various dialects of Tibetan. Like the Madhesi, the Bhotiya are doubly excluded: they have been economically deprived and denied ownership of the national identity, the latter historically having been a mid-hill (Pahade) caste-ethnic monopoly. The difference between the mountain- and the plains-dweller is that the former are a much smaller group and are constrained by rugged topography from organising a social or political movement across the sacred high valleys, or *beyuls*. Fortunately, the very terrain which was considered remote and unproductive throughout history is now in the process of being converted into a tourist haven; it is also the repository of hope for the nation's hydropower production. The Bhotiya inhabitants of the Himalayan highlands of Nepal – those who live in the regions of Humla, Dolpo, Mustang, Manang, Gorkha-Dhading-Rasuwa, Helambu, Rolwaling, Solu-Khumbu, Makalu and Kanchenjunga – thus stand to prosper per capita much more than their Madhesi compatriots in the future.

Muslims are divided into three communities: the plains people, who share a cultural heritage with the Muslims across the border; the 'Kashmiri' of Kathmandu Valley, who arrived two to three centuries ago; and the hill Muslim, whose lifestyle matches that of the mid-hill communities of central Nepal. The Muslims are a larger community than many other population groups, their political voice has been far more muted because the state called itself a 'Hindu kingdom'. Even so, Muslims have been afforded relative protection in Nepal, and the Hindu-Muslim conflict that has erupted at times across the open border in Uttar Pradesh and Bihar has not shaken Nepali society as it might have. There have been communal clashes since Panchayat times, but local community elders and the government have always moved quickly to prevent an inferno from developing. Recent events in Kapilvastu in 2007 and Nepalganj in 2008, for example, have shown how a vigilant local civil society, including community elders and political activists, can help extinguish communal sparks before they lead to an explosion. In this context, the successful spread of FM radio transmission in Nepal, for all its capacity to raise awareness, must not be allowed to be misused as an incendiary tool in times of tension.

While women of many ethnic communities have a higher status than the women of the hill and plains caste groups, on the whole, all Nepali women suffer the repression of patriarchy. The relatively egalitarian nature of hill ethnicities suffers when urban middle-class mores kick in. The absence of women in the hierarchies of political power and the double burden faced by working women forced to raise children and perform household chores almost single-handedly are matters that affect women grievously. The fact that girl children are fed less nutritious diets and receive a poorer standard of education than boy children remains a challenge, and maternal and infant mortality rates of 280 per 100,000 live births and 41 per 1000 live births respectively are a shameful indicator of how far Nepal has to progress. Young girls robbed of their reproductive rights and health because of social mores and early marriage and the scourge of uterus prolapse highlight other of the myriad subjugations the women of Nepal face. From the disproportional incidence of women with spinal injuries (incurred from falling out of trees while collecting fodder) to the poverty that pushes a large number of women into sex work both in the country and in India – the status of women of Nepal is a dark reminder of a society that is truly 'backward'. Over the past two decades, the huge outflow of male migrants to India and overseas has increased the burden of wives, mothers, sisters and daughters-in-law. Meanwhile, women, too, have begun to migrate in large numbers to the Gulf and farther afield in search of jobs. While all these changes are happening, the power of political feminism has weakened considerably as some activists have been diverted by the new focus on awareness-raising 'gender workshops'.

Amidst the challenges faced by marginalised communities large and small and by women, who, of course, form part of all communities, we can take heart in the fact that Nepali society has the ability to adapt to new realities and take rapid strides when there is a proper mix of activism, peace, political stability and democracy. Because of the adaptability and flexibility of Nepali society, there is reason to realistically hope that in the coming era of peace and democracy all communities will rise above the exploitation and marginalisation that have dogged them throughout history. Some of this reversal is already evident in the representation of a large cross-section of Nepal's rainbow society in the Constituent Assembly's 601 members.

While the Constituent Assembly's own work has been in shambles throughout nearly all of its three years of existence, there is no doubt that many of its members will help make the egalitarian future of Nepal a reality. As participants in constitution-writing and individuals well educated about the critical issues of the day, many of these women and men, who today represent the grassroots at the national level, will emerge as the political front rank of the future. The fact that the Nepali state has accepted 'third gender' legislation indicates the ability of Nepalis in all categories – including the intelligentsia, civil society, the legislature, the judiciary and the public – to adjust to modern-day demands. Some laws may have been pushed by enthusiastic donor agencies, others may be adopted without adequate homework in the rush of populism, but on the whole the legislation adopted is the kind that will push the country ahead. In just a handful of years, terms once used to denigrate communities have been replaced in common Kathmandu parlance by more acceptable terms;, 'Madhise', for example, has been replaced by 'Madhesi', 'Bhote' by 'Bhotiya' or, more recently, 'Himali'. These changes are more than an easy linguistic switch: they indicate the social adaptability of a society marked by diversity.

19

Being Bahun

The pecking order
One must seek an explanation for the dominance of the Bahun in modern-day Nepal, in politics, education, academia, the bureaucracy, the judiciary, the law and the media. Bahuns (hill Brahmins, including this writer) form a caste group that migrated into the Western hills many centuries – or, some suggest, millennia – ago, either moving eastward along the mid-hills or up from the plains. They adjusted to the areas where they settled, which were often inhabited by ethnic groups which had arrived earlier. As the custodians of liturgy and learning, the Bahun were close to the Thakuri rulers of pre-unification days. The main societal advantages of the Bahun, those which explain their present-day dominance, seem to be a) the spread of their settlements across the country, which helped promote networking; b) their tradition of learning, which was useful in a modernising state requiring scribes, administrators and judges; and, c) their command of Sanskrit and Nepali, the evolving lingua franca, which helped them represent the state in numerous capacities.

There is competition among Bahun sub-identities, including the Purbiya easterner, the Kumai westerner, the Jainsi hybrid and others, and divisions among various clans, but, by and large, this has been a community whose inter-connectedness has helped it to get ahead. Once they arrived in Kathmandu Thakuri rulers utilised both the Bahun and the Newar as associates and advisors, but the Bahun had the advantage of being part of a large community extending beyond Kathmandu Valley, so while a few Newars moved around to conduct trade and commerce, the Bahun did so in large numbers as state functionaries. The limited job options available to ethnic communities like the Tamang and the Rai in the small Valley-centric state forced them to migrate to India in search of menial labour or to join the brigade of Gurkhas set up by the colonial British. In contrast, Bahuns, with their Sanskrit learning providing a deep learning base, gravitated towards state administration, teaching and ritual punditry. In the modern era, with the advantage of Nepali language, both spoken and written, they found easy access to the fields of law, academia, civil service and politics.

Together with other caste groups, the Bahun pandits were the drivers of Khaskura, which was later called Nepali. In other circumstance, the lingua franca that evolved could have been Maithili or Newa Bhay, but Nepali it was, which meant that the Bahun had an advantage even without the state policy of marginalising other languages. In the modern period, to address the perceived need for a unitary nation-state, the Panchayat state establishment patronised and propagated Nepali, and other languages grew weaker. This loss of language explains in great part the deep animosity of ethnic activists towards Bahuns: it is they who were the main propagators of the Nepali imperial language. The fact that the eclipse of one's language signifies a loss of heritage and identity and generates a panic among many was not sufficiently understood by the Bahun-Chhetri establishment of Nepal. Interestingly, soldiers returning home from the Brigade of Gurkhas upon retirement were a major force in the spread of the Nepali language over the past two centuries: they took the language, which was used in the regiments, to the far corners of mid-hill Nepal. Other than by a few scholars and academics, the contribution of the hill ethnic groups in developing Nepal's lingua franca is not appreciated enough. Scholar-activists who harbour a rigid view of cultural transformation are particularly oblivious.

The Chhetri
In the ethno-political discourse, the Chhetri as a caste tends to be hyphenated with the Bahun as part of the political establishment – 'Bahun-Chhetri'. The warrior caste has a trajectory of movement and settlement similar to that of the Bahun – indeed it led the process – but as rulers, fighters and administrators. The rulers of the principalities that existed prior to national unification as well as the kings and Rana oligarchs who reigned afterwards have been Thakuri, an 'upgraded' branch of the Chhetri. The Thakuri, have been, therefore, the most privileged of

communities over the last two centuries, with the Bahun, the Newar and others serving as its courtiers and supplicants. The long reign of the Ranas and the continuation of an active Thakuri kingship through the Panchayat period as well as the grip of the Chhetri over the Royal Nepal Army and strong presence in the Nepal Police continued and augmented this community's access to state power. Across the western hills, the descendants of princelings continued to enjoy at least recognition, if not treatment, as royalty well into the 2000s.

The Chhetri front rank wielded enormous power during the Panchayat regime beyond that which accrued due to being from the same 'warrior' caste as the Thakuri royalty. However, the position of the Chhetri in governance changed drastically with the arrival of representational politics, when the Bahun pushed ahead with near-exclusive control of the two largest political parties, the Nepali Congress and the CPN (UML). The Bahun also continued to be better represented than the Chhetri in all institutions of state other than the security forces. Thus, the constant repetition of the 'Bahun-Chhetri control of the state' does not reflect the reality after 1990. The presence of Chhetris among the uppermost national power elite has been almost completely undone by Bahuns. The credit and blame for the last two decades of rule and misrule of the country, if it is to be laid on the shoulders of any one community, should fall on the Bahun, with the Chhetri released from the burden. If the UCPN (Maoist) has introduced great challenges to the democratic and peaceful growth of Nepali society, that party, too, has been led at the top by Bahuns (Dahal, Vaidya/Pokhrel and Bhattarai), with the Chhetri relegated to the lower ranks.

B.P. Koirala and friends
A study of the ethnicity and background of the democratic leaders jailed for eight long years in Sundarijal jail by King Mahendra in 1960 reveals a fine representation of Nepal's demographic diversity among those who would have been rulers in of modern Nepal had the nascent democracy not been quashed. Besides B.P. and Krishna Prasad Bhattarai, both Bahuns, the jailed leaders included Ganesh Man Singh, a Newar; Yogendra Man Sherchan, a Thakali; Ram Narayan Mishra, a Madhesi; and Diwan Singh Rai and Jamaan Singh Gurung, both from hill ethnic groups. It was the Panchayat system that negated the possibilities for inclusion heralded by the fight of these social demo-

crats against the Rana regime. Led by an autocratic monarchy which sought legitimacy by developing ultra-nationalism, the Panchayat regime concentrated on developing a pan-Nepal identity based on the top-down diktat of one country, one people, one national dress, one national language. Working for unity from the bottom up would have required democracy, which was of course, not possible under Mahendra's authoritarian regime. The Panchayat superstructure made a show of representing the ethnicities, castes and regions, but that was selective tokenism. It would require the return of open society in 1990 for identity assertion to become an effective tool in fighting exclusivity at the top.

The possibility of developing an inclusive democracy early in the modern era was thus lost when King Mahendra conducted his 1960 coup and converted Nepal into an absolute monarchy. Other than token inclusion of the elite from the ethnic groups and the Tarai communities, the Panchayat kept state power very much within the Bahun-Chhetri fold, with some Newar representation. The aspirations of the educated, the able and the ambitious among marginalised communities were to remain bottled up for three long decades. Only representational politics in an open society could begin the process of creating a level playing field, with each community represented according to its proportion in the total population.

As it turned out, the advent of democracy in the last decade of the 20th century made it possible for voices to rise, demanding an inclusive polity and rightful representation in the political hierarchy. The situation rapidly turned so that ethnic activists who demanded community rights and asserted their identities were no longer ostracised by the mainstream nor labelled anti-national or separatist as had been the case for decades. But things did not move fast enough, with leaders engaged in the hustle and bustle of competitive politics neglecting the manifest unfairness of one community taking all of the topmost public positions. Belying the principle of inclusion, it began to look as if the Bahun were taking over all the top positions in the democratic society. Bahuns manned the front ranks of politics, covering the full spectrum from royalist to liberal democrat to progressive to radical. Today, each of the three topmost leaders of the Maoist, Nepali Congress and UML parties are Bahun males. Sher Bahadur Deuba of the Congress is the only exception: he is a Chhetri.

Communities in democracy

With the advent of open society, the Bahun found their tradition of learning and command of both Nepali and Sanskrit provided them with leverage in all major sectors other than business and security. As they got into the game of political competition within and between parties, the rulers who happened to be Bahun, such as long-time prime minister Girija Prasad Koirala, failed to notice the resentment brewing among others who saw the Bahun ascend at the cost of their own aspirations. The concern multiplied as Nepal's hundred-plus other tongues were weakened at a time of rapid economic globalisation, while Nepali grew in strength as the language of government, was embraced by the marketplace, and became the language of choice for the media and advertising.

At 12% of the population, Bahuns make up the second largest community in Nepal (after the Chhetri at 16%), but they are grossly over-represented in all significant areas of the polity. Resentment grew, therefore, as other ambitious, educated youth from other communities came into the mainstream and found their path blocked. The Bahun in the upper reaches of politics and civil society alike failed to understand the need to proactively promote inclusion in a democracy, as the arguments made by many Bahuns for merit-based advance did not address the matter of historical marginalisation.

The brief but successful experiment in local governance in the late 1990s and early 2000s showed that members of marginalised communities had achieved the learning and political ambition needed to convert Nepali politics into a level playing field. If representational politics at the local level had continued, it would by now have delivered a veritable army of non-Bahun politicians into the upper echelons, and the exclusive face of today's national politics would be drastically different. Tragically, representative local government was disbanded after its first term, and a corrupting 'all-party mechanism' came up to take its place.

The local government initiative was also a move towards developing inclusive politics from below, as it opened the door for activists and party workers from many demographic groups to get elected to positions at the village and district levels. The cancellation of the planned 2002 local government elections to local government bodies and the endless hurdles in front of us when it comes to reviving the system not only weakened grassroots democracy but also sent an arrow into the heart of inclusive politics. Rule at the district and village levels by unelected party bosses in the name of 'all-party mechanisms', supported by government-appointed secretaries, has made a mockery of both inclusion and representation. For nearly a decade now, it has robbed the grassroots-level broad-based identities the opportunity to gain political experience. The entire realm of national politics has thus been made poorer, paradoxically when everyone is talking of inclusion and representation. It is a wonder that activist-scholars so actively seeking ethnically defined federalism have not bothered to demand the revival of local government as one of the places where inclusive politics should be energised.

A system of affirmative action with time-bound reservations carefully adjusted to the realities of Nepal's social fabric of micro-communities and its historical inequities is required to bring all communities to the forefront of national politics, the bureaucracy and the judiciary. Efforts must also be made to ensure inclusive representation in the media, the courts, the education sector, academia and the security forces. While working to institute such a practice, the state must be careful not to create a culture of entitlement and dependence; in this, lessons both positive and negative can be learnt from India. There is no denying the Bahun lock-hold on government echelons and a special effort must be made to break it, but the spread of opportunities in the private sector, including commerce and tourism, shows that the goals of inclusion can be achieved. Overall, the future of inclusion should not be tied to government jobs – though Nepal should aim for full proportionality in this realm; the concentration should instead be on creating a vibrant economy which opens up the job market all over the country at all levels.

Bahuns do dominate the government and politics of Nepal, but neither by conspiracy nor design. This community's ascendance was not state-mandated social engineering, meant to create an *apartheid* state in which the Bahun control all the levers of society. On the contrary, the catapulting of the Bahun to the political frontline was the result of a series of politico-demographic historical realities. Inevitably, these realities changed as Nepal evolved into an open society post-1990 and the market and the world entered its villages. Indeed, the Bahun were first to rush in to exploit the new opportunities because of their dispersal, their tradition of learning, and their proficiency in Nepali. At the same time, there has been a palpable acceleration in the spread of education, opportunity and ambition among all castes and ethnicities of mountain, hill and plain. The Bahuns were fast on the uptake, primed as they were to take advantage of competitive politics in 1990; however, the constant push for inclusion since then and the added momentum after 2006 means that the Bahun representation in positions of authority will progressively decline to reflect their proportion in society.

The hoary picture of conspiratorial societal exclusivity sought by the Bahun-Chhetri that is propagated by some prejudiced scholar-activists does not do justice either to the complexities of inter-community relations in Nepal or to the possibilities of course correction. It also neglects the sad reality that a large proportion of Bahun-Chhetris are mired in poverty and marginalisation, though few acknowledge that fact. The upheavals of the last few years have certainly shaken up society, and the revival of local government, the implementation of federalism, and the opening up of the national-level arena will see all communities rising to participate proudly in a polity they can call their own.

20

The People's Movement

The Movement of April 2006

If there is one grand episode that proves to the world the political style and sophistication of the Nepali masses, it is the People's Movement of April 2006, which reflected an entire population's extraordinary commitment to democracy and peace. Some call it the second People's Movement; the first was in the spring of 1990 and brought an end to three decades of rule under the Panchayat regime. The 2006 People's Movement was a coming together of the public, starting in the districts and culminating in massive daily rallies over 19 days in Kathmandu Valley to bring down the absolute monarchy Gyanendra put in place with his putsch of February 2005, which followed the 'creeping coup' he had initiated in October 2002. The movement was also a direct message to the Maoist insurgents that true revolutions require the peaceful participation of the people as a whole.

Resistance to Gyanendra began in June 2002 with his dismissal of Sher Bahadur Deuba as elected prime minister and dissolution of Parliament. Donning the crown after the murder of his brother Birendra, Gyanendra had begun to build the ground for a royal takeover by questioning the abilities, motives and nationalist commitment of the political parties. His tactics were like those of his father, Mahendra, four decades earlier, and, indeed, Gyanendra seemed to suffer from the delusion that time had stood still and that a second royal coup would also succeed. After dismissing Deuba, Gyanendra began appointing and dismissing governments on his own until, in February 2005, he himself took over as head of government. His excuse was tackling the Maoist insurgency, but, as became evident later on, Gyanendra had been holding secret talks with the rebels to sideline the political parties before he decided to go his own way.

The leaders of civil society came into their own during this period of royal autocracy, keeping the flame of liberty alive at a time when the political parties had lost status and energy and were finding it difficult to challenge Gyanendra. Having been charged with mal-governance from 1990 to 2002, the image of the political parties was further tarnished as many of the topmost political leaders made compromises with Gyanendra, some even 'applying' at the Narayanhiti for the post of prime ministership.

Even after Gyanendra's naked ambition became clear, the leadership of the parties found it difficult to spark a democratic people's movement. Instead, it was unaffiliated civil society stalwarts such as Padma Ratna Tuladhar, Daman Nath Dhungana, Devendra Raj Panday, Dr Mathura Shrestha, Krishna Pahadi and Shyam Shrestha who rallied the public. Other stalwarts included Sambhu Thapa of the Nepal Bar Association and Bishnu Nisthuri of the Federation of Nepali Journalists, political scientist Krishna Khanal of Tribhuvan University, the entertainer duo Madan Krishna Shrestha and Hari Bamsha Acharya, the young minstrel Rubin Gandharva, and many poets and singers. Numerous unsung leaders in Kathmandu and the districts, including those affiliated to trade unions, professional groups and academia, added depth to the movement. Eventually, many of the stalwart activists were apprehended by the royal regime, but by then the public at large had taken matters into its own hands.

Though unable to generate crowds on their own, the party leaders decided to send their own cadre to join the civil society meetings and swell participation. Octogenarian Girija Prasad Koirala crisscrossed the country with a simple message for the people: there must be civilian supremacy vis-à-vis the military, the people are sovereign, and the Parliament must be reinstated. Starting after Gyanendra's takeover, Koirala's Congress leaders and those of the CPN (UML) began to reach out to the top-level Maoists, who tended to hover in and around the Indian capital. Meanwhile, officials in New Delhi started turning the screws on the rebels to negotiate and come above ground. The Maoists ultimately proved willing, for they needed a parachute out of the 'people's war' to a 'soft landing'. However, they agreed to an alliance with the parliamentary parties only after Gyanendra tricked them, denying them their planned collaboration, with his coup of 1 February 2005.

The early attempt of the alliance of the seven parliamentary parties (the SPA) to challenge the royal regime was a non-starter because its platform was limited to the reinstatement of democracy and was silent on peace, both of which the people wanted in tandem. During negotiations in New Delhi, the rebels initially insisted on a parallel movement, retaining their own violent campaign. However, they realised soon enough that this would not be accepted. It was only when the SPA signed the 12-Point Agreement with the Maoists for a peaceful movement that public participation was galvanised against Gyanendra. The people arose in a spontaneous mass movement, which culminated in 19 days of protests between 6 April and 27 April 2006.

Hundreds of thousands of Nepali citizens appeared in the streets and fields to demand non-violent politics and an end to royal autocracy, and, in doing so, paved the way for peace and democracy. The demonstrations by ordinary, non-political citizens grew by the day even as many of the civil society stalwarts who had helped trigger the movement were arrested. The People's Movement culminated in demonstrations so massive that they stretched the entire circumference of the 27 km Ring Road that encircles Kathmandu and Lalitpur. On 21 April 2006, Gyanendra offered a half-way measure of capitulation: he would establish a government as proposed by the political parties. That move was initially supported by Indian and Western diplomats, but the public rejected the suggestionand the political parties, headed by Girija Prasad Koirala, stood their ground. Three days after his partial capitulation, Gyanendra relented and agreed to reinstate the dissolved Parliament. Nearly two dozen people died during the People's Movement and many more were maimed. Thankfully, many head-on collisions between the massive demonstrations and the security forces, including the army, were avoided or many more would have lost their lives.

Rhododendron Revolution

Few events in Southasia during the last six decades can be compared to the People's Movement of 2006 in terms of the sheer size of participation in a peaceful protest for regime change. It was a show of people power somewhat larger than the movements in Eastern Europe of the previous decade, whether the Rose Revolution of Georgia or the Orange Revolution of the Ukraine. The People's Movement was of the kind that overtook North Africa and parts of the Persian Gulf in the spring of

2011, a mass call for democracy and non-violence in politics. Nepal's 'Rhododendron Revolution' stands as the voice and directive of the people today, even as the above-ground Maoists have sought to hijack the polity by foisting their own definition on the Movement. For this and other reasons, much of what has transpired after 2006 is not owned by the population at large, representing instead sometimes a deviation, if not an outright betrayal, of what the people sought. The Maoists' refusal to complete the peace process five years after the People's Movement ended the 'people's war' is one such treachery. Others include the weakening of the representativeness of Parliament by allowing 83 Maoists to enter wholesale as members rather than as consultants until they could be elected. Moreover, the declarations that Nepal would adopt federalism and be a republic were political decisions taken by a partially elected body in order to reward the Maoists and keep them in the peace process. Many far-reaching decisions have been taken under populist pressure or in an attempt to keep the peace process active and the Maoists appeased, and though they have no connection to the People's Movement, these decisions are justified in its name. The countrywide trickery practiced by the Maoist party during the Constituent Assembly elections of April 2008 constituted a grave violation of the values espoused by the People's Movement. The Maoists could now claim to be speaking on behalf of the 'people' through the ballot and try to erase the values that had driven the masses in April 2006. It bears repeating that the unrehearsed, spontaneous uprising of the Nepali public was for two simple demands – peaceful politics and an end to autocracy.

It is the People's Movement itself, not subsequent events and claims, which we must study to understand the underlying values of Nepali society. The people voiced their desire for a peaceful means of political transformation, said 'no' to the armed insurgency, and demanded a return from absolute monarchy to absolute democracy. In short, the People's Movement laid out a general pathway for a return to both peace and democracy. The discourse of the intervening years, however, has suggested that the People's Movement demanded more specific terms, i.e., a republic, a constituent assembly and federalism. Any study of newspaper archives will show clearly that the people did not set out such a detailed road map; they merely set out the broad guideline to our future. It was the power of Maoist propaganda and the weaknesses of the parliamentary parties and civil society to confront that propaganda which allowed departures beyond what the people had contemplated when they walked the streets and trails. To review the series of decisions taken after the People's Movement is not to try and undo them – many were taken out of evolving political necessity – but only to clarify what the People's Movement was about and what it was not about. The republic, for example, is a political *fait accompli*, and fealty to the People's Movement requires that we fight to keep it democratic through the writing and implementation of the new constitution.

One thing is clear: the people showed their ability to crush the autocratic ambitions of a foolish monarch who used the national army as his tool. They were also able to force the insurgents to adapt to a civilised, popular way of securing a political transformation. The People's Movement made clear to anyone, of either the radical left or the radical right, who harboured autocratic inclinations that the Nepali public would ultimately dash such hopes. The people as a whole cannot always rise up, but when they do speak up *en masse*, they trust the politicians and civil society to heed their bidding. Sadly, the directives of the People's Movement of April 2006 have been ignored by both politicians and civil society stalwarts. Most importantly, those in charge have not worked to push the peace process through to a successful conclusion. With the cantonments and the 'PLA' still in place, the all-important task of constitution-writing has stalled. The Maoists have sought to hijack the polity and the democrat-politicians of the parliamentary parties have been either too trusting or too lacking in dynamism to challenge them.

In the middle of the political recriminations and wrangling, it is important to remember that the People's Movement is the guiding light for the drafting of the new constitution and the evolution of the polity. In defining the new political landscape of Nepal as a federal republic through the new constitution, we must remember that when they arose in April 2006, the people made two simple demands – liberty and politics without violence. Though they also participated in the People's Movement, the Maoists were humbled enough by the show of people power not to use their firearms during the 19 continuous days of demonstrations. While the Maoist leaders like to claim the movement as their own, more credit goes to the SPA, civil society and the public at large. Given the fraud that marked the April 2008 elections which gave the Maoists such a presence in the Constituent Assembly and associated parliament, it is the People's Movement of two years earlier which is a better measure of the desires of the Nepali citizenry. If the shenanigans of the Maoists take the polity away from pluralism and non-violence, the people will have no choice other than to once again express their collective will.

Ganatantra, prajatantra, loktantra

Ganatantra, prajatantra, loktantra – these terms are not interchangeable though they are often used as if they were, especially the last two. Each carries a specific meaning in contemporary parlance. *Ganatantra* means, simply, republic. Nepal was declared a *ganatantra* by the Interim Constitution of 2007, which abolished the monarchy through a political act undertaken by the revived Parliament, including its new Maoists members. The idealised goal of the Maoists, as the draft constitution they have made public reveals, is to establish a *jana-ganatantra*, or people's republic, ostensibly modelled on the People's Republic of China. *Prajatantra* was the term used by one and all during the modern era, from 1951 till 2006, to mean democracy. The term remained extant after 1990, when Nepal became a constitutional monarchy.

When King Gyanendra started his creeping coup in 2002, civil society activists decided to abandon the use of *prajatantra* because *praja*, or subjects, derive their existence from the presence of a king. Instead, they used *loktantra*, a term used extensively in Hindi. In Nepal, the new term was taken to mean democracy without reference to monarchy. The claim of some conservative commentators that *loktantra* was introduced by the Maoists does not stand up to scrutiny. Though older democrats such as Girija Prasad Koirala continued to use *prajatantra* out of habit, others have by now adopted *loktantra*. Amidst the transitional etymology, one could say that *prajatantra* connotes the Nepali practice of democracy under a constitutional monarchy, while *loktantra* refers to representative democracy in a republic. As far as it concerns pluralism, human rights and fundamental freedoms, there is no difference between the two. The move from *prajatantra* to *loktantra* simply marks the transition from a constitutional monarchy to republic.

Democratic republic or people's republic?

It is important to get history right, even if the story sounds better otherwise. The People's Movement of 2006 did not demand a republic, and retaining the kingship remained a possibility for at least a year after the uprising dismantled Gyanendra's autocracy. As the people understood it, the goal was to stand up for democracy, pluralism and non-violent politics, and under the right circumstances these principles could very well have been preserved under a constitutional monarchy. After the people showed their ability to crush autocratic designs, no one need have feared the monarchy after April 2006. However, the personage of Gyanendra made it difficult to build the trust needed to restore constitutional monarchy and he, so went the argument, would always be there to block the democratic exercise. Girija Prasad Koirala mounted a rearguard effort to preserve the institution, suggesting either an infant monarch or a ceremonial monarchy be adopted, but it was the royal palace itself that posed a hurdle. Gyanendra just did not have the ability to apologise, to show humility before the people, or to accept a relative (other than his wayward son Paras) as successor. Gyanendra was the biggest republican of all, as the man who ushered the monarchy out the door through his escapades between 2002 and 2006, and his inability to apologise in the year following the People's Movement. A show of humility and a request for forgiveness would probably have turned the public mood in favour of retaining the kingship.

Though the royal palace repeatedly interfered with and disrupted the democratic evolution of Nepal, the public, in the hope that democracy could be preserved under a constitutional monarchy, showed much forbearance. Retaining the two-and-a-half century-old monarchy was still a possibility for months until the democrat-politicians agreed to a republic, a political concession to the Maoists for giving up their 'people's war'. Now that we are a republic, however, all effort must be concentrated on making that republic a robust, caring democracy. With the kingship dissolved, the polity is released from the constant interference it had to contend with earlier. At the same time, the political parties no longer have a royal palace on which to pin the blame for their mistakes and incapacities. The key value within the republic must be pluralism, even though the UCPN (Maoist) documents and declarations make it clear that their goal is 'revolutionary republicanism', meaning a top-down, centralised, non-federal, one-party communist state – whatever spin they may give the public.

While accepting the political decisions which converted Nepal into a republic from a constitutional monarchy and declared the country 'federal', it is important to resist the populist pressures to accept republic and federalism as representing universal values such as democracy, pluralism, non-violence and human rights. Federalism and republicanism are political choices that societies make; they do not necessarily represent a 'universal good'. Some constitutional monarchies, such as Norway, Japan, the United Kingdom and the Netherlands, because they are transparent democracies, are much more preferable to authoritarian republics like Zimbabwe, Burma and Uzbekistan. Some unitary states, such as Japan, Sweden and South Africa, are better governed than some federal countries, such as Nigeria, the former USSR and present-day Bosnia. In resisting the Maoist attempts to define the Federal Democratic Republic of Nepal according to its own image, we must understand that the country with which the party is most closely aligned ideologically is the Democratic People's Republic of Korea, which is neither democratic nor republican and one would be hard pressed say that it is owned by the people. In addition, some members of two nations share a disturbing affinity for using violence to get what they want. Let not the people of the Republic of Nepal face the same fate as the beleaguered citizens of DPRK.

21

Madhes, Arise!

Movement of 2007

The Madhesi people of the Tarai plains have long felt doubly disfranchised. Like the other hill and plains ethnic communities, they have been kept out of the national mainstream; in addition, they have not been allowed to lay claim to the state, whose identity, as reflected in the national dress, faith and language, has long been along the lines of the mid-hill culture shared by the major ethnicities and castes. The Nepali *topi* crosses the country from the Mechi to the Mahakali rivers along the mid-hill chain, irrespective of community, and Nepali is a lingua franca that was propagated not only by the hill castes and the Nepali state, but also by returning Gurkha soldiers. The 'hilly' nature of Nepali nationalism almost completely excluded Madhesis, who felt that their own cultural heritage was compromised. Indignant at being thus kept at arm's length deep into the democratic era, the Madhesi were primed for an uprising against the state and neither the political leadership, the development community nor Kathmandu's civil society were sufficiently sensitive to the discontent brewing in the Tarai.

While the movement of ethnic assertion gathered momentum in the hills after 1990, Madhesi distress remained bottled up. Nepal continued to be presented as a mountainous Shangri La even as the size of the population of the plains (including people of hill origin) overtook that of the hills and mountains. The nationalist icons have remained hill-centred: the new government seal of the republic is adorned with the mountain rhododendron and Sagarmatha/Chomolongma (only half of which, incidentally, is in Nepal). The Chitwan and Bardia jungles were developed as tourism sites in the plains, but they are linked to the forest livelihood of the Tharu rather than to the Madhesi cultural frame. Lumbini, the birthplace of Siddhartha Gautam, has become the pre-eminent site in the Tarai, but Buddhism is rather remote from the present-day plains culture. Only lately has Janakpur, the birthplace of Sita and the seat of her father, Dasrath, been recognised as a national heritage site, and the national cultural elite has allowed the great archaeological site of Simraungarh in the central Tarai to be desecrated without voicing an iota of concern.

Donor agencies, too, for decades neglected the Tarai, where poverty is as entrenched as it is in many parts of the hills but affects many more people per square mile. In the Kathmandu imagination, which influenced the international and donor agency perception, the Tarai communities were seen as appendages of the Indian plains. Ironically, it was this very neglect that ensured the strength of the Madhesi political activism when it erupted in 2007. Often, discovery by the donor sidetracks movements away from grassroots political organisation and towards workshops and seminars, as has happened with much feminist, Dalit and even ethnic activism. The distance of the Madhesi community from Kathmandu-centric and international thinking allowed it to emerge as a potent challenge to the state establishment in the early months of 2007, triggered by the writing of the Interim Constitution. It was only after the Madhesi people rose up in a mass movement that international funders finally discovered plains-based organisations and individuals to support. Workshops and seminars are now all the rage in Nepalganj, Birganj and Janakpur.

When the Interim Constitution was being drafted in 2007, the Madhesi intelligentsia felt that it was an opportunity to rewrite the relationship of the plains population with the state. When it was learnt that the drafters of the Interim Constitution, including the Maoists, were not going to mention federalism in the text, there was protest. The Madhesi intelligentsia believed that they would be protected in the 'new Nepal' only if there were a federal structure with an adequate devolution of power. When the national political classes seemed reluctant to incorporate federalism, the Madhes erupted in a movement which saw the death of nearly twice as many citizens as had died during the People's Movement of 2006. It is instructive that all the dead were protesting civilians; there were no casualties among the security personnel.

The outcome of the Madhes Movement was the inclusion of federalism in the Interim Constitution. This was seen as a boon by the other hill and plains communities of Nepal, which would otherwise probably have let the opportunity pass, given that the Maoists themselves were pulling back on it. The actual advantages of federalism will depend upon how it is defined and whether the Madhesi intelligentsia is able rise above identity-based populism and ensure that the future provinces are defined in such a way that they will promote the social and economic interests of the citizens of the Tarai. While the advantages of federalism lie somewhere in the future, the most impressive outcome of the Madhes uprising was that it upturned historical definitions and demanded and received their right to be considered first-class citizens of the country. This was an achievement from which no power centre can retract. People of Tarai origin, who constitute a large proportion of the total population, have finally begun to feel a sense of ownership of the nation-state of Nepal.

Post-movement issues
The Madhes Movement was the beginning of the political inclusion of the people of Tarai origin, and it was its momentum that ensured that both the first President and the first vice-President of the Federal Democratic Republic of Nepal are of eastern Madhesi origin. The state establishment has been appropriately chastened. While the promise of inclusion must be fully discharged by the state, there are challenges before the Madhesi civil society and leadership. Perhaps the largest challenge is that Madhes parochialism, which is pushed by the newly-established parties relying on identity-based populism, seems to neglect the social and economic interests of the plains population itself. Powerful plains politicians, who themselves represent various clan and caste interests, have found it difficult to rise above the amorphous and indeterminate identity of being Madhesi and assume the proportions of national politicians. The one shining exception is the Nepali Congress leader Ram Baran Yadav of Dhanusha District, who stood his ground against the more chauvinistic aspects of the Madhesi populism during the elections of April 2008, won a seat in the Constituent Assembly, and was endorsed by the country as a whole as the first President of the republic.

The definition of Madhesi is hazy but refers generally to caste people of plains origin who speak the Maithili, Avadhi or Bhojpuri tongues and use Hindi as their link language. Among those who identify themselves as Madhesi, the Maithili-speakers, who are concentrated between the towns of Gaur and Rajbiraj in the central Tarai, have the highest national profile and have taken the lead in representing the plains in national politics. However, not all people of Tarai origin accept the Madhesi identity all the time; those who reject it include many Tharu, the largest ethnic group of the plains and one spread across its length, other plains ethnic communities, and Muslims. Certainly, the term 'Madhesi' does not cover those hill communities, both caste and ethnic, which migrated to the plains early on or recently. To many, the Madhesi engine seems over-bearing though others, like some Muslims, have decided to join the train even if they do not consider themselves 'Madhesi' per se. Dissatisfaction with Madhesi hegemony spawned the Tharu Movement, which took off in March 2009, and it can be said that the Madhesi identity is still a work in progress in terms of how many Tarai-dwelling communities it will be able to bring within its fold. It is also possible that the term 'Madhesi' will revert to a loose politico-cultural signifier, and that we will see a return to the geographically neutral term 'Tarai' that has been sidelined since 2007.

One Madhes
During the transitional period in which the new constitution is being written, the single concentration of the many competing Madhesi politicians has been in consolidating their hold on the plains populace by loudly declaring their populist agenda, at whose heart resides the unworkable demand for 'One Madhes, One Pradesh'. The proposal is to demarcate a province that would include the entire Tarai plain, a region roughly 500 miles long and 20 miles wide which incorporates dozens of population groups varying greatly by faith, ethnicity, language and geographical origin, not all of which wish to be labelled Madhesi. This insistence on a single plains province is based on the supposition that all in the Tarai share a common identity and an apparent willingness to forgo the possibility of economic and social advance for the sake of this nebulous identity.

Over time, the demand for one federal province covering the entire plains region has given way to proposals for three or more, but even these would have to pass the test of people-friendliness. Why would the plains leadership want to give up the income of the adjacent hills and mountains, including tourism, hydropower, agro-forestry and service industries? If it is true that a significant part of Nepal's economic growth in coming decades will happen in the hills (and this is likely) then it would be less than wise for Madhesi parties to separate their population from the future largesse. A study of any of the plains districts, take, for example, Bara in the central Tarai, will show that the quality of life is better towards the north because access to resources increases. Getting the electricity and water that industrial and agricultural growth rely on will be far easier if the hills which hold these resources are part of the same 'Tarai-hill-mountain' province than if their purchase has to be negotiated with a different province altogether. As the newly formed Madhesi parties consolidate their presence, or as the national parties (the CPN (UML), the UCPN (Maoist) and the Nepali Congress) make a comeback in the plains after the debacle of the April 2008 elections, geography and economics will probably become more a part of the state-restructuring debates in the Tarai towns than it currently is.

Madhesi parties will doubtless emerge over the next few years as more 'political', rising above identity-based populism to speak up for democratic values and fundamental freedoms in the Tarai as well for what makes best economic sense for the plains citizenry. The relationship that has developed between some of these parties and the cross-border criminal gangs will probably be downgraded as the people demand more accountability. A class character is bound to emerge, forcing the parties to tackle the enormous economic disparities and deprivation in the Tarai. There is a need for Madhesi parties to bring public health and basic services into their agenda and to seek, for example, a doubling of the number of primary school teachers in the Tarai so that the teacher-student ratio in the classroom is brought down from 1:90 to 1:40.

As they consolidate their base of support, one expects the Madhesi parties will become more national and less parochial; they will, for example, advocate proportional representation in the national army but not through group entry, seek a north-south definition of federal units that will help bring prosperity to plains households, and persuade the hill people who were forced out of the Tarai after 2007 to return. Beyond demanding representation in state institutions, the Madhesi parties must evolve to become more representative of the caste and ethnic groups of the plains, and recognise the discrimination that keeps, for example, the Tarai Dalit and the Muslim the most marginalised groups in the entire country. As time passes, Madhesi parties will also start to represent the people of hill origin in the plains and ultimately emerge as national parties.

The mid-eastern Tarai

Even though the population elsewhere has seen a slow return to peace and tranquility following the end of the 'people's war' in 2006, this has not been the case for the plains, especially the mid-eastern Tarai, which, for several years now, has been the most violent part of Nepal. Maoist splinter groups and newborn politico-criminal outfits take advantage of the open border to find refuge in Uttar Pradesh and Bihar and conduct militancy in Nepal. There has been a heart-stopping rise in targeted killings, kidnappings and extortion by militants and extra-judicial killings by the state. The intimidation of media organisations as well as of print and radio reporters is higher in this region than in any other, and the degree of self-censorship practiced is of grave concern.

The newborn Madhesi parties have not tried to block this violent trend and some even provide undeclared support to militant groups. Many politicians pressure the state administration and the judiciary to release militants who are arrested, and, in response to this demand, the police have resorted to 'encounter killings'. When human rights groups from Kathmandu have protested, some community leaders have gone as far as to ask them to desist, saying that the situation would spiral out of control if the criminal gangs were not checked in this manner.

One of the most unremarked aspects of the law-and-order situation in the mid-eastern plains is the departure of Pahade people from towns like Janakpur and Rajbiraj and the surrounding villages between 2007 and 2009. Because the human rights community and the national media are manned mostly by people of hill origin, they 'over-corrected' by doing less than necessary to protest against this exodus by challenging the Madhesi politicians. A related trend is the evolution of the East-West Highway, which runs close to the Chure hills, as a demarcation line between the Madhesi and Pahade regions of the Tarai. Even though great tragedy has visited the hill people living amidst the plains communities, the people most extensively affected by the Tarai-based militancy – the killings, kidnappings, extortions – have been the Madhesi. Unfortunately, the parties which have emerged since the Madhes Movement have not, in the present stage of their growth, shown sufficient humanitarian concern for the victims.

The Madhes Movement of 2007 helped the Nepali citizens of the plains wrest full ownership of the state for themselves. Now the plains people ask the Madhesi political leadership to work for their economic uplift, eschewing parochialism, defining federalism beyond nebulous identities, seeking linkages with the adjoining hills, abandoning all nexus with criminal gangs, and being alert to the class and communal divides in the Tarai. To do this and to secure their own political futures, Madhesi politicians must represent all the plains people – the Tharu and other ethnicities, Muslims, the Dalit, the 'other backwards castes', as well as the Pahade. A Tarai population which has been eyeing the sudden rise of Bihar, once the 'basket case' of Southasia, and expects the same to happen in the Purvanchal region of eastern Uttar Pradesh, India, wants nothing less for itself.

22

Republican Nepal

The new constitution and the republic
The parliamentary parties agreed to hold elections for the Constituent Assembly as part of the peace package to end the 'people's war' and bring the CPN (Maoist) into open politics. The reason for abolishing the monarchy and declaring Nepal a republic was the same, though, of course, things are a bit more nuanced than that. The political parties and civil society came to the conclusion that even though the Maoist defeat in the war had begun, with the army able to hold its ground, their complete subjugation would demand the blood of too many innocents. Thus, going against the advice of the diplomatic corps, the parliamentary parties decided to reach out to the underground rebels. The UML leadership held parleys in several cities of India, including Siliguri and Lucknow, and the President of the Nepali Congress, Girija Prasad Koirala, sent emissaries to meet the Maoist leaders in New Delhi.

During the negotiations with what came to be the seven party alliance, the Maoists asked what they would receive in return (or what they could tell their cadre they got) for abandoning the 'people's war' and its accompanying rhetoric of revolt. The SPA suggested that the Maoists could have elections to a constituent assembly, which was one of their 40 demands when they went underground in 1996. The Nepali Congress itself had sought a constituent assembly in the 1950s, a demand it had let lapse over the decades, particularly after the establishment of a constitutional monarchy under the Constitution of 1990. The Maoists offered this agreement to their followers as evidence of their success. What was originally meant as a face-saving measure for the leadership was used to maximum advantage once they came above ground, when the Maoist leadership discovered the power of propaganda and its ability to manipulate the media, commentators and the political parties. After the idea of a constituent assembly had been accepted by the Maoists, it was embraced by marginalised communities, including ethnicities and the Madhesi, in the hope that a new constitution would help eradicate discrimination and provide a fast track to social and economic advancement.

As suggested earlier, the removal of the monarchy was not a demand of the People's Movement. When the movement ended, Gyanendra remained in Narayanhiti, though he was more a ceremonial or cultural monarch than a constitutional head of state. For almost a full year, until the Maoists entered the interim Legislature Parliament (named so because the Maoists wanted to camouflage 'parliament' with a qualifier), the king did his state-mandated cultural rounds by visiting the Kumari, Nepal's 'living goddess' during the Indra Jatra festival, worshipping at temples and shrines on Shivaratri and Krishna Astami and during Dasain, and attending the Bungdeo (Machendranath/Avalokiteshwar) chariot festival of Lalitpur. However, with the number of Maoist members of parliament equalling that of the CPN (UML), the outcome of Girija Prasad Koirala's tactical benevolence designed to control the power of the UML, it became apparent that the kingship would go. Just out of the jungle and still requiring an enemy to keep the flock together, the Maoist leadership drummed up a phobia of the de-fanged kingship. Of course, this fear-mongering was used to cover up its discomfiture at having abandoned the 'people's war'. In reality, the party had conspired with the 'dreaded enemy' Gyanendra before his February 2005 takeover and had been in an undeclared alliance with Birendra earlier. Even so, the Maoist propaganda machine was able to make the Kathmandu intelligentsia look at things its way. For their part, the parliamentary parties were willing to go along with the Maoists. The memory of Gyanendra's autocracy was still raw, and the monarchy had been a thorn in the side of democracy for six decades – a spoilsport institution which promoted ultra-nationalism in order to build its own space, pitted political parties against each other, and maintained a facade of inclusion and pluralism even while promoting the Kathmandu diktat.

Republicanism had remained the unstated foundational demand of many in the democratic left even as they had adjusted to constitutional monarchy. The Nepali Congress had suffered most under the ambitious monarchs of the past, Tribhuvan, first, and then Mahendra, Birendra and Gyanendra. Haunted by the spectre of the arrogant Gyanendra remaining on the throne to be followed by his wild and unruly son Paras, few leaders objected to the advent of *ganatantra* even though it would be seen as part of the Maoist rather than the parliamentary party agenda and the former rebels would be sure to reap the propaganda advantage. At least the spoiler in the royal palace would be removed, is what the democrat-politicians thought.

Goodbye, monarchy
After 1990, regional super-power India supported the twin-pillar arrangement in Nepal – a multi-party democracy supported by a constitutional monarchy. The primary concern of New Delhi, as of Beijing, is a politically stable Nepal, and in their eyes the monarchy helped steady the polity. This position was jettisoned by New Delhi when adventurist King Gyanendra sought to turn geopolitics on its head by leaning towards Beijing. The February 2005 coup by Gyanendra was the last straw for New Delhi, which saw that the constitutional monarchy was in its last throes. Even with New Delhi on board, though, there would have been no republic without the acquiescence of Girija Prasad Koirala, in declining health but still the unquestioned power centre. Prime Minister Koirala suggested the options of ceremonial king and even a baby king, but Gyanendra's stubbornness even in the face of the republican tsunami meant that the octogenarian politician could not halt the tide of events.

During that crucial year after the People's Movement, Gyanendra had ample opportunity to lay himself bare before the people, to apologise for his autocratic designs and thus to save the throne, if not his own place on it. In the end, the last king of the Shah Dynasty turned out to be the most republican of them all, creating the conditions for ending the lineage through his stupidity and hubris. Gyanendra can be considered more responsible for the advent of republican Nepal than even the Maoists, taking, as he did, actions that robbed the monarchy of the goodwill of the democrat-politicians and the people. To begin with, he should have realised that the royal palace massacre of 2001, for which he was unjustly blamed, had weakened the kingship terribly and for that reason he should have reined in his adventurism. In the year's grace period he had before the Maoists joined the Interim Parliament, Gyanendra could have testified before the Rayamajhi Commission set up to investigate the excesses during the People's Movement or made a public declaration, expressing remorse for all his actions since 2002. Instead, he maintained a stony royal silence. Thus, when the time came, the institution had to go.

Man in Narayanhiti

The mistake that Gyanendra made was to believe that the monarchy was a plaything of the sitting monarch, whereas, in fact, its ownership lay with the people of Nepal. It was Gyanendra's direct ancestor of 12 generations ago, Prithvi Naryayan Shah, who unified Nepal and established the Shah dynasty. Prithvi Narayan gets credit for establishing what became the oldest nation-state in the Subcontinent, established when the prototypical European nation-states also were just beginning to form.

The history of Nepal is inextricably linked to the institution of the monarchy dating as far back as when real-life events collide with mythology, to the Gopala dynasty and the ancient aboriginal kings who worshipped the sun god. In terms of recorded history, kingship is tied to periods even before the Shah dynasty, including the Lichchhavi and Malla rulers of Kathmandu Valley, scores of ethnic and Thakuri principalities all over the country, and the Sen dynasties of Udayapur, Palpa and elsewhere. It is noteworthy that several ceremonial kinglets who had been subjugated by Gorkha, including the Raja of Mustang Jigme Parbal Bista, continued to receive token disbursements from the Kathmandu state well into the 21st century. The abolition of the Nepali kingship was thus a matter of historical significance far beyond the collapse of the Shah dynasty, even though the public and intelligentsia have not had time to mull over this fact in the rush and reverberations of constitution-writing, the peace process, and power-sharing.

The People's Movement of 2006 proved that the populace had the will and the agency to bring the autocratic monarchy to heel within a democratic framework. Thus, it would have been possible to retain a constitutional monarchy if not for the fact that the Maoists desperately needed to abolish it, that they manipulated the media and the intelligentsia to make it happen, and the fact that the democratic parties had no love left for the institution. The removal of the monarchy was thus a political decision taken for the sake of the peace process. That much is history, and must be stated. However, even though the republic was not a demand of the People's Movement, the absence of the royal palace that was an obtrusive force against democracy throughout six decades of the modern era, including during King Birendra's constitutional monarchy, will force the Nepali polity to mature and allow democracy to consolidate. For this, the first challenge is the very party which forced through the republic, the UCPN (Maoist), which hopes to establish a much more rigid, autocratic and centralised state than the monarchy could have ever managed in the modern era. Against Maoist wishes, which would be to create a 'people's republic', the democratic republic must now be used to strengthen democracy rather than weaken it. The advantage of the republican polity is that one does not now have to be on constant guard against the machinations of the royal palace, pitting political parties against each other or using the army against civilian will. Nor can politicians use the royal palace as a convenient scapegoat for their own mistakes and incompetence.

The departure of the man in the Narayanhiti royal palace is a *fait accompli*, a step to be used to build representative democracy. A return of a cultural monarchy with an official stamp, which the Maoists leadership has now been mulling as an opportunistic way of garnering support, would give more power to the institution than the polity could sustain. Gyanendra's departure from Narayanhiti was, other than the rowdiness of the press in attendance, the epitome of decorum: he left with the dignity befitting a member of a historical monarchy, the 12th descendent of the great unifier of Nepal, Prithvi Narayan. His departure was something to marvel at and is an indication of how much more refined the Nepali polity and its democrat-politicians are than friends near and far give them credit for. It was at the press conference that Gyanendra finally defended himself against the charge of complicity in his brother Birendra's murder though the media and opinion-makers cruelly ignores his plaintive defence.

The place of ex-royalty

The first important thing is to strengthen pluralism, democracy and non-violent politics, and, with the departure of the monarchy, this step will be made within the new republic. It is also important to set the historical record straight, to record how the republic was achieved and not be carried away by the breathless rendition of events presented by commentators under the thrall of Maoist populism. A proper description of the run of events, after all, will strengthen democracy within the republic that Nepal has become. Given the modern history of Nepal, in which the radical left has been close to the royalist right wing, in a tradition that goes back to the early Panchayat era, when some 'Russian communists' became royal apologists, and given that the republic is a reality, it is important now to nurture the republic, to let democracy consolidate, and to prevent a comeback by the kingship in any form that is recognised by the constitution and state.

As the peace process and constitution-writing have faltered, the hopes of some kind of a restoration of monarchy has flickered in the mind of ex-king Gyanendra and his cohort. He harbours expectations that the growing political confusion will create the conditions required for reinstating the monarchy and that domestic acceptance will garner international recognition. The ex-king sees his main allies as the conservative Hindus of Nepal, backed by the large Hindutva lobby in India, which loudly regretted the collapse of the 'world's only Hindu kingdom'. Ironically, even though he seeks the support of the religious right in India, Gyanendra, too, relies on the anti-India ultra-nationalism which was developed by his father Mahendra and which puts him on the same page as the UCPN (Maoist). Meanwhile, the Maoist party reaches out to the royalists in its calls for the unity of all forces, including 'patriots' and 'nationalists', in the fight for national integrity. Gyanendra obviously sees the Maoists, and especially its utilitarian chieftain, Pushpa Kamal Dahal, as presenting the most viable route back to reinstatement of the monarchy.

Incidentally, the main building of the Narayanhiti royal palace has been converted into a museum, but the exhibits are nothing more than the royalty's living quarters suspended in time, frozen in June 2008, when Gyanendra departed. A sense of unreality pervades the bedrooms and dining rooms, which look as if they are awaiting the return of their occupants, belying the decisiveness with which the Nepali monarchy was ended. It is possible that some members of the political class still believe that the kingship will return and do not want to take the initiative to convert the former royal palace into productive use on behalf of the people. This may be why the new President of Nepal was not moved into Narayanhiti but has to make do with the former state guest house, Shital Niwas. The expansive grounds of the former royal palace provide one of the few open spaces in a crowded city and must be opened up as a park and green for the population to enjoy. The main Narayanhiti building, if it is not to house the President of the Republic, must be made a national museum of the arts.

As part of the shenanigans related to the election of the prime minister in the summer of 2010, Chairman Dahal reached out to royalists for support, even offering to reinstate a cultural kingship. There was a history to this, for there are certain issues on which the Maoists and the royalty of Nepal, the latter representing the right wing of Nepali politics, come together. Most importantly, the ultra-nationalism developed by King Mahendra to bolster his regime in the 1960s was used by the CPN (Maoist) to develop its base both during the insurgency and in the period since. This ultra-nationalism is a switch that can be flicked, an easy tool to rouse youths who are unable to think critically because of an exploitatively poor education, both at the school and the college level. Both the monarchy and the Maoists have relied on the under-education of Nepal's youth to exploit ultra-nationalism, and they have been helped in this endeavour by the pusillanimity of the Kathmandu intelligentsia.

Being efficient utilitarians, with the ability to easily convince the cadre to espouse a drastic change of course, the Maoists, after they came above ground, saw the former royalist apparatchiks as allies and had no compunction in publicly taking them on as advisors and nominating them to the Constituent Assembly. The royalists, left out in the cold following the People's Movement, were more than happy to accommodate the Maoist demands. This was how, soon after the People's Movement, the man who was foreign minister during Gyanendra's autocracy became an advisor to the Maoist party on international affairs, and several Panchayat-era individuals – including one who had earned a name as the most despotic royal administrators of the time – were inducted into the Constituent Assembly as nominated members of the UCPN (Maoist).

Over the summer of 2010, the Maoists' reaching out to the former royals took on a more urgent turn. In his desperation to get back to the prime ministerial seat which he had vacated in May 2009, Dahal sought the support of the royalist Kamal Thapa, the chair of the Rastriya Prajatantra Party-Nepal, suggesting that the reinstatement of a cultural kingship would be fine by him. Among reports of collaboration between the former royals, the ex-king's son-in-law, businessman Raj Bahadur Singh, is said to have helped raise funds for the Maoist party, and even gone to New Delhi to as an interlocutor with the Indian political class. When Dahal made a dash to Malaysia in October 2010, he twice met the former crown prince, Paras Shah. He is said to have met the latter again in Singapore in March 2011. Meanwhile, Gyanendra plays a dangerous game with his dalliance with Hindutva, hoping to revive the monarchy on the back of religious conservatives, particularly those of the Tarai. While the Maoists and former royals draw near and drift apart according to their political needs, there is no doubt that one side will betray the other at the first opportunity should they ever even get together.

An alert polity will surely stymie the ex-king's and the Maoists' plans for cohabitation. In terms of how the life and times of the Nepali ex-royalty might evolve, there should be no recognition of kingship in any shape or form in state documents. Individual citizens are, of course, free to regard Gyanendra or his descendents as commoners or as royals as they wished. This would be the appropriate response to the end of the monarchy in a country that is and will remain an open society. It is likely, as has happened in those parts of India which had princelings till Independence in 1947, that the ex-royalty of Nepal will continue to be regarded as royal by some sections of the populace; the state and constitution, however, should not recognise or acknowledge its existence in any way. A return of any kind of formally recognised monarchy would give rise to an interventionist kingship that would retard democratic evolution much more than if the institution had never been abolished. A proper evolution of the constitutional monarchy before it was manhandled by Gyanendra and killed off by the Maoist momentum would have been the way to go, but that was back then. Now that the Nepali monarchy is gone, it is better to keep it so permanently.

23

April 2006 – April 2011 Review

Interim Parliament to republic
With the success of the People's Movement of 2006, the Parliament – dissolved by King Gyanendra on Prime Minister Sher Bahadur Deuba's recommendation in May 2002 – was reinstated. Girija Prasad Koirala, the only frontline leader who had not compromised in his opposition to Gyanendra's autocratic agenda, was propelled to the forefront as the only person with the credibility and power to define the peace process and the road back to democracy. There was debate for a while about how to accommodate the Maoists in the power structure, with some suggesting that they be included in a consultative body attached to Parliament. Instead, Koirala decided that they be included in what became the Interim Parliament as full-fledged members, giving them 83 seats, the same number the CPN (UML) had won through election. The royalty had its wings clipped by the Interim Parliament, which used republican symbolism to remove the term 'royal' from the national army, the national airline, the state-owned pharmaceutical company, and other state institutions.

While the Interim Constitution was being drafted, the Madhesi population of the Tarai rose up, demanding the declaration of a 'federal republic', a demand supported vociferously on the ground by the leadership of ethnic communities, particularly those of the east. The Nepali Congress lost its age-old foothold in the Tarai and at least three parties expressing a Madhesi agenda emerged. Militancy picked up in the middle-eastern Tarai as gun-wielding bands took advantage of the open border and safe houses in Bihar and Uttar Pradesh. The Maoists, too, were forced to retreat from the Tarai as other forces, including many former-Maoist Madhesis, took control of both politics and militancy.

The massacre of 26 Maoist activists in March 2007 in the Tarai town of Gaur showed how vulnerable even the ex-rebels became to violence in the post-'people's war' period.

The Interim Constitution declared Nepal a secular, federal republic, and left the job of defining federalism and the provinces to the forthcoming Constituent Assembly. UNMIN was invited to monitor the Assembly elections and the peace process. The Maoists established the Young Communist League, incorporating into it many of their hardened fighters. They claimed they had over 32,000 combatants in total, though UNMIN ultimately verified just over 19,000, all of whom were placed in seven main and 21 satellite cantonments across the country.

The interim government with Girija Prasad Koirala as the head of both the state and the government acted curiously in allowing the UCPN (Maoist) cadre leeway in their violent ways. The degree of impunity the Maoists enjoyed encouraged other groups to take advantage of the deteriorating rule of law to further weaken the state, particularly in the Tarai and the eastern hills. The Constituent Assembly elections of April 2008 saw the UCPN (Maoist) become the largest party, with more seats than the Nepali Congress and CPN (UML) combined. The Madhesi parties of the Tarai also became a significant force.

Immediately after the elections, the Maoists received their first setback in competitive politics: their candidate for President of the republic, Ram Raja Prasad Singh, was defeated by Ram Baran Yadav of the Nepali Congress, behind whom the other parties rallied. Singh was a former radical who had been involved in bombings and killings back in the Panchayat era and who had taught bomb-making to the Maoists during the conflict. He had floated his own party, which got so few votes in the Constituent Assembly elections they could be counted in the hundreds. After the elections, the Maoists believed they had complete control of who would be the first President of the republic, and they used the carrot of the presidency to try and waylay various leaders. Before they nominated Singh, they offered the position to both Madhav Kumar Nepal and Girija Prasad Koirala. Koirala's record in chaperoning society since 1990 and his leadership during the royal palace massacre crisis, the People's Movement and the declaration of republic certainly made him a deserving candidate, but perhaps Dahal's fear that Koirala's national and international stature, as well as his forceful personality would create a parallel power centre made him change his mind.

The Interim Constitution proposed establishing a consensus government of the kind that had been in place before the elections, on the premise that such a government would help in the drafting of a new constitution. However, with the Maoists creating hurdles to its joining the government, the Nepali Congress decided to stay in opposition. Its decision required amending the Interim Constitution to allow a majority government, which was done. As the caretaker prime minister, Girija Prasad Koirala asked the other parties to start consultations to form a government; for the delay that ensued he was accused of trying to hold on to the prime ministership. Ultimately, a coalition government was formed, led by the UCPN (Maoist) in an enviable all-powerful position and including the CPN (UML) and the Madhesi Janadhikar Forum.

The fact that a force which till just two years previously had been engaged in insurgency was suddenly at the helm of government indicated the strength of the peace process and the forbearance of the other parties, especially given that there had been significant Maoist malfeasance both before and during day of election. The UCPN (Maoist) held all the powerful ministries, including those of prime minister, finance, defence, peace and reconstruction, information, tourism, transport, labour and local government. The Ministry of Home Affairs was held by a Maoist-oriented UML leader, and the Ministry of Foreign Affairs went to the leader of the Madhesi Janadhikar Forum, a former member of the Maoist party. The ex-rebels were in a position to make the most of their control of the state machinery, but this required understanding parliamentary procedures and regional geopolitics and controlling the ambitions and waywardness of the cadre. Such wisdom was lacking, however, and the Maoists over-reached. Dahal's evident lack of principles and his inability to manage his own party meant that the Maoists were unable to use their time in government to present a responsible face to either the public, its neighbours, or the larger international community.

Maoist in government and out

The Maoists' period in government did serve to educate the party, to some extent, about the challenges of statecraft. At the same time, the public came to realise that the former rebels were neophytes when it came to governance, state administration and the parliamentary process and that, in addition, they harboured a veritable cache of ill intentions.

Maoist adventurism was rife, with the leadership egging on the cadre and looking the other way in the face of countrywide extortion, attacks on cultural traditions and media organisations, attempts to compromise the bureaucracy, a rush to above-ground impunity in the activities of the newly organised Young Communist League, a rise in the ostentatious lifestyles of the ex-rebel leadership, and – the final straw – an attempt to manipulate the chain-of-command of the national army. Dahal complained to confidantes that internal pressure within the party forced him to take action against the army chief, Rookmangud Katawal. Whether this was true or not, he acted unilaterally and against due process to dismiss General Katawal. President Yadav rejected the instruction and told Katawal to remain in his post.

Following the President's action, Dahal resigned as prime minister even though the other parties had not demanded his resignation. He may have quit due to pressures from within his own party, whose leadership may have believed that it had the numbers to get back into government with, perhaps, a prime minister other than Dahal. It did not quite work out that way: 22 out of 25 parties in the Constituent Assembly immediately got together, not only to ask the President to reject Katawal's termination but also to form a new majority coalition government. Madhav Kumar Nepal of the UML became the new head of government. The Maoists were to spend the next year, till the expiration and the subsequent renewal of the term of the Constituent Assembly in May 2010, vainly trying to bring down the Nepal government through street protests.

The President's action
On 4 May 2009, amidst tension that continued late into the night, President Ram Baran Yadav reversed Dahal's decision to dismiss the chief of army staff. He acted carefully and correctly throughout the episode, keeping this one remaining national institution outside the marauding reach of the UCPN (Maoist). His action could be justified both legally and constitutionally, though the opinion-makers in Kathmandu were curiously non-committal about his action in the following months and years, when their views would have made a difference. The Presidential move was precipitated by the *ultra vires* actions of the head of government. There was no other way to avert a grave national crisis – but to truly understand President Yadav's action one needs a bit of background.

The Maoist leadership had suggested to its cadre that there would be full integration of Maoist fighters into the national army, directly refuting the 12-Point Agreement, which called for partial integration into the national security forces and for rehabilitation of the remaining ex-combatants. In the Shaktikhor cantonment videotape Dahal himself assured cantonment residents of full integration. Over several months, Prime Minister Dahal sought to convince General Katawal to accept full integration but the general proved recalcitrant. When second-in-command Kul Bahadur Khadka, however, expressed his willingness to do the prime minister's bidding, Dahal decided to oust Katawal immediately so that Khadka could take charge.

With his action, President Yadav obviated the possibility of what could have been a blunderbuss Maoist move towards autocratic governance, one step on the way to creating a one-party state. After all, here was a prime minister from a party which retained its own private army trying to bring the national army within its political ambit as well. Alert to Prime Minister Dahal's nefarious plan of action, the President both met him in person and sent him official memos reminding him of the constitutional process. The Interim Constitution, the President told the prime minister, required decisions on important matters related to the peace process to be made by consensus. After dithering for a while and complaining to some confidantes that he was being cornered within his own party, Prime Minister Dahal decided to oust the army chief without seeking approval from the non-Maoists partners in his coalition. He sent the letter of dismissal directly to army headquarters rather than to the President, who is the supreme commander-in-chief and who had formally appointed the latter.

Not only had Dahal sought to destabilise the army by interfering with the chain-of-command but he had also introduced the possibility of bloodshed by creating a condition in which two generals were in command at the Bhadrakali army headquarters. Had he instead sent the letter to the President recommending Katawal's dismissal, the former could, at most, have sent it back once for review before approving the decision. But Dahal's hasty action forced the President's hand and the latter sent a note to Katawal ordering him to stay put. The Prime Minister was sent a copy of the order. Before making his move, however, the President had protected his flanks: he had a letter of support signed by 17 parties in the opposition and some in the ruling coalition. CPN

(UML) Chairman Jhala Nath Khanal, who later seemed to backtrack, signed that letter at the very top. There was a standoff at the army headquarters and the war of nerves between generals Katawal and Khadka lasted late into the night of the fourth May. Katawal's control of the senior officers and the President's directive helped him prevail, putting paid to the Maoists' plan to make Khadka chief.

Immediately, a writ petition submitted to the Supreme Court challenged President Yadav's action, but the justices dallied till a decision became moot. The Maoist leadership, in the meantime, spent the following year castigating the President as its newly anointed enemy. At a time when the new republic needed the office of the presidency to bring the increasingly divided national society together, the Maoists succeeded in bringing down the stature of the first incumbent. The polarisation between the President and the largest and loudest party in the Constituent Assembly weakened the presidency at a time when it should have evolved as a symbol of national unity in the fledgling republic. For President Yadav, a senior Nepali Congress politician who had stood up against the populism of the Madhes Movement, it would be a slow journey back to the spontaneous applause he had enjoyed immediately after being appointed head of state.

President Yadav would have regained his stature quicker had the intelligentsia been bold in analysing his move, but it maintained a studied silence. Some intellectuals, in fact, joined the Maoists in vociferously condemning the President's action. But even though they and the Maoists flayed President Yadav for pandering to the military, it was, in fact, his move to quash Prime Minister Dahal's summary action against the army chief that had helped maintain civilian supremacy in the country. Dahal's action was a bid to compromise the army and make it subservient to the whims of the Maoist party. To suggest that the President should have accepted the prime minister's unconstitutional action is to be blind to a situation about to severely compromise pluralism, peace and democracy. To condemn President Yadav without questioning Prime Minister Dahal's motives is tantamount to endorsing prejudice and radicalism.

President Yadav acted on behalf of the people of Nepal when he rejected, remaining within the constitution and with political endorsement, Dahal's dismissal of Katawal. His move was against an unconstitutional act, it was supported by the overwhelming majority of parties in Parliament, and its intention was to protect a society in political transition and undergoing a peace process. Those who suggest that President Yadav should have followed the dictates of the elected prime minister forget a) the elected prime minister could easily have forced the President to agree to his decision by following due process; b) the elected prime minister had violated the constitution's stricture on consensus decision-making; and c) the country was in the middle of an incomplete peace process and the Maoists still had their own armed force. At the very least, critics must consider the illegality of Prime Minister Dahal's action before challenging that of President Yadav.

The Nepal cabinet
The cabinet of Prime Minister Nepal, who succeeded Prime Minister Dahal, was weakened at the very start when the aging Nepali Congress President Girija Prasad Koirala insisted that his neophyte daughter Sujata lead his party in the cabinet. Koirala's directive saw other parties also send untested juniors to the cabinet at a time when tackling the Maoist challenge and providing good governance amidst the reigning impunity required political skill and experience. Nepal had lost to the Maoists in both the constituencies from which he contested the Assembly elections, and the Maoists and others used this failure to claim that he was an 'illegal occupant' of the Singha Durbar secretariat. Coming from them, this accusation rang hollow because it was Chairman Dahal himself who, according to the provisions of the Interim Constitution, had lobbied for Nepal's nomination to the House to serve as the chair of the important Constitutional Committee. Nevertheless, the 'loser' label, which was also applied to several other ministers in the cabinet, dogged Nepal and made him a diffident prime minister from the start. Nepal was also weakened by the surprising activism of his party chairman, Jhala Nath Khanal, who embarked on a clandestine campaign to bring down the government his own party was leading with a majority in the House. His campaign finally succeeded in February 2011, when Chairman Khanal was elevated to the post of prime minister after making a secret deal with Maoist Chairman Dahal.

Even as the Maoists sought to force out the government using non-parliamentary methods, the chiefs of each of the three major parties sought to bypass the Constituent Assembly. In a clear attempt to challenge the position of the prime minister's as well as that of the

Constituent Assembly, Pushpa Kamal Dahal, Jhala Nath Khanal and Girija Prasad Koirala established a 'high-level mechanism' to direct political affairs made up of themselves. Parliamentary functions were continuously compromised, mainly by Maoist action, and while their filibustering need not have affected the constitution-writing functions of the Constituent Assembly, it did. After all, both constitution-writing and law-making were to be done by the same 601 members, so the issue of power-sharing would and did affect the drafting process. The suggestion that the functions of Parliament and those of the Constituent Assembly be divided between those directly elected and those nominated through the proportional representation system looked attractive in retrospect, but the damage had been done.

Dangerous draftsmanship
The Constituent Assembly was (and remains) a house of 601 members representing the breadth of Nepal's demography. Its promulgating a democratic constitution that underwrites the evolution of an inclusive society working towards social justice will ensure that all the people of Nepal feel they own the document. However, the political leadership of each party has largely bypassed the Assembly and the writing of a democratic constitution has been hampered by the introduction of un-democratic and downright dangerous provisions into the drafts produced by the Maoist leadership. These include clauses which deny separation of powers, call for the subservience of the judiciary to the legislature, undemocratically exclude political parties from standing for elections on, and define the federalist unit by ethnicity. The draft constitution made public by the Maoist Vice-Chairman Baburam Bhattarai at a public meeting on 29 May 2010 clearly indicates that the Maoists plan to create a one-party communist state, a 'people's republic of Nepal'. Fortunately, the Maoists do not have the two-thirds majority required to ram their own version through the House. Interestingly, the deep deadlock in constitution-making did not become apparent because all the political forces, as well as the media and intelligentsia, were riveted on the attempts by Chairman Dahal over 2009 and 2010 to resume government leadership using ultra-nationalism and 'civilian supremacy' over the army as his call to arms.

Constitution-drafting became an increasingly unrealistic exercise because the mandated first two years of existence of the Constituent

Assembly was clearly being seen as a cooling-off period for the UCPN (Maoist) and other new forces in the field. Besides, no one could take the writing seriously when one party in the Assembly held on to its fighting force, reneging on its promise to disband it within six months of the elections of April 2008. Moreover, it became clear that Maoist and non-Maoist forces did not share a common understanding of the nature of the Nepali state and they had not agreed on its fundamental principles either. An exercise to reach such a consensus would have revealed that it was not then even possible to draft a democratic constitution because of the Maoist leadership's refusal to agree to the universal values of pluralism, fundamental freedoms, the separation of powers and human rights.

Because no single party had a two-thirds majority, it was important for all to agree on the foundational principles of the new constitution and structure of the state first, before starting work on drafting it, Unfortunately, no such attempt was made. While some were claiming by the spring of 2010 that 80% of the drafting work had been completed, this clearly was not the case. There might have been that much verbiage in the agreed-upon draft, but there was no agreement on the key provisions which would make Nepal both democratic and federal. The position of those civil society stalwarts who were most vociferous did not help either the peace process or the constitution-writing, for all they demanded was that the constitution be written on time. Because civil society stalwarts made little effort to promote agreement on fundamental guiding principles or to require that the conclusion of the peace process be a prerequisite of its drafting, they inadvertently helped Maoist attempts to railroad through an undemocratic constitution. The first two years of the Constituent Assembly's mandate, to give them a positive spin, could be described as an important sacrifice to appease the Maoists and keep the peace process alive. Simply put, this period kept the former rebels engaged above ground and allowed the wheel of time to eat away at the party's radicalism and keep it from taking up arms again.

Street action, state capture
Immediately after Prime Minister Dahal resigned in May 2009, the Maoist leadership realised its blunder. They had given away control of the state machinery, with not just one bird, but all birds, in the hand. Despite its internal weaknesses, this 22-party coalition which entered

Singha Durbar was so alert to the possibility of a Maoist takeover that it fended off every attempt by to break its unity. For their part, the Maoists spent the remaining six months of 2009 and the first five months of 2010, up to the expiration of the Constituent Assembly's term on 28 May – the time that should have been set aside for constitution writing – on a one-point agenda: force Prime Minister Nepal to resign. Nepal, however, continued to command a majority in the House, and the Maoists were not able to win over a single party, large or small, that formed part of the coalition.

A national unity government comprising all parties in the Assembly would have been ideal for constitution-drafting, but achieving such a unity would have required a meeting of minds on constitutionalism as well as on power-sharing, and that was not to be had. In the Constituent Assembly, the Maoists' proclivity for railroading the various committees into adopting un-democratic measures did not inspire much confidence. On the streets, the attempts of the largest party in Parliament to bring down the government through calls of revolt and state capture inspired still less. Mainly because of the suspicions that arose due to the Maoists' words and deeds, it became impossible to reach the consensus required for a national consensus government. How could the other parties agree to let the Maoists lead such a government when, to begin with, they insisted on keeping their armed force? This simple question was not asked either by the vociferous civil society stalwarts nor by those Western diplomats who maintained a somewhat low regard for Nepali democracy.

Unable to muster a no-confidence motion to bring down the coalition government, Chairman Dahal resorted to agitation, hoping to get into the government through sheer obstruction. His party blocked the work of Parliament for five months, not even allowing it to debate the budget of the fiscal year of 2009-2010. After abandoning his campaign to become prime minister when winning it began to look impossible, Chairman Dahal decided to concentrate on consolidating his hold on his party by starting an ultra-nationalist campaign aimed at India. He launched the campaign at a mass meeting at Kathmandu's Naya Baneswor on 22 December 2009 in which he also addressed a country-wide audience through live television, claiming that the political parties in government were all servants of India, which was the lord and master of the Nepali polity, the *'prabhu'*.

May Day, May Day

Nothing seemed to be able to dislodge the Madhav Kumar Nepal government. In the early spring of 2010, the UCPN (Maoist) leadership momentarily mulled over the idea of introducing a no-confidence motion but, realising it would go nowhere, decided to use the springtime (traditionally the season of political upheaval in Nepal) to launch an indefinite nationwide general strike following its May Day show of strength. The Maoist leaders called up their supporters and cowed many thousands of other hapless villagers into attending a workers' rally in Kathmandu, bussing them there to ensure compliance. The participants were then trapped in the Valley and forced to participate in the ensuing days of demonstrations because the general strike had halted all road transport and they could not return home.

The indefinite forced closure was labelled a 'peaceful' protest by many commentators and diplomats, a terrible misnomer because its staging was backed by the threat of violence. According to one calculation, eight million children and youth were kept from attending school and the economy lost 20 million Euro a day. Besides, the opportunity costs of continued instability, capital flight, and lost foreign direct investment were demonstrably immense, and the impact on the forthcoming 'Visit Nepal Year 2011' could not have been insignificant. By massing its supporters and luckless villagers in Kathmandu, and priming them with talk of a 'third people's movement' and 'state capture', the Maoist leadership deliberately set about creating conditions ripe for the eruption of violence. Seeking to reap benefit from chaos, the party hoped something untoward would happen. Fortunately, nothing did.

The indefinite strike began to crumble as the public began to chafe under the restrictions. It became clear that the Maoists would have to call off the strike to rescue their cadre from public wrath and to save face in a rapidly deteriorating situation. The final straw was a peace rally rivalling the Maoists' May Day rally in size, which was spontaneously organised by the citizens of Kathmandu Valley. Called with barely a day's notice and in the face of menacing threats from the topmost Maoist leaders, some of the organisers got cold feet and announced a cancellation. However, others went on overdrive to make it happen, utilising phones and texting. The seventh of May dawned with tens of thousands of citizens all over the Valley making their way to Basantapur Durbar Square in the centre of Kathmandu city. Many were blocked by stick-wielding Maoist cadre en route, but the rally nonetheless was able to issue a resounding message: call off the strike which hurts the people. Photographs of the Basantapur peace rally and the May Day Maoist rally demonstrate that the spontaneous, voluntary gathering of the people was at least as large as the orchestrated, conscripted attendance of the Maoists. Needless to say, the UCPN (Maoist) called off its 'indefinite' strike the very next day.

Even though the strike organisers and some starry-eyed members of the Kathmandu intelligentsia sought to juxtapose the 'well-heeled' (*sukila mukila*) of the peace rally with the 'unwashed masses' on the streets representing Maoist supporters, there was no doubt that the Kathmandu public had spoken up on behalf of the population as a whole against the Maoist bullying. The Maoists were alerted to the silent majority that was watching their every move and had the wherewithal to rise up in a true people's movement as and when required. After first identifying the peace rally participants as members of the 'well-heeled' upper classes and labelling them all as 'vigilantes', Chairman Dahal later apologised publicly and retracted his accusations at least, in his words, 'as far as 99 percent are concerned'. Amidst such a dire situation, with the naked ambition of the Maoist leaders so clear, there were still commentators willing to go on live television asking Chairman Dahal, as one of them put it, 'not to become a civilian party'.

The strike period was fraught with danger for the Madhav Kumar Nepal government due to the propensity of the more extreme among Nepal's political players to play politics with corpses. Indeed, the death of just one demonstrator could have turned the tide and led to the fall of the government; this tantalising possibility was why the Maoists were so willing to play the game of brinkmanship. Some diplomats and donor agency heads lauded the Maoists for their peaceful conduct during the strike, though it is hard to see how an indefinite strike enforced by the threat of violence can be called peaceful. These expatriates should have given credit to the government and to the police force for their forbearance, but it took an Asian ambassador to say that it was not the UCPN (Maoist) but the government which had shown restraint. By their peaceful show of force on the seventh of May, the people of Kathmandu indicated their ability to speak for the silent masses and reminded all autocratic-minded leaders that the zest of the People's Movement of April 2006 could be recalled for the sake of democracy and peace.

By refusing to bow down to street pressure for a full 14 months, Prime Minister Nepal was able to notch up one grand success for his otherwise weak government: he stood by the principles of the constitutional and did not let extra-parliamentary action bring down his government. If the Presidential election was the first debacle in parliamentary politics to strike the elected Maoists, the failure of its year-long agitation, culminating in the collapse of the indefinite strike, was yet another sobering reminder to the former rebels of how not to conduct politics in open society. The Maoist leadership, especially its chairman, slowly but surely lost credibility among the followers – having promised revolt they delivered a dud. Of course, the leader of a politico-military organisation would not be sidelined easily, but Chairman Dahal steadily built a case against himself even as he dragged the party down with his personal agenda and his 'triplespeak', all the while raising the bogey of ultra-nationalism, reaching out to rightist royalists, and promoting ostentatious living.

The constitutional extension

Soon after the lifting of the general strike, the Constituent Assembly deadline arrived. Some politicians arrayed against the Maoists felt it was important to let the Assembly term lapse on 28 May 2010, following the letter of the Interim Constitution, which mandated a two-year term for the constitution-drafting exercise. Their point was also that the Maoists drew strength from their strong elected presence in the Assembly and used that strength to prevaricate about the peace process and to insist on a constitutional draft that threw democratic tenets out the window. It was best not to renew the term of the Assembly, they argued; the Interim Constitution did not have a provision for extension, so why allow it? Other democrat-politicians, afraid of being accused of being against a new constitution, favoured a six-month extension. The Maoist leaders continued to insist that Nepal resign before they would cooperate on anything – the extension, the peace process, constitution-writing, or the passage of the upcoming budget. The UCPN (Maoist), the very force which wanted a renewed life for the Constituent Assembly more than anyone else, was able to fool many of its opponents into believing that it did not care for its revival. The irony was lost on everyone, and no one was willing to call the Maoists' bluff.

In the high drama that played out on the night of 28 May 2010, a compromise three-point formula was worked out to extend the Assembly's term by a year. Those in the Nepali Congress who wanted the Assembly term to lapse could make no headway, while within the UML rumours of a signature campaign led by the supporters of Chairman Jhala Nath Khanal made the other leaders seek compromise rather than challenge the Maoists. The three-point formula, which the Nepali Congress agreed to during tension-ridden hours late in the night, confirmed that 1) work towards concluding the peace process and writing the constitution would begin immediately, 2) the Constituent Assembly would be extended by a year; and 3) the prime minister would resign. The other parties had agreed that the resignation would be activated simultaneously with the Maoists' providing a credible and time-bound timetable for cantonment dissolution. In a farce all too familiar, the agreement was signed though Chairman Dahal obviously had no intention of fulfilling his part of the deal even if the prime minister did resign.

Indeed, before the ink on the three-point agreement had dried, the Maoist leaders had launched internal discussions which yielded the demand that all their ex-combatants be integrated into the security forces, thereby thumbing their nose at all previous agreements on combatant management. Even though it was the Maoists violated the terms of the three-point agreement, a good part of the Kathmandu intelligentsia accused Prime Minister Nepal of greedily trying to hold on to his position. This was part and parcel of their habit of looking at a change of government as a source of entertainment rather than as a way to provide better governance and greater stability. While the opinion-makers were sniping at Prime Minister Nepal's heels, the Maoist leaders insisted that the peace process would be put on track within hours of his resignation. UML Chairman Khanal said the same. In fact, both Dahal and Khanal made a big show of seeking a national consensus government, but it was clear that that was the last thing they wanted.

The rest of 2010 was devoted to power-sharing, which had a grave impact on constitution-writing. Even as Chairman Dahal was coming under fire for the various shenanigans he carried out between the summer and winter of 2010, he regained some of his credibility by forming a senior all-party task force on constitution-making. Made up of members of the Constituent Assembly but functioning outside the Assembly and its rules and procedures, this task force concentrated on publicising exaggerated claims of progress made on the various sticking points. Once more the Constituent Assembly, as well as the masses, were manipulated by Chairman Dahal, who switched on hope and hopelessness as part of his personal agenda.

The resignation of Nepal
At the end of it all, it was not Maoist pressures but fear of the break-up of his own party that forced Nepal to hand in his resignation and serve thereafter as caretaker head of government. Unable to bring down the 22-party coalition through parliamentary processes or run the government to ground through state capture methods despite a year of effort, the UCPN (Maoist) had no recourse but to go back to Parliament. They were able to generate momentum in the media with the suggestion – easily ingested by many opinion-makers – that they were the rightful claimants to government leadership because of their numbers in the House. Many internationals, including the redoubtable UNMIN and the prescriptive ICG, thought that the Maoists had been unfairly sidelined by the other parties, given that their involvement was crucial for the writing of the constitution. The latter point was of course true, but it was up to the Maoists to convince the others of the need for a national all-party government led by their party. They were unable to build the requisite trust.

When it came time for the budget of the fiscal year of 2010-2011 to be presented and passed, the Maoist leadership decided that it would oppose the move. The inability of the government to pass the budget, it reasoned, would be tantamount to a show of loss of confidence in the House and Prime Minister Nepal's government would fall. The Maoists did not have the numbers to reject the budget, however, and the government may well have passed it if not for the Jhala Nath Khanal factor.

UML Chairman Khanal nursed a grudge against Nepal and everyone connected to him for having been bypassed for the prime ministership when the UML's turn rolled around in May 2009. After all, Khanal was the elected chair and had, exceptionally among the UML's top ranks, won the Constituent Assembly elections. Moreover, his faction had a majority in the UML's parliamentary party. Even so, Girija Prasad Koirala had proposed Nepal as prime minister, and the majority within the UML's central leadership had gone along with his proposal. For this reason, from the very day Nepal formed his government, Khanal predicted its imminent collapse and, when it did not fall, continuously sought to undermine it, claiming that it was a failure.

The result was the irony of the chairman trying his utmost to bring down a government led by his own party, aligning with the Maoists as required. Chairman Khanal did not speak up for cantonment disbandment with the vigour expected of the head of a democratic party, he had personally okayed Chairman Dahal's plans to unconstitutionally oust General Katawal, and more often than not repeated Maoist Chairman Dahal's views on different matters related to the government's functioning. Once, at the funeral of a UML party worker killed by Maoists, Chairman Khanal invited hooting when he referred it to a 'death' rather than a 'killing'. There was increasing polarisation within the UML, with the Madhav Kumar Nepal and Khadga Prasad Oli factions uniting against Khanal. Meanwhile, the UML chairman's ambitions soared as the parliamentary numbers and the geopolitical situation created a barrier to Maoist Chairman Dahal's being elected, with the latter not about to make way for his deputy Baburam Bhattarai.

In the mid-summer of 2010, Nepal became convinced that he would be embarrassed by his own UML party colleagues – the 'young turk' followers of the Khanal line – who, he feared, would publicly reject the budget. On 30 June 2010 a prime minister who had ridden the Maoist storm for his resignation resigned without consulting even his closest allies within the party or outside. Oli was peeved by this action, as was the Nepali Congress party, which had backed Nepal to the hilt, particularly after the demise of the patriarch Girija Prasad Koirala in mid-2010. Meanwhile, Nepal felt that he had done his own career a favour, especially after it became clear that a government would not be formed that easily. He had suffered great insults from the Maoists, the intelligentsia and the columnists and cartoonists, all of whom accused him of hanging on to the prime minister's seat, and he was happy to publicly prove them wrong and coast along as caretaker prime minister.

Caretaker Prime Minister Nepal looked more pleased as the summer of his resignation turned into autumn and then winter, for those who had sought his ouster had been exposed. The promises of the chairmen Dahal and Khanal that his resignation would lead to immediate consensus on an all-party government and progress on the peace process were belied. While Chairman Dahal was clearly fighting for his political career, it must be said that the main 'democratic' person to blame for political instability throughout 2010 was UML Chairman Khanal. His refusal to confront the Maoists regarding the peace process and his ambition to become prime minister with Maoist support rather than let the Nepali Congress take its rightful place is what led to the continuous political deadlock. The resulting bad blood also affected the constitution-writing.

The election exercises
The left-democratic alliance of the CPN (UML) and the Nepali Congress, started in the prelude to the 12-Point Agreement of 2005 and revived with the Maoist resignation from government in May 2009, was in tatters as the election exercise for the prime ministership proceeded. Those proposing a Maoist-UML coalition, representing a so-called left alliance, once again went into overdrive. Their rationale was that since the leftists would never again achieve such a majority in Parliament, this was the time to join forces. However, this proposal neglected the ideological distance between the two – the UML was a mainstream left political party which did not espouse violence and believed in multiparty democracy and the Maoists had in word, deed and constitution-drafting showed that it was firmly for a people's democratic republic despite earlier promises to efface the 'revolt' mentality. The reason Khanal's 'establishment' faction within the UML even considered a left alliance was rooted in the relatively weak commitment to non-violent politics of the individuals involved. Khanal was a relative latecomer to 'people's multiparty democracy', the line developed by the late UML leader Madan Bhandari in 1990. This line accepted multi-party competitive politics and made it possible for his party, despite its being communist in name, to garner international support even in the inhospitable environment of the 1990s following the fall of the Soviet Union.

After Prime Minister Nepal resigned, President Yadav asked the parties to form a consensus government within seven days. When they could not manage that, he extended the deadline by five days. When a consensus government still could not be formed, according to the terms of the Interim Constitution, the field was opened for a majority coalition. In the beginning, the UCPN (Maoist), the Nepali Congress and the CPN (UML) fielded candidates, Pushpa Kamal Dahal, Ram Chandra Poudel and Jhala Nath Khanal respectively.

Between the summer and winter of 2010, the parliament held 16 rounds of elections to try to elect a prime minister. At first it was a three-sided contest among Khanal, Dahal and Poudel. The Nepal and Oli groups of the UML believed it should be the turn of the Nepali Congress to lead the government, given that the UML had already had an opportunity and that the Maoists had not yet disbanded the cantonments. During the year of Maoist discontent following its May 2009 resignation, the Nepali Congress party had stood stolidly behind Nepal's UML-led government. Nepal and Oli were resolute that the job should not go to the Maoists given their poor record in the peace process. And yet, after Chairman Khanal had thrown his hat into the ring, they could hardly support the Nepali Congress against their own party's candidate.

Instead Nepal and Oli did the logical thing, which was to raise the bar for the eager party chairman: the CPN (UML) Central Committee, where Khanal was in a minority, decided that he had to muster a two-thirds majority in the House, or 401 votes, and not the simple majority which had made Nepal prime minister. The logic behind this was elementary: if Chairman Khanal could only secure a simple majority as Nepal had, there was no sense in bringing the Nepal government down. Two-thirds also was also seen as an appropriate proportion to ensure adoption of the constitution. On the day of the first vote, 21 July, the UML Chairman was unable to muster the required number of votes and was forced to withdraw, leaving him even more resentful of his party cohort. The next dozen and more rounds of election also proved inconclusive, mainly because Poudel of the Nepali Congress could not get the support of the Madhesi and UML parties to make a majority of 301. The Maoist party, for its part, needed either the Madhesi coalition or the UML on its side. The repeated voting made a mockery of the parliamentary process: over and over the members of Parliament went through the ballot exercise to try to make the major number 301 when there were not even that many present in the chamber because of the Madhesi parties, UML and Maoist staying away.

Chairman Dahal pulled out all the stops, tried every stratagem in the books, to get elected prime minister. Increasingly, it began to look like a Dahal candidacy rather than a UCPN (Maoist) candidacy, with the Chairman seeming capable of degrading his own party's credibility and fortunes in his personal bid for Singha Durbar. To buttress his own position, he reignited long-term Indian displeasure with his party by promoting anti-India ultra-nationalism. To neutralise the challenge within his own party, he spread the word that Baburam Bhattarai was

India's candidate for prime minister. He sought to get the Madhesi parties on his side by promising their leaders all manner of positions, including multiple deputy prime minister-ships. He sought to raise funds internationally to pay 50 members of Parliament the sum of ten million rupees each; ignominiously labelled 'Maharagate', this episode saw his deputy Krishna Bahadur Mahara caught red-handed on audiotape talking to a Chinese-sounding voice. Dahal even reached out to the royalists by promising to revive a 'cultural kingship'. While much of the skulduggery during the prime ministerial elections was within the bounds of the Nepali polity, once a worried New Delhi sent foreign secretary (and former ambassador to Nepal) Shyam Saran on a 'damage control' exercise to keep the Madhesi parties out of Chairman Dahal's grasp; another time during the interminable election process, Indian operatives seemed to be active in seeing that the 'Maharagate' audiotape reached the media.

Despite Shyam Saran's efforts, Chairman Dahal's overtures were steadily weakening resistance among the Madhesi parties, as was well appreciated by Deputy Prime Minister Bijay Kumar Gachhedar of the Madhesi Janadhikar Forum (Loktantrik). He told his counterparts in the Nepali Congress and CPN (UML) that he could not, in the face of the lollipops being offered by the Maoists, keep his members of Parliament together much longer. But it was also the case that the audiotape exposé, the inter-party mudslinging and other matters had taken a toll on Chairman Dahal's personalised campaign. He was feeling vulnerable, and the wily UML leaders decided to act. They asked Dahal to take back his candidacy, assuring him that the UML would remain neutral in the vote for the lone remaining candidate, Poudel of the Nepali Congress. This agreement peeved the Nepali Congress, which saw it as a betrayal of the consistent support it had accorded the Nepal-led UML government. However, Nepal and Oli maintained that the priority was to make Dahal withdraw, for his unprincipled campaign could well succeed in putting a Maoist-led government in place and thereby take the polity in an undesirable direction. Based on this agreement with the UML, Chairman Dahal withdrew his candidacy on 26 September 2010.

The 16 rounds of elections which ultimately led to the election of a new prime minister were indeed a farce, but not for the reason media commentators, who tended to blame Congress candidate Poudel for salivating after the post of prime minister, gave. What they failed to see was that Poudel's withdrawal would have created a politics-without-process situation and, under pressure from the Maoists, completely destroyed the parliamentary procedure. The ex-rebels would have succeeded in derailing one more process, in their campaign to steam-roll the institutions of state. While Chairman Dahal at least had reason to desperately seek the position, it was the lack of principle evident in Chairman Khanal's machinations throughout the prime ministerial term of Nepal which made politics so directionless during 2010.

'Maharagate' and 'Mr. Prachanda Path'
In early September 2010, the media got its hands on an audiotape which contained two separate conversations between the Maoist international affairs-in-charge, former information minister Krishna Bahadur Mahara and an unidentified man with a Chinese accent. The conversation suggested the latter would provide all of Rs. 500 million (50 crore- 'one crore per member of Parliament') to buy the election in favour of Dahal. The Chinese-sounding speaker on the other end insisted that the transfer had to be implemented with the knowledge and approval of the Maoist chairman. The tape exposed Dahal's Machiavellian scheme, and coming on top of a year of agitations and incendiary allegations mean to topple a constitutionally elected government, it should have provoked outrage in Kathmandu salons. Yet, as with the reaction to the release of the Shaktikhor tapes, the response to the 'Maharagate' tapes was also was muted. Most Kathmandu opinion-makers ignored this latest attempt to derail the democratic process.

The Maoists did not deny that it was indeed Mahara speaking in the tape, but offered several lame explanations for it, such as a technological splicing together of words spoken at different times. For their part, media commentators, rather than going into the substance of the tape, suggested that the Maoist leader had been entrapped, his right to privacy infringed. While the apparent ease of access to a political leader's phone conversations should indeed be a matter of concern, and it is important to know who did the eavesdropping, the central matter should have been the content of the conversation. Thus, despite the Maharagate scandal, Dahal continued to remain an aspirant for prime minister and Mahara remained by his side, including when the two went on an official trip to the People's Republic of China in October 2010. In the medium term, it seems that the Maoist party has been able to ride out the Maharagate storm – even to ride the wave and get Mahara made deputy prime minister in Khanal's cabinet – but it is unlikely that the polity will forget this attempt to corrupt the process of governance by a party that has abandoned all of its revolutionary spirit and its opposition to the 'dirty parliamentary politics' which purportedly sent it underground.

Dahal made a lightning visit to Kuala Lumpur, Malaysia in the first week of October 2010. Why he went and whom he met is not clear. Perhaps his intention was to meet ex-crown prince Paras Shah, which he did twice, it is said, or maybe he had arranged to meet Chinese officials or Indian intelligence operatives – or all of the above. Any of these meetings, even the rumour of meetings, would have been a political embarrassment to any other leader, but not to Chairman Dahal. By now he had managed to so completely befuddle the media and the intelligentsia that any threshold of expectations had almost vanished. It is likely that, in addition to the meetings he may or may not have had, he was in Kuala Lumpur to manage banking and financial matters – Chairman Dahal controls his party mainly through the cantonment commanders and his monopoly over the party's purse strings. Knowing he would be queried by journalists upon return to Kathmandu, the chairman came armed with a brass plaque 'appointment letter' as an alibi. The plaque said that he had attended a meeting of an Asia-Pacific entity to which he had been elected co-chairman. In poor English, the plaque read, 'We are honour To Appointment Mr Prachanda Path as the Co-Chairman of Asia Pacific Exchange & Cooperation Foundation.' The only time the Foundation shows up in an English internet seach is in relation to Chairman Dahal's 'honour'.

Perhaps Dahal knew the Nepali commentator brigade too well, for the whopping lie barely concealed by the Malaysian plaque did not create more than a ripple in the pond of Nepali politics. The mis-naming of Dahal himself, calling him by the title of his 'ideology' Prachanda Path, was clearly part of a shoddy scam meant to deflect attention from the real reason behind the Malaysia trip. However, commentators did not make much of the 'Mr. Prachanda Path' plaque, just as they had said little about the Shaktikhor videotape, the Maharagate audiotape, and many other opportunistic acts and pronouncements which emerged from the UCPN (Maoist). When the Chairman made a lightning dash to Singapore again in March 2011, supposedly on the invitation of the same murky entity that got him over to Kuala Lumpur, no one was even asking questions any more. Dahal added yet one more layer of impunity for himself, but one wonders what toll the cumulative burden of these excesses will take on his party.

Ram Chandra Poudel
With Chairman Dahal out of the picture, and the UML and the Madhesi parties abstaining from the vote, the Constituent Assembly continued to hold elections with the Nepali Congress' Poudel as the sole candidate. The Maoists were intent on denigrating the parliamentary process, so the farcical repetition of the vote on the floor of the House was fine with them. The Speaker of the House, Subhas Chandra Nembang, chose to play it safe: he failed to use his prerogative and stand up to the charade and acceded meekly to the decision to continue with the voting. Even the Nepali Congress team in the parliament seemed willing to be led by the nose through the successive election dates, which were called in the full knowledge that with the Maoists and the UML abstaining there were not even enough members present in the house to garner the 301 votes needed for anyone to win.

In the beginning, Poudel did indeed cut a sorry figure as he 'lost' election after election and cartoonists and commentators had a field day lampooning him. Just as the vocal intelligentsia and civil society vanguard in Kathmandu had called for the resignation of Madhav Kumar Nepal without seeking a consensus candidate before the resignation was tendered, they insisted on Poudel's withdrawal without a care for his principled stand. Curiously, many Nepali Congress leaders themselves did not speak publicly on behalf of the Poudel candidacy; some were from the rival Deuba faction of the divided party, others who had easy access to the media were unwilling to swim against the tide of populism. Fortunately, Poudel was willing to stand up for principle, reminding the political class and the public at large that the refusal of the UCPN (Maoist) to reform, democratise and conclude the peace process required continuing the 'left-democratic alliance' not rewarding Dahal with the prime ministership. Poudel took a brave stand despite the mordant ridicule and lack of support and deserves commendation.

Among the Nepali intelligentsia and members of the international community in Kathmandu, there were loud expressions of exasperation regarding a political class which could not elect a prime minister after more than a dozen tries. Yet these smug thinkers ignored the real problem holding up agreement on everything, including government formation: the deadlocked peace process, which was the doing of the Maoist party. In fact, Poudel's candidacy was a challenge from the left-democratic front (including politicians within the Congress, UML, Madhesi and other parties) to force the Maoists to live up to their commitments as outlined in the 12-Point Agreement of 2005 and the Comprehensive Peace Accord of 2006 the following year, and the three-point agreement which had extended the life of the Constituent Assembly. Dahal was seeking to become prime minister without fulfilling the demands of the peace process which were part of the Interim Constitution, and Poudel's refusal to withdraw his candidacy was a bulwark against his overweening ambition.

The Poudel candidacy ended up in limbo in the middle of November 2010, when a constitutional crisis related to the passage of the budget for the fiscal year of 2010-2011 overtook the state. Though the UCPN (Maoist) was unwilling to allow the budget to be presented during the regular session in July, a 'one-third budget' was approved. When things came to a head in November, the Maoists said they would agree to the adoption of the full budget by the caretaker government by amending the constitution. The other political parties agreed to this controversial suggestion, yet more proof that they were succumbing to the constant drive by the Maoists to destroy process and procedure and would even have allowed the Maoists to adjust the rules for the election of the prime minister through constitutional amendment as per their liking. At the last moment, however, the Maoist leaders decided not to push the matter. On 19 November 2010, as Finance Minister Surendra Pandey walked up to the podium to present the budget, in a pre-planned exercise, the Maoist members of Parliament rose in unison, blocked his path and battered him. They snatched the briefcase holding the budget document, kicked it, and tore it open. The house was adjourned amidst the pandemonium.

The next day, the government brought out the budget through ordinance. The prime minister recommended the dissolution of the parliamentary session. The candidacy of Ram Chandra Poudel was pushed into limbo as the Maoists busied themselves for their sixth plenum in Palungtar village of Gorkha District, while the caretaker prime minister, Madhav Kumar Nepal, headed off for an international conference on tiger conservation hosted by Vadimir Putin in St. Petersburg.

Three roads from Palungtar

It was becoming important for the Maoists that the cadre speak with one voice, and so the 'sixth extended plenum' was called in November 2010. Some 6000 members of the party gathered in the village of Palungtar in Gorkha District, including hundreds of ex-fighters from the 28 cantonments across Nepal, joining against the advice of both the government and UNMIN. Instead of demonstrating a unified stance, however, the Palungtar plenum made plain that the leaders Dahal, Vaidya and Bhattarai diverged in strategies and tactics. This was evident in the official reports each submitted, in comments and press leaks, and in their body language at the conclave.

The divide actually harked back to the latter half of the insurgency, when Dahal wanted to collaborate with the kingship against India and the other parties, while Bhattarai sought to keep the line with New Delhi open. Vaidya, meanwhile, languished in an Indian jail. At the 2003 Chunbang meeting in the mid-western hills, Bhattarai had weaned Dahal away from the 'people's war' agenda and towards collaboration with the seven party alliance. Four years later, and after emerging above ground, Vaidya, at the Kharipati national conclave of November 2008, managed to get the party to officially reject the Chunbang position and work towards a 'people's federal democratic republic'. At Palungtar, Vaidya advocated immediate revolt, Bhattarai said revolt was an option if peace and constitution-writing failed, and Dahal tried to have it both ways. In the search for a principal enemy or 'contradiction' against which to rally, Bhattarai identified the national feudal class, Vaidya took straight aim at New Delhi, and Dahal named the enemy as 'the fusion of domestic feudalism and Indian expansionism'.

Benefitting from factional sources more than willing to spill the beans, the media was a strong presence in Palungtar, and the chairman spoke on the need for 'artistic evasion in placing the party's plans before the public, now that the party was no longer underground. That did not help, and the papers reported how the two vice-chairmen tore into Dahal, accusing him of financial irregularities, power-hunger, ideological abandonment and nouveau-riche leanings. Vaidya claimed Dahal was using 'power, authority and finances' as well as control of the cantonments to keep the party in his grip. In response, Dahal called Vaidya a radical and Bhattarai a rightist, and sought to protect himself under the mantle of ultra-nationalism: 'We should be prepared for retaliation against foreign domination through a people's revolt. For this we will use the fronts of the street, the government and parliament.' Taking aim at India, he said, 'What started as a civil war must now end as a national war.'

The trinity was one only on how to nullify the peace process, standing firmly against the dismantling of the Maoist cantonments and demanding full integration of ex-combatants into the national security forces. Bhattarai demanded a 'strong rejection of any attempt to disband, disable or humiliate' the Maoist fighting force. Though publicly perceived in different ways as radical (Vaidya), pragmatist (Bhattarai) and opportunist (Dahal), the three concurred that the peace agreements of the past, going back to the 12-Point Agreement negotiated in New Delhi in 2005, were mere tactics (*karya-niti*) meant to support the party's strategy (*rana-niti*) of 'state capture'.

Unable to decide on a single concluding document, the week-long plenum papered over the differences by announcing three goals simultaneously: 'peace process, constitution and revolt'. The chairman's attempt at producing a synthesis document was shot down by the other two leaders, Bhattarai likening the document unkindly as 'a bowl of rice mixed with dung'. The plenum disbanded asking the Central Committee to formulate the party's working policy, leaving it to a future general convention to address the evident ideological differences. In early December 2011, the central committee met and endorsed Chairman Dahal's position: revolt if there was a conspiracy against peace and the new constitution – a conspiracy as defined by the UCPN (Maoist), of course. Vaidya went along but Bhattarai expressed his disagreement, saying Dahal's line would only encourage counter-revolution.

Pushpa Kamal, Baburam and New Delhi
Pushpa Kamal Dahal urgently needed to sideline Baburam Bhattarai from the competition for leadership, as the latter's popularity was rising among the cadre and the public, owing both to a very partial media as well as to his competent handling of the Ministry of Finance during the time of the Maoist government. Dahal could not risk the fate of being upstaged by his deputy, for in a militaristic, un-democratised party that could mean oblivion. For his part, since the time he had been hustled into house arrest, Bhattarai had been biding his time. To make a move

for leadership, Bhattarai required the cadres to begin to understand that the chairman's public misdemeanours were now affecting their own individual advancement. Dahal desperate campaign to become prime minister between 2009 and 2010 opened their eyes even as the opportunists swarmed about him.

With the party faithful increasingly sceptical about Dahal's ability to lead, Bhattarai decided in the spring of 2011 to strike out on his own by going public. When the chairman suddenly announced that the party would vote for Jhala Nath Khanal as prime minister in February 2011, Bhattarai and 50 of his supporters dissented with a signature drive on the floor of Parliament. At a 'rafting retreat' in early April in Kavre District, called to discuss intra-party polarisation that was affecting the organisation down to the grassroots, one newspaper reported how Baburam Bhattarai had preferred to remain aloof, eating alone and maintaining a faraway gaze at meetings. Meanwhile, Dahal made another lighting dash overseas, this time to Singapore, ostensibly for a meeting once again with the elusive 'Asia Pacific Exchange & Cooperation Foundation'. Though rumours flew about his having met Chinese officials or Indian operatives or both, in all likelihood Dahal was in the city-state to manage the party's financial matters. That was important because, beyond the fealty he still enjoyed among the cantonment commandants, his power lay in the control of the bank accounts, important for a party which paid salaries to the membership.

The chairman had managed to remain on top also because of his ability to be everything to everyone, his penchant for intimate eye contact in meetings and his show of gesticulating earnestness. While in India as prime minister, he had even tried to ingratiate himself to the Indian authorities by confiding in public that the Pakistni intelligence agency ISI had offered the Maoists weaponry, but that the Maoists had refused. However, the law of diminishing returns was beginning to work on Chairman Dahal five years into open society. Forced to publicly spout anti-Indian venom to stay on top, Dahal got stuck ever deeper in a quagmire of his own making as the cadre took up the line with alacrity. Having painted himself into a corner, the chairman sent messages via intermediaries to South Block that he was keen to mend fences – even as he was splashing more kerosene on the anti-India ire he had ignited. Dahal reassured his confidantes, that the dual game was viable, recounting how he had been preparing the cadre for an Indian invasion in 2005, building tunnels and bunkers, even while participating in the negotiations in Delhi with the seven party alliance. He seemed not to understand that the rules had changed when the UCPN (Maoist) entered open politics, with newspapers unlikely to let transgressions go unreported. By exaggerating India's role in Nepali politics, by the spring of 2011, the chairman found himself in a self-created quicksand when it came to India, and the developing Chinese position of 'strategic friendship' with Nepal had not yet matured enough to rescue him. In January 2011, Baburam Bhattarai was treated to meetings with the pantheon of Indian leaders in New Delhi while Chairman Dahal was left cooling his heels in Kathmandu.

Three parties, three divides
If the publicly visible growing rift within the UCPN (Maoist) was the most significant trend at the start of the new year 2068 BS (14 April 2011 CE), the two other major parties were also riven with dissension. In the Nepali Congress, it became clear that the reunification of the Girija Prasad Koirala and Sher Bahadur Deuba factions had been achieved with nothing more than band-aid. With Chairman Dahal throwing fodder to Deuba, the latter became less than enthusiastic about Ram Chandra Poudel as the party's candidate for prime minister. He had formally proposed Poudel, but neither Deuba nor the so-called independents in the party rallied to the side of their candidate as the interminable elections continued throughout the fall and winter of 2010. The divisions between Congress President Sushil Koirala and Deuba escalated in the 2011 spring, with the result that the organisation was unable to fill any its important departmental positions. The party president's situation was full of irony – Koirala's democratic credentials were impeccable and of just the kind required to take on the Maoists when the CPN (UML) was floundering, but he was unable to rally the rank-and-file.

Within the UML, the rupture had its roots in the grudge Party Chairman Jhala Nath Khanal bore against all and sundry for having bypassed him for prime ministership in 2009 in favour of Madhav Kumar Nepal. With a small coterie of friends, Khanal began working with the Maoist leadership in order to undermine Nepal's government since the day it was formed. The factions of Nepal and K.P. Oli came together to resist, but they were constrained by Khanal's seeming willingness to even risk break-up of the party to get into Singha Durbar himself. Khanal got what he wanted when Maoist Chairman Dahal decided to abandon his own impossible candidacy and push for Khanal, but only after signing on the dotted line of a secret deal.

Peace process at the brink
Unable to do much in other arenas of governance, especially since his cabinet of junior politicians was weak, Prime Minister Madhav Kumar Nepal had, early on, decided to concentrate on bringing about a semblance of law and order in the country and to force the UCPN (Maoist) to fulfil their commitments according to the Comprehensive Peace Accord. Nepal's doggedness in confronting the Maoists during the 'indefinite strike' of May 2010 was a turning point: for the first time Dahal had failed publicly, nationally in his use of bluster and chicanery. Even as he became caretaker prime minister after 30 June 2010, Nepal tenaciously clung to the peace agenda. As chair of the Special Committee meant to oversee the integration and rehabilitation of the Maoist ex-fighters, the prime minister brought in retired General Balananda Sharma to coordinate the secretariat to plan the modality for the dissolution of the cantonments. Prime Minister Nepal insisted on the departure of UNMIN to ensure progress towards conclusion of the peace process and oversaw the flag-lowering ceremony which should have signalled the handover of the chain-of-command of the ex-fighters to the Special Committee. That did not happen, but Nepal persevered.

Prime Minister Nepal did not allow the vile epithets hurled at him by the Maoists to divert his attention. He maintained good relations with Pushpa Kamal Dahal, knowing well the latter's habit of breathing fire on the pulpit and being cloyingly friendly on the couch. Above all, Nepal had learnt to beware of the charm that Dahal could turn on at will, using it to convert into putty his political opponents, civil society stalwarts and 'the diplo-donors'. This ability to understand the camouflaged insincerity of Pushpa Kamal Dahal was an asset for the prime minister as chaperone of the peace process, and in his penultimate days at Singha Durbar he nearly achieved success.

Alternately challenging and cajoling the Maoist chairman, Nepal sought to push Dahal to agree on the number of ex-combatants for integration. When the Maoist side, including the influential commandant Barsha Man Pun, proposed 7000 and the other parties said 4000, it seemed, at a crucial meeting at the Gokarna Forest Resort on 26

January 2011, that a median number could be found and that peace was at hand. At that point, the parliamentary parties would have agreed to a Maoist-led all-party government, and a swift conclusion of the constitution-drafting by 28 May 2011 suddenly looked tantalisingly possible. But it was not to be, for over the lunch intermission the Maoist chairman met his party colleagues and came back a rejectionist – he was not going to agree to a integration number 'just to become prime minister'.

The momentum the peace process had achieved collapsed that day and it sent a flurry of alarm across the polity. The constitution-drafting was as good as stalled. It was at this very point that the secret seven point deal between Dahal and Khanal catapulted the latter into the prime ministerial seat. While Madhav Kumar Nepal had stood firmly by the letter and the spirit of the peace agreements, going back to the text of the 12-Point Agreement, Khanal ascended the steps of Singha Durbar by agreeing with Dahal to essentially destroy the peace process.

Over at the Constituent Assembly, the 17th attempt to elect a prime minister was suspended as the House bowed to pressure from the Supreme Court, which issued a directive to end the 'meaningless election process'. The voting had been rendered farcical by the absence of the Maoists and the UML and the Madhesi parties to leave less than 301 members in attendance. A new election process was started with Khanal, Dahal and Poudel in the running. The date for the election was set for 3 February 2011. There was a possibility that there would be a runoff between Poudel and Dahal, but in the first round of the election itself the Maoist chairman made the dramatic announcement that his party would support Khanal of the rival CPN (UML) for the prime ministership.

The seven secret points
The Nepali political landscape is littered with unimplemented deals, each titled with a number identifying the range of points within. The latest to keep the populace in thrall was the secret seven point deal crafted a few hours before Jhala Nath Khanal became prime minister on 3 February 2011. Khanal did not share the deal with his own colleagues, who got to know about it at a meeting with the Maoists the following day meant to discuss portfolio divisions. Khanal had essentially agreed to language which could be interpreted by the Maoists as allowing them to set up a separate fighting force of all ex-combatants; he also agreed to

Maoist verbiage with definitive connotations of a 'peoples' democracy'. Going against parliamentary process, the two chairmen also decided to share the prime ministership turn by turn. There were also two unwritten points to the secret deal: Khanal would give the Home Affairs portfolio to the Maoist party and Dahal would take over as prime minister around the time the new constitution was promulgated.

Khanal had gambled the future of his party to fulfil his ambition and Dahal had decided that, as long as he could not be the prime minister, he would keep his deputy Bhattarai out of the honey-pot and work instead with the malleable UML chairman. Though supporting Khanal was of course a mortifying course of action, Dahal sought to justify it before his cadre by giving it the ultimate spin – Khanal's election was a nationalistic victory over New Delhi, denying the latter the ability to influence government-formation in Kathmandu. However, the deal stayed close to the UCPN (Maoist) strategy of wanting control of the state administration when the constitution was promulgated. With the party in control of the Home Ministry and the two police forces, with its war chest full and muscle power at the ready, Dahal could easily accept the promulgation of a fully democratic constitution and call immediate elections. Taking the cue from the last elections, the Maoists seemed confident that ready cash, threat of violence and and control of state mechanisms would deliver them a two-thirds majority to the forthcoming Parliament. The Maoists would then be able to amend the constitution to their liking.

Pushpa Kamal Dahal and Jhala Nath Khanal, chairmen of the radical and democratic communist parties in Nepal respectively, together hold responsibility for having led society towards extreme polarisation for the last two years. Both did their utmost to become prime minister, throwing decorum, values and due process to the wind. The left-democratic alliance between the UML, the Nepali Congress, the Madhesi and other parties, which were united for the peace process and a democratic constitution, was shattered after Khanal embraced Dahal.

The secret deal shook the UML down to its very foundations, with some fearing that it may even fracture due to the marauding Maoists. Confronted by the seven point agreed to by their own chairman, the UML Central Committee went into paroxysms of interpretation. The Maoists saw no irony in publicly demanding the implementation of the secret deal – some of it not even written down – especially the Home Affairs having to go to them. With Khanal safely in the prime minister's chair, the UML leadership announced baldly that the seven points did in fact allow the peace process to proceed under the Special Committee and that the Home Ministry would be kept by the prime minister himself 'for the moment'. Both the Standing Committee and the Central Committee of the party forbade Prime Minister Khanal to give the Home Ministry to the UCPN (Maoist). Thus it was that as the country entered the new year 2068 BS, the country lost one prime minister who held a majority in Parliament, from the ranks of the CPN (UML), and got another from the same party.

24

Kingdom of Conspiracy

How did Madan Bhandari die?
While every society has its conspiracy-seeking traditions and sometimes unbelievable conspiracies are indeed hatched and implemented, certain home-grown factors seem to make Nepal a world centre for wild rumour and supposed diabolic plots. One factor is poor scholarship, which leads to a paucity of critical thinking among opinion-makers and a resultant susceptibility to populist pressures. In such an environment, the number of individuals who try to speak on the basis of evidence, facts and logic is limited. Conspiracy-seeking, after all, is the recourse of educated individuals who are too lazy or have too few tools to go after the facts. Again and again, it becomes clear that Kathmandu's intelligentsia fails to take advantage of the information available and, for reasons of ideological expediency or sheer indolence, allows false notions to take root among the populace.

The national proclivity to accept conspiracies in turn forces the foreign diplomat, scholar and journalist, constrained as they are by the language barrier, to give credence to the conspiracy theories that are popularised. The ease with which imagined stories relating to the Narayanhiti royal palace massacre of 2001 and the death of CPN (UML) General Secretary Madan Bhandari and an associate in 1993 have captured the public imagination is something that needs study, if only to explain the intelligentsia's inability to lead opinion. Such investigation is important because a society that falls easy prey to conspiracy-led explanations of major events is bound to face hurdles along the path to progress. Both the Dasdhunga highway tragedy which took the life of Madan Bhandari and the royal palace massacre show the proclivity of the Nepali intellectual class for conveniently eschewing logic and ignoring the evidence available in order to latch on to the lowest common denominator explaining specific happenings.

In May 1993, UML General Secretary Bhandari and another senior party leader, Jeev Raj Ashrit, were travelling from Pokhara to Narayanghat in central Nepal. The jeep was driven by Amar Lama, a highly regarded party cadre. The best one can make out is that there was heavy rain on the road heading southwest from the rest stop of Mugling and that the jeep carrying the UML leaders slipped off the road and fell into the Trisuli River in Dasdhunga. Ashrit's body was found in the smashed vehicle when it was fished out of the river, while Bhandari's body was located many kilometres downstream. Lama managed to save himself by jumping out as the vehicle plunged off the road, and reported the incident.

For the first couple of days after the accident, the UML party leadership seems to have accepted Lama's story, and he was presented as a dedicated party worker. Soon, however, the UML leaders were presenting the incident as a political assassination, evidently seeking to take populist advantage of the angry protest which erupted to boost the party's positioning and put Prime Minister Girija Prasad Koirala on the defensive. In wanton disregard of the lack of evidence – unable to point to a possible assassin or even a possible motive – the party pushed ahead to fashion a conspiracy theory. This fiction of Bhandari's assassination and the associated societal burden has been perpetuated to this day. Lama spent time in jail and then years afterward trying to clear his name until, ten years after the accident, he died in mysterious circumstances in the Valley town of Kirtipur. Though Lama's death has been presented by some UML leaders as further proof of the assassination of Bhandari, it seems to have been the result of a botched attempt by some underground Maoist cadre to question him about the Dasdhunga event. By all accounts, when the vehicle carrying Lama was stopped unexpectedly at an army checkpoint near the town of Kirtipur, he tried to escape and was shot dead by his Maoist captors before they themselves fled.

Bhandari was one of the path-breaking politicians of Nepal's modern era, a communist leader who devised the ideology that enabled his party to participate and succeed in competitive politics after 1990. His foresightedness and sagacity are of a kind that is at a premium among the Maoist leaders who came above ground after 2006. Tragically, Bhandari's memory is now associated in the public's mind not with statesmanship, but with the murkiness of his supposed assassination. Before long, the CPN (UML) party will have to abandon the assassination conspiracy as one unsupported by fact and reason. It will have to reinstate Bhandari's high stature without the tag on the side reading 'victim of assassination'.

By allowing the conspiracy theory to remain unchallenged, the Kathmandu intelligentsia exhibited a singular lack of concern for the rules of evidence and showed its inability to challenge the excessive opportunism of the UML and its propaganda machinery. Indeed, the UML was able to raise the bogey of assassination without credible evidence only because of the silence of the intellectual class. Worse, this silence conditioned the Nepali public to accept the possibility of political assassination and conspiracies in general. The overall weakness of the intellectual class in challenging popular beliefs and the demagogic agenda was most exposed by its failure to challenge the Maoist's rationale for starting a 'people's war' barely three years after Bhandari's death. It is interesting, though, that while all and sundry have been accused of plotting the assassination of the UML leader, the finger was never pointed at the Maoists, even though it was they who benefited more than others by the loss of a charismatic leader of the democratic left. As Nepali scholarship gains depth and the courage to be dispassionate, we will arrive at a time when the public will be presented with rigorous research and presentation on how Madan Bhandari died and who killed Amar Lama.

Who killed King Birendra?

Using the evidence available, both direct and circumstantial, reports of those in the know, as well as the capacity of reasoning, there can be no doubt that Crown Prince Dipendra went on a shooting binge on the night of 1 June 2001, taking the life of his father Birendra, his mother Aishwarya, two siblings, aunt, uncle, and others. This was the conclusion of the commission set up under the leadership of the very respected chief justice of the time, Keshav Prasad Upadhyay, to probe into the murders. There were 24 people in a room of the Tribhuvan Sadan mansion in Narayanhiti royal palace, attending a party called by the crown prince. Eight were killed that early monsoon night, and detailed testimony about what happened is available to the public from the surviving witnesses, including children. The commission's report confirms that Dipendra had ingested some whisky (the Famous Grouse brand) and smoked cigarettes with 'certain black particles' (hashish). Dipendra was either inebriated or acting so and was escorted to his bed chamber upstairs. A while later, he descended carrying three automatic rifles; after that, mayhem ensued.

The public at large, including the non-royal elites of Kathmandu, were unaware of the deep tensions developing within the immediate royal family of King Birendra. A rift had developed between mother and son after Queen Aishwarya threatened to cancel the royal succession if Dipendra followed through, as he intended, and married Devyani Rana, whose family had nursed a multi-generational family feud against the queen's own Rana clan. The queen had already shown her ability to follow through on her threats: she had defrocked King Birendra's youngest brother Dhirendra, who was married to her sister, for alleged matrimonial misdemeanours. The crown prince had a love for guns and regularly used the pistol he had been given at the age of eight to do target practice around the palace grounds. At the time of the massacre, as colonel-in-chief of the Royal Nepal Army, the crown prince had been testing three automatic rifles, all kept in a rack in his bedroom.

That night, inebriated by alcohol or hashish or both, or making everyone believe so, Dipendra descended from his bed chamber with the three rifles slung over his shoulder. He first targeted his father, shooting him in the abdomen. Exiting the room momentarily, he returned to shoot the downed Birendra again and then proceed to kill his other relatives in a hail of automatic gunfire. Why Gyanendra's family was spared – a matter which has fed the conspiracy theories – can be answered simply enough. Gyanendra was in Pokhara. His son Paras had helped shield and save the children in the room by appealing to his buddy and cousin Dipendra to spare them. Gyanendra's wife Komal was, in fact, hit: a bullet pierced her lungs and exited from her back, just missing her heart.

Gyanendra's autocratic ways became clear soon after he ascended the throne, but neither his authoritarianism nor his praise for the Panchayat era nor the past record of his son, the n'er-do-well Paras, can justify the attempt to blame father and son for the multiple murders at Narayanhiti. Gyanendra's idiocy ultimately led to the demise of the monarchy itself and the stories of his past misdemeanours do ring true, but no credible proof or believable argument has been presented to support the conspiracy theory; the juxtapositions, coincidences and supposed reports just do not add up. The reports of a murderer wearing a Dipendra lookalike rubber mask are the product of fevered imaginations impacted by Bollywood potboilers featuring masked impersonator-villains causing bedlam. Reports that scores of people were murdered within the palace grounds in order to permanently silence witnesses were never borne out either.

The public sought an answer to one simple question: 'Why Dipendra would do something as dastardly as kill his own father?' Unfortunately, the only answer that the commentators could provide was the conspiratorial one. The tendency of society's 'gate-keepers' to accept and even promote conspiracy as an explanation affects various areas of public life, from economics to geopolitics. To take just one example, the opinion-making class of Kathmandu likes to create the impression that the Indian government is constantly out to get Nepal, whether it in regard to water resources, border matters, the printing of machine-readable passports (a recent instance), government turnover or regime change. It may well be that, at any given time, a few Indian government agencies are indeed working to undermine Nepal, but equally true is that there are events that happen on the ground, across the border, and among citizens, about which New Delhi is quite unaware. To present an elaborate web of intrigue in which Nepal is always without agency against a malign Indian state power is a falsification of reality and a damaging one at that. Few would disagree that Nepal's hydropower development has been held hostage by the anti-Indianism extant in Nepali society, especially among the intellectual classes, a sentiment traceable to conspiracy theories about how India cheated Nepal on the Gandak and the Kosi river treaties.

The low intellectual benchmark maintained by the Kathmandu cognoscenti is seen in how it reacted to Gyanendra's statement of innocence in relation to the 2001 Narayanhiti massacre as he vacated the royal palace on 11 June, 2008. After having maintained a lengthy royal silence despite the barrage of accusations, in his last press conference as king and as he was about to depart Narayanhiti, Gyanendra finally defended himself. He said that he had been unable to do so earlier because, as king and head of state, he had had to maintain a certain regal decorum. He referred to the living witnesses who could testify about the event and, on an uncharacteristically personal note, mentioned the injury suffered by his wife, the former queen Komal. He asked the public plaintively to believe he was innocent. Shockingly, in the papers the next day and later, media commentators and opinion-makers studiously avoided reference to that lengthy segment of the ex-king's press conference. In this neglect, one sees once again the unwillingness of opinion-makers to challenge populist notions, even when a deep injustice is done.

An intellectual class which lunges at fanciful conspiracy theories is weak-kneed when it comes to accepting evidence that stares it in the face. Thus it was that the intellectuals preferred to keep a studied silence on the audiotape that revealed Maoist leader Krishna Bahadur Mahara trying to fix a Rs 500 million deal to buy the prime ministerial elections for his boss Chairman Dahal, and did not raise any objection when he was elevated to the position of deputy prime minister in the Jhala Nath Khanal cabinet in March 2011. There is no doubt that the inability of Kathmandu's opinion-makers to challenge conspiracies theories about either Gyanendra's complicity in the royal massacre or the 'assassination' of Madan Bhandari, made society poorer and less prepared to tackle other challenges thrown its way.

25

Civilising Society

Civilian deconstruction
The civil society of Nepal, as elsewhere, is a broad-based, countrywide group made up of trade unionists, community leaders, lawyers, professionals, academics, school teachers, human rights activists, entertainers, journalists, business people and others. However, those who are presently identified as 'civil society stalwarts' *(nagarik samaj aguwa)* by the media are about a dozen national-level individuals who came to the forefront in challenging King Gyanendra's autocracy and have been engaged full-time in activism ever since. This group played an important role in ensuring that Gyanendra did not take us back to where we came from, that is, an updated version of the autocratic Panchayat era. These leaders were critical in maintaining resistance against the king when the public was in a wait-and-see mode with respect its backing of the political parties. They held the fort until the democrat-politicians regained a footing following Gyanendra's disastrous performance and gained momentum after signing the 12-Point Agreement in November 2005. For their pains, most of these stalwarts were detained for varying periods, only to be released on the exhilarating day Gyanendra surrendered to the people's will, 24 April 2006.

In addition to these stalwarts, the people of Nepal can count on groups dedicated to democracy to come to the forefront whenever there is a threat. In Southasia, those who organise to fight autocratic trends tend to be scholars, journalists, activists, lawyers, doctors, student leaders and trade unionists. In Nepal, it was the bar, the media, the medical profession and unionists who stood up first. Of course, college students are also active, but they tend to be directed more by political party agendas than by a concern for human rights and democratic freedoms. Although there are certainly exceptional individuals, the academia can be credited neither for providing cutting-edge opinion to lead the political discourse nor for descending to the street when democracy and peace were endangered. Lately, many academics have been compromised by their acceptance of a surfeit of consultancies from donor organisations, though, in theory, such affiliations should not prevent them from speaking up.

The matter of appeasement
That society as a whole appeased the Maoists during the peace process to the long-term detriment of the people is a familiar charge. It must be clarified, firstly, that those who worked with the parliamentary parties to help the Maoists come above ground did so because the civilian toll associated with trying to secure the military defeat of the Maoists would have been unacceptable, leaving many more than the 13,000 who had already lost their lives dead. Also, because the army was under the command of the autocrat Gyanendra, Nepal would have entered a right-wing phase that would have set society back several years in its evolution into a liberal democracy. The resulting 'un-democracy' would have delivered top-down (rather than participatory) development, centralised government, crony capitalism, and all the other banes of the Panchayat regime. Bringing the Maoists into open society and challenging them to convert themselves into a democratic party was a better option than continuing the fight, even if it meant that that the other political parties would lose some momentum.

Together with the responsible politicians of the seven party alliance, therefore, civil society felt it was important to make compromises and to guide the Maoist to a 'safe landing'. For their pains, those civil society members in the thick of things were simultaneously called 'royalist' and 'Maoist', depending on the proclivities of the accuser. And it is true that things did not work out quite as expected: the Maoists reneged on their commitments to evolve as a civilian party and to disband their armed force through integration and rehabilitation. The interim government of Girija Prasad Koirala, with his confidante Krishna Prasad Sitaula as home minister, took a weak line with the politico-military Maoist organisation, which took full advantage of their leniency and continued to feed visions of state capture to their cadre.

Uncivil people

After the exhilaration of bringing down the autocrat Gyanendra, the civil society stalwarts were unable to take on the next challenge, which was to wrestle the Maoist violent agenda to the ground. Reaching out to bring the Maoists above ground was not appeasement, but not challenging the UCPN (Maoist) to convert to peaceful politics thereafter was. The failure of democrat-politicians to hold the Maoists to account lost them crucial support and put the peace process on hold, thereby delaying reconstruction and deepening the loss to economy and society. Deceived by the social justice agenda mouthed by the Maoist party, the stalwarts were carried away by the wave of populism that marked the Maoist arrival into open politics and responded weakly to a whole range of issues being pushed rather brazenly by the Maoists, from their proposal for ethnic federalism to the un-democratic elements in their draft constitution. Most critically, they did not challenge the Maoist party's lack of commitment to the peace process. Their present mollycoddling of the Maoists is part of much longer trend: at the very start of the insurgency they failed to question the logic behind the start of insurgency, preferring to believe the simplistic notion that its origins lay in marginalisation and poverty

The Kathmandu-based, full-time stalwarts seemed to lose their bearing after the People's Movement of April 2006. Well-protected by national and international recognition, they should have challenged Maoist Chairman Dahal to conclude the peace process in the six months allotted and in the terms specified. Upon challenging the king the worst that could have happened to the Kathmandu stalwart was to be converted into a well-recognised 'prisoner of conscience' – they did not have to face the dangers the activists in the districts did. However, insisting that the Maoists' violent means destroyed the credibility of their professed social justice agenda is more difficult than keeping mum and the stalwarts did not rise to the challenge. They feared a Maoist backlash and the burdensome 'rightist' label. Stalwarts who have not insisted the UCPN (Maoist) fulfil its commitment to conclude the peace process and to democratise have worked against the interests of the average Nepali citizen. They must be challenged for having ignored the pain and suffering of the conflict and post-conflict periods and the central role of the Maoist party in creating that pain and suffering.

The black-and-white fight against royal autocracy united civil society because the threshold for understanding and unity was relatively low. In terms of taking on the Maoists, however, matters became more complex as the stalwarts' values, principles and ideology came into play. Naturally, these complications put an end to unity. The stalwarts, some 'failed politicians' who had unsuccessfully tried their hand at electoral politics and others with ties to the royalist Panchayat era, were vehemently opposed to the parliamentary parties. Their vehemence blinded them to the gaping chasm between Maoist promises and Maoist actions and to the difference between political parties which, decades ago, engaged in minor violence against an autocratic regime and one fought a bloody ten-year-long war against a democratic system. Perhaps the fact that many in the civil society front rank spent their productive years as professionals in the Panchayat regime has generated a romantic submission to ostentatious displays of power and demagoguery, even if it is on the radical left.

Thus it was that, after April 2006, the stalwarts relinquished their role as public watchdogs though, with the king vanquished, it was their responsibility to ensure that the Maoist army disbanded and a democratic constitution was written. In the process, they should have assisted the UCPN (Maoist) in transitioning into a democratic civilian party. In their inactivity, the stalwarts did an injustice not just to the people but to the Maoist party itself: their watch-dogging would have promoted the transition.

Two examples, one to do with constitution-writing, the other with the peace process, will help describe the pro-Maoist bias of the civil leadership after 2006. The focus of the stalwarts' activism was nothing more than writing the constitution, *on time*. They did not call for a *democratic* constitution and, in fact, acted as if the matter of democracy was a closed affair though the Maoist position made it clear it was not. Society, they seemed to think, could get by with a constitution that was complicated and contradictory and which undermined the universal principles of pluralism and representational politics. Neither the intelligentsia or civil society objected to the flagrantly non-democratic proposals of the Maoists, including ethnic federalism with political 'prior rights' to a few designated communities; a faulty separation of powers placing the judiciary subservient to the legislature; restrictions on the right to form parties and on the various freedoms based on the vague notion of 'nationalism'; and so on. The best the stalwarts could do was to spread banners on the ground before the Singha Durbar southern gate demanding that the constitution be written on time – and wait for the television cameras to arrive. They may have looked committed and caring, but their narrow-minded unconcern for the values and principles involved in constitution-writing did a disservice to democracy.

As far as the peace process is concerned, for six long years the stalwarts kept silent about the need for the Maoists to live up to the commitments they made in the Comprehensive Peace Accord of 2006. Not once during the two-year term and one-year extension of the Constituent Assembly did the stalwarts effectively question whether a constitution could be written when one party retained its 'liberation army'. This crucial issue did not even figure into their discourse. The Maoists have sometimes come in for reluctant criticism by civil society but never the kind of castigation that the democratic parties suffer. Whether about the Maoists' involvement in killings and extortion, their hijacking of state resources, or their adventurism during the nine months of Maoist rule, criticism, when it was even voiced, was always muted. In early May 2010, when the Maoists called an indefinite nation-wide strike, a move designed to bring down the government but which would cripple society, the *aguwas* were quiet. Unable to wait for civil society to wake up, the Kathmandu public took matters into its own hands: there was a massive show of people power on the streets of Kathmandu on 7 May 2010, rejecting the indefinite nationwide closure. Recognised civil society stalwarts were not among them. Since then, they have refused to acknowledge the rally for what it was – a sign of solidarity among all Nepalis who suffered the Maoists' bullying – and have promoted instead the Maoist canard that this was a gathering of 'well-heeled' vigilantes. Deep down, the *aguwa* may just feel that they missed the bus on this one.

'The well-heeled' versus 'the unwashed masses'
The peace rally was projected by some commentators and by the radical left as an anti-people gathering of the urban gentry, an attempt to suppress the 'unwashed masses' that hoped to see the future built by the UCPN (Maoist). For their 2010 May Day celebrations and the indefinite strike to follow, the Maoists bussed in thousands of supporters and lay villagers from across the country to start what they very publicly

announced was the 'third people's movement' to capture state power. When the pre-monsoon rains arrived, many farmers in the Maoist ranks wanted to head homewards to plant the maize even if the strike meant they would have to walk. In defiance of the cadre's exhortations to stay put, a train of villagers began to head out through various Valley passes. Those who remained were kept in check when they marched by cadres wielding heavy bamboo batons. They were lodged in inadequate accommodations short on sanitation facilities. These were the 'unwashed masses'. Many were certainly Maoist supporters but there is no denying that the majority was kept forcibly in Kathmandu to carry out daily demonstrations which could easily have given way to violence and injury. The demonstrators did indeed showcase the terrible reality of poverty in the country, but they were exploited by the Maoist leadership, which thought nothing of the distress it was causing.

All over the country, in response to the Maoists' extortions, violent ways, and arrogance, a silent rage had been building up. In the districts and villages it was difficult for this rage to express itself: there was too much danger involved in challenging violent bands of Maoist cadre uncontrolled by ideology or hierarchy. Under the circumstances, it was the moral obligation of Kathmandu's protected civil society to raise its voice; the stalwarts, however, chose to parrot the fashionable and ultimately elitist comments about the 'well-heeled' *(sukila mukila)* of the Valley versus the 'unwashed masses' *(maila dhaila)* of the countryside, supposedly all UCPN (Maoist) supporters. Although elite commentators remained silent, the middle class of the Valley began to understand that the entire country was being held hostage by one party and its chairman.

On the sixth day of the general strike, the business community and professional organisations decided to conduct a peace rally the following day. The call was given by the entertainer duo Madan Krishna Shrestha and Hari Bamsha Acharya, who had played critical roles in voicing the public's feelings in the people's uprisings of 1990 and 2006 as well. They were part of the 'Roll Back Violence' campaign *(Himsa Antya Abhiyan)* of 2008-2010, whose well-attended rallies called for a rejection of violence in public life. The call for the rally saw an electric response as informal networks, both by word-of-mouth and through electronic messaging, blossomed. At the last minute, after Maoist Chairman Dahal made his displeasure known, some organisers got cold feet and word went out in the evening that the peace rally had been cancelled. However, enough people insisted it had to happen and the campaign was renewed that night.

The next day, Maoist demonstrators sought to block access to Basantapur Durbar Square, but enough locals made it through the dragnet to send a resounding message to the UCPN (Maoist) as well as to all the sceptics in civil society and the international community. The spontaneous gathering rivalled the size of the massive Maoist rally of May Day; it was a peaceful show of strength, mostly of Kathmandu Valley's middle class, in solidarity with the masses in the rest of the country, all of whom had suffered at the hands of general strike. The address by entertainer Madan Krishna Shrestha was a classic example of strong opinion expressed to a mass gathering with maturity and decorum and stood in stark contrast to the vile language that Maoist Chairman Dahal favoured in the days immediately before and after. A large group of young participants, many political party members, led an impromptu march out of Basantapur, where they were confronted by Maoist demonstrators. The clash that resulted was a made-for-television melee and Maoist leaders claimed that the rally had been organised and managed by 'vigilantes'.

A major regression from peace, democracy and political stability had been averted by the spontaneous participation of the people of Kathmandu Valley in a rally representing citizens across the country. Not to forget, there were other examples of defiance of the Maoist closure all over the country, not as well covered by the media. The stalwarts stayed home, but the larger, more genuine civil society was firmly in place and able and willing to organise a 'people's movement' against demagoguery. The people had sent a message loud and clear – enough is enough. Confronted by the possibility of an avalanche of reaction against them all over the country, the Maoists submitted to this show of people's power and withdrew the strike.

26

Community Power, Local Government

The localisation discourse
The fact that local governance has not been a part of the national discourse since 2003 is worrisome as it ignores the foundational hope of the People's Movement: to see people empowered at the grassroots level so they could direct their own affairs. The lack of discussion about local governance indicates, once again, that Kathmandu's 'gatekeepers' have little regard for citizens' rights and responsibilities. It also reflects a neglect Nepal's great heritage of community-based organising. The members of the Constituent Assembly, despite their being very representative of Nepal's rainbow community, have not been attentive to the importance of representational governance at the village and district levels, neither in their parliamentary oversight nor in their constitution-writing.

The society's traditional system of managing the commons, particularly in the mid-hills, was progressively weakened during the modern era as the centralised state sought to develop its network of controls. Representative democracy, which would have guaranteed some level of power-sharing with the grassroots, was stifled during the decades of Panchayat autocracy. Villagers were free only where they remained outside the reach of governmental authority, and they did pretty well with traditional means of managing the commons. There were bombastic programmes such as the Back-to-the-Village *(Gaun Pharka Abhiyaan)* campaign initiated by King Mahendra, and the Panchayat era leadership never tired of talking about decentralisation, but there was no commitment. It was only after 1990, when representatives were elected to a sovereign parliament that the public at large began to feel linked to state power. The enactment of the Local Self-Governance Act of 1999 empowered citizens in the country's 3913 village development committees (VDCs) and 75 district development committees (DDCs), giving them the ability to decide on development projects and disburse governmental funds.

The arrival of genuine local government was a major departure, with the local population able to experience the push and pull of competitive politics for the first time. It was natural that local governance would see the participation of more communities than ever before, as differentiated by caste, ethnicity, faith, gender and language. While the initiative was not equally successful everywhere, the Local Governance Act did take democracy to the grassroots through the medium of VDCs and DDCs, and successive party-led governments competed with each other to provide support to the villages and districts. The CPN(UML), for example, launched the Making-Our-Villages-Ourselves *(Aphno Gaun Aphai Banaun)* programme and both the UML and the Nepali Congress began, for the first time ever, to provide grants directly to villages. For most part, the funds were used wisely, providing a fillip to local development. Nepal's heritage of community organisation was finally being utilised for participatory development.

While many developing countries, including India, whose Panchayti Raj programme has taken time to take hold, have struggled for decades to make a success of local governance, Nepal achieved relative success within the first five-year cycle of local government. The exclusive power of the central government, exercised through the offices of the central district and local development officers, was diluted as VDC and DDC chairs and committees were empowered to take decisions and administrators and government functionaries became supportive personnel. The concept of decentralisation, bandied about for years but never applied, was coming true because elected representatives trusted the people.

Sadly, the local government experiment was cancelled at the end of the first five-year term in 2002. The turbulence introduced by the Maoists as well as intra- and inter-party conflicts resulted in the decision of the government of Sher Bahadur Deuba to cancel the local government elections scheduled for 2002. This proved to be a boon for the CPN (Maoist), which had viewed the rapid success of local governance with alarm, energising as it did local leadership that stood as an obstacle to the party's spread and to its plans to rule through commissars. The targets of the rebels in their maiming and killing of civilians were school teachers and local government leaders; it was by making an example of them that the Maoists were able to cow the populace. The abandonment of representative local government by Prime Minister Deuba and the weakening of local elected leadership provided fertile ground for the CPN (Maoist) to extend its network around the country without much resistance.

It says something of the quality of the national political discourse that neither the political leadership nor civil society has raised the absence of local government as a matter of serious concern, if not outright panic. As the peace process was extended and political stability became a mirage after the 2006 People's Movement, the issue of local government elections lost all priority. Local development and disbursement of government funds are now farcical, with government-appointed secretaries to the VDCs and DDCs acting under the dictates of local-level all-party *samyantra* (mechanisms). The result is a local-level division of the spoils, with the most vociferous and violent enjoying all the clout.

For nearly a decade now the citizenry, which for five years experienced and enjoyed the advantages of local governance, has been forced to function in an unrepresentative system where power rules. This loss has been one of the most significant for the polity, and the inattention of Kathmandu opinion-makers to healing it acts like salt in the wound of the rural populace. Even the very fact that local governance is a travesty has not emerged as a matter of public debate. Not only has this neglect mocked the success of our local democracy, it has also corrupted local-level politicians and activists and killed the possibility of a healthy democracy developing from the grassroots up. It is with regret that one looks back at the lost decade, which could have been spent building participatory representative democracy at the local level, for many of the demographically diverse participants of the various political parties would by now have moved from village and district-level politics to national level politics. Even if it were absent from efforts at the top, egalitarian governance would have been guaranteed through the rising tide from below. Instead, by denying the evolution of genuine and inclusive local democracy, one could say that the CPN (Maoist), with the other political parties as well as the activist-scholars in tow, have created the conditions for continued non-inclusive national politics at the top as politicians fail to be groomed from the ranks. By not rushing to protect the local government as they jumped on the community-specific federalism bandwagon, the activist-scholars who speak so vigorously for ethnic and Madhesi rights have been complicit in the disempowerment of Village Nepal and its marginalised communities.

Local government and federal structure
During the last five years of populist politics, the voice in favour of local governance structures has been muted almost to the point of silence. Politicians, analysts and the media were intimidated by the demand for a federated republic, as if the creation of provinces would negate the need for village- and district-level government. For a couple of years after 2006, even uttering the word *bikendrikaran* (decentralisation) was enough to invite the charge of being anti-federal, an accusation almost tantamount to being a traitor. During this period, the three federations of local bodies – DDCs, VDCs and municipalities – sought to remind one and all of the decentralisation successes of the Local Governance Act, but there few were listening. Many development agencies, including multilateral and bilateral organisations and international and national non-governmental organisations, forgot local governance even though it was the resplendent jewel of the democratic era which allowed those organisations to make a success of participatory development. The reason for this forgetfulness in the development community was obvious: reviving interest in local government would lead to the charge of being against federalism, which would needlessly open a three-pronged attack from the Maoists, the scholar-activists and Madhesi politicos.

The decentralisation of the Panchayat era was, of course, a sham, but now the home-grown arrangement of local governance created by the politicians, bureaucrats, development workers and scholars of Nepal was being regarded as anathema, even by some of its creators. The abandonment of participatory government by many international non-government organisations was most notable after the Maoists won the elections of April 2008, when national and international staff acted as if their presence required a new paradigm of development, one in which local government need not be pursued. The very organisations involved in building awareness for social change over the previous decades, such as Care, ActonAid and Oxfam, became diffident as if they felt guilty for having used the 1990-2002 era to reach out and energise people at the grassroots. They did little to raise the alarm as the process of participatory development was weakened by the momentum of a party that sought to rule by commisars rather than by elected local representatives. Encouragingly, despite the neglect of the large and well-endowed development community and the Kathmandu commentators, the spread of community forestry user groups kept the idea of participatory local action alive.

The suggestion that there is a dichotomy between decentralisation and federalism was unfortunate, because both are necessary under the Federal Republic of Nepal that the new constitution seeks to fashion and concretise. The Interim Constitution has already proclaimed Nepal a federal state and local government is vital to preserve the people's power to choose their leaders in the villages and districts. Experience of local governance has already been acquired, and the Nepali polity is in a position to fine-tune the system and learn from the mistakes and weaknesses, such as areas in which marginalised local communities have lost out. There is no need to hold back on planning local government structures while simultaneously working to define the federal provinces and their power vis-á-vis the centre as the VDC and DDC boundaries are expected to remain more or less intact within the provinces. The fact that Constituent Assembly has not discussed local governance and seems to think it is a matter for individual federal units to decide upon when they are formed is dangerous because without constitutional strictures to bind the provinces to guarantee maximum devolution to the local units, autocratically-minded provincial leaders or groups may wrest power from locals.

Both Nepal's civil society and the international community must revive institutional memory of local governance and give due credit to the democrat-politicians, bureaucrats, scholars and local and international experts who made it happen. They must insist that local governments be made a strong element of the state re-structuring exercise and include provisions for doing so in the new constitution. A democratic, representative, inclusive Nepal begins at the level of local politics, and we already have the experience in district- and village-level governance to prove the point and to improve upon. Local governance represents Nepali originality at its best; why should it be sacrificed on the altar of cowardice and expediency?

Participatory development
While local government was an experiment of the post-1990 democratic era, it builds on the particular ability of Nepali village communities to

manage the commons. To our credit, the cooperative spirit of Nepali hill farmers formed the basis of Nobel Prize-winning Elinor Ostrom's foundational work on the management of the commons. It is our heritage of local-level cooperation that came to the fore and made 'development' genuinely 'participatory' after Nepal became an open society in 1990. The propensity for cooperation at the local level is due particularly to the village-level blend of demographic groups. This genius of cooperative society was repressed for at least a century by autocratic regimes which would not allow citizens the freedom to organise and make decisions for themselves. Despite the repression, systems to manage all sorts of local resources, from forests to livestock to water for irrigation, persisted wherever they were out of reach of the state administration. The Panchayat government's unwillingness to trust citizens rendered development a top-down effort and people, expecting the government to act, stopped initiating efforts to build bridges, manage conflict, organise irrigation, control forestry, and so on. The easy provision of foreign-aided development projects also eroded the independent rural can-do spirit, replacing it with supplication and dependence.

Some genuinely participatory efforts at development did energise the grassroots even during the Panchayat regime, however. These included the National Development Service and the Seti Project, both of which sought to help villages progress, particularly through education. But both were cancelled even as they succeeded, precisely because their success meant they had the potential to threaten the autocratic state. A definitive move towards decentralisation (or federalisation, in current parlance) was attempted during the Panchayat era under the supervision of well-known geographer Harka Gurung. The country was separated into five development regions, regional capitals were assigned and divisions into 75 districts made. However, this effort was doomed from the start because of the central government's unwillingness to provide autonomy to the development regions; they had no fiscal, political or administrative powers. In addition, the central government retained the 14 zones *(anchals)* so the Panchayat could maintain political control. Naturally, deprived of both raison d'étre and power, the development regions were weak. The fact that Kathmandu was placed in the central development region though the Valley lies squarely in the east demonstrates how fundamental centralisation was to the Panchayat state.

It was after 1990, often in spite of the weakness in leadership among the political parties, that the advent of open society allowed participatory development to flower in Nepal. Fortunately, there was a 'green army' of grassroots development workers, supported by national and international organisations and ready and willing to use the political opening to promote bottom-up development. There was a surge in genuine, catalytic development: local irrigation systems; village roads, trails and bridges; and community forestry all made great advances, as did the vast arena of social development. The ability of the citizens to question authority was the most significant change that came about with the 1990 makeover: this change, *ipso facto*, helped energise local-level efforts. The national heritage of community management was revived on all fronts after a long dormancy and it was grassroots development workers – largely unrecognised for their cumulative contribution – who were the trail-blazers. Even amidst the Maoist monopoly of the discourse, we must never let the memory die, that in the 1990s and 2000s it was individual experts (foreign and national), bureaucrats (senior and junior), local level actors (politicians and activists), and grassroots development workers in fields from health to agricultural extension who helped blaze the trail of true development in Nepal.

When the government conceded in 1995 to media activists' suggestion that the transmission of radio programming should not remain a monopoly of the state, local journalists, business leaders and community activists all over the country responded by fuelling a FM radio movement which enabled the public to fulfill its right to information and entertainment and set an example for the rest of Southasia. When the successive governments of the Nepali Congress and CPN (UML) showed that they trusted elected VDC and DDC office-bearers to decide how to disburse funds sent from the centre, there was a sudden energising of local initiatives countrywide. The take-off of community forestry in the democratic era, on the basis of legislation adopted during the last years of the Panchayat era, proved that there was still dynamism left in the local sphere. The success of the community forestry soon became tangible: a sharp delineation began to be seen between fields and forests; no longer did shrubs and scrub make up the margins. The credit for Nepal's world-renowned effort in afforestation goes to the villagers and their ability to orgainse and to the democratic state's faith in their ability to do so. If anything has weakened the community forestry movement, it is the donor community, which has wanted to participate in that success by pouring in money, in the process robbing the movement of dynamism.

Debates in and around the Constituent Assembly have failed to recognise the importance of community participation and local government. Carried away by the populist discourse that sought to deny all history, the members of the Assembly have not given credit where it is due or preserved the great advances made by the state and citizenry working in concert. Even the very development organisations which achieved success in participatory development after long decades of failure during the Panchayat era have failed to stand up to the above-ground Maoists or to emphasise the link between democracy and participatory development. Even as it became clear before and during the Maoists' nine months in government that the ex-rebels intended to devastate the achievements and possibilities of local government, it was hard to hear a single voice in the vast development community of Nepal defending democracy as a precondition to development. The silence indicates a great degree of disinterest among the phalanx of development professionals and national and international non-governmental organisation heads, most of whom overlooked the genuine contributions of grassroots workers when confronted by the tsunami of Maoist propaganda.

The failure of development practitioners and scholars to raise the flag of alarm and its terrible consequence – the neglect of local governance (and, with it, participatory development) – can be attributed to the fear of federalist populism promoted by Maoists, activist-scholars and Madhesi politicians. This is a travesty because, even under a federal structure, local government is required. Opinion-makers and politicians must be alert to the need to safeguard the autonomy of local government in the future federation; the provincial elite should not be allowed to manipulate the people at will. There must be guarantees for local initiatives in the text of the new constitution so that the citizenry, which has already seen and experienced the promised land of local governance, is not cheated. Even though the debate in the Constituent Assembly is marked by ignorance and disinterest, the text of the new constitution will hopefully give due importance to local governance and participatory development even as the country goes federal.

Local governance is seen as a 'rural affair' by the opinion-makers in the capital, and they fail to consider that it is the absence of elected local officials that has led to the devastation of the Valley's urbanscape over the last decade. The intellectuals who lament Kathmandu's destroyed environment and diminishing quality of life, with the lack of planning and infrastructure guaranteeing a future of urban chaos, do not pause to consider that the city is by national line ministries rather than elected representatives. They do not consider that the municipality, such as it is, has not had an elected council or mayor since 2002. Kathmandu's urban elite fail to realise that the absence of elected local government affects them every single day of their lives through the bad traffic, poor water quality, load-shedding and air pollution that plague them. Clearly, representative local government and participatory development is not just something for villages and districts.

The American Peace Corps served Nepal from the 1970s till 2004, when it was disbanded due to insecurity related to the Maoist insurgency. Young Americans who spent a year or two in the villages working as teachers, agricultural extension workers and in other vocations, helped bring the ideas and methods of a transforming world to remote hamlets. These young volunteers helped support the villagers in their community action, with critical and catalytic input that went far beyond the modest costs involved for the American authorities. Interestingly, there was nary a voice from the Kathmandu intelligentsia seeking the return of the Peace Corps, showing once again a lack of sensitivity to the inhabitants of rural Nepal. Encouraged by the American Embassy in Kathmandu, the Government of Jhala Nath Khanal approached the US Government and the good news from Washington DC in mid-April 2011, coinciding with the New Year 2068, was that the programme would be re-started.

27

The Evolving Political Spectrum

Terminology of politics
In UCPN (Maoist) usage, whoever is not present in the radical left fringe, even within the party itself, is a *rightist*. Since many observers make the mistake of applying this Maoist-defined placement to the larger political spectrum, they stick the label 'rightist' on those very democrat-politicians within the CPN (UML), the Nepali Congress, Madhesi parties and members of civil society who most effectively exhort the Maoists to abide by their promises with respect to the peace process and plural politics. This labelling also provides a cover for the true rightists of Nepali society, who seek to utilise the present anarchy and ultra-left activism to organise amidst the semantic confusion. Besides the 'rightist' marker, the Maoists use other terms, such as *feudal*, *royalist*, *revisionist*, *elite*, *anti-national* and *'bideshi dalal'* (foreign agent), as a way to keep commentators and critics on the defensive. Only the most stout-hearted are able resist such name-calling and maintain their stance against the Maoist vis-à-vis peace and democracy.

Nepali is a relatively new language of Southasia, and plural politics is so new and recent that the lexicon has not yet evolved enough to address all aspects. There is, for example, no word extant to describe a politically conservative person, for example those within the Rastriya Prajatanra Party and some within the Nepali Congress who might correctly be so termed. Only recently has liberal democracy come to be called *udaar loktantra*; however, it is so close to *uadar arthatantra* (liberal economy) that, really, a new term is required to communicate the nuance. It is under such conditions that use of 'rightist' *(daksinpanthi)* from the Maoist manual came to be a catch-all. Thus, the Panchayat era politicians who have energetically engaged in multiparty politics should be called 'political conservatives', and there are 'fiscal conservatives' to be found within the Nepali Congress, but for the want of a term both tend to be called 'rightists'. At a still the more simplistic level, those who urge the Maoists not to cheat on the peace process are also 'rightists'.

Traditionally, all the political formations of Nepal's modern era have laid claim to the social democratic space, which forms the middle ground of Nepali politics. Such was the pull of social democratic ideology developed by the Nepali Congress together with the leadership of newly independent India, with its promise of equity within democracy and capitalism, that even the Panchayat regime mouthed the same ethos. This chameleon opportunism in declaring something other than what one is also applies to the Maoists; and when they came above ground they sought to be everything to everyone, telling the Nepali and Indian chambers of commerce that they stood for 'capitalism'; among the Western European diplomats in Kathmandu in particular, they presented themselves as 'social democrats'. Only those alert to the ways of the communist regimes of Eastern Europe have recognised the Maoist 'triplespeak'.

In the as yet developing polity, positions are taken on and discarded as per political expediency, but it is nevertheless significant that social democratic values are seen as paramount, whether the parties concerned follow them or not. As the spectrum evolves in the very real platform of competitive politics, we will probably see political parties large and small proceed to find their positions in the rainbow – radical left, mainstream left, social democratic centre, conservative and right. But one hopes that even as the rampant radicalism of the Maoist proceeds to energise the incipient right in Nepal, social democracy will continue to command the centre of the political spectrum.

Rightward drift
During the decades of the modern era, the existence of a monarchy as the central political institution and its full command over the national army obviated the development of a right wing in Nepal's politics. The abolition of the kingship has now created space for this flank to evolve, but for some time since 2006 it was unclear which force would lead the emerging right – fundamentalist Hindu elements, royalists, the Panchayat era nobility, the ultra-conservatives of the hills and plains, Kathmandu's uppermmost classes, ultra-conservative elements within

existing political parties, former and serving army officers, or the ultra-nationalists. In the rapidly transforming landscape, it has become evident that the main platform of rightist politics will be faith-based, i.e. radical Hindutva, and supported by other ultra-conservative elements. The organisation of rightists is spurred by opposition to the secularism declared in the Interim Constitution and expected to be incorporated in the forthcoming constitution. Simultaneously, while seeking to restore Nepal's status as a 'Hindu state', the right wing will seek to restore monarchy in some form. The former king, Gyanendra, seems more than willing to be used for this purpose, hoping to be the fulcrum for the ultra-conservatives of the mid-hills and the Tarai. He has been testing the waters, particularly in the towns of the Tarai, while interest in the monarchy's return among the ultra-conservatives seems to wax and wane according to the immediate needs of the Maoist leadership. Meanwhile, the Maoists continue to cast a line in that direction with their enthusiastic use of the term *desbhakta*, whose intended meaning is 'royalist patriot'.

The Hindu right was not able to infiltrate Nepal during the height of Hindutva activism in India in the 1980s and 1990s, not even during the rage surrounding the 1992 demolition of the Babri Masjid in Ayodhya, a town close to the Nepali border in Uttar Pradesh. The fact that Nepali identity is a composite of multiples, including language, caste, ethnicity and geographical origin in addition to faith – and that it evolved syncretistically – seems to have made it difficult for the religious right to strike root. After the political changes of 1990, rather than move to the right as some may have expected, Panchayat era politicians largely joined the multiparty political mainstream and today make up a small but erudite democratic force.

It was after the People's Movement of 2006, amidst the dramatic declaration of a republic and the abolishing of the monarchy that the dormant right found a conducive environment to develop, giving continuity to the clear right-wing agenda of Gyanendra during the last years of the monarchy. Those who believed the state should have retained its definition as 'Hindu' and livid that the monarchy had been finished off without a referendum are in the process of gravitating towards this new right. The Panchayat era nobility, which had never reconciled to the loss of power and prestige in 1990, seems to be egging this process along. The religious-cum-feudal elements among the Madhesi community, meanwhile, have emerged as a potent force of the emerging right, with former king Gyanendra pandering to it with frequent visits to temples and to 'power places' (*shakti peeth*) across the length of the Tarai. More than anything else, it is the continued radicalism of the above-ground Maoists that has helped develop a base of support for the rightist agenda: the exasperation with the Maoists' endless calls for revolt and the inability of the mainstream political parties to respond effectively has doubtless helped build a base for a rightist rise.

Ideally, if peace and stability can be ensured over the next few years, the mainstream of Nepal's polity will develop left-liberal, centrist and conservative flanks and the energetic radical left of today and the emerging right would then be relegated to the fringe. At the very time when the radical left should be challenged and forced to abandon its anti-plural, self-serving, ultra-nationalist demagoguery, it would be a tragic failure if the absence of a strong challenge gave momentum to a right wing in reaction. A right wing regime in Kathmandu would be much more welcome to both neighbours to the north and south, as 30 years of the Panchayat has proven. Such a development would once again set us on the road of long-term political instability and put an end to the hopes of the present generations for growth and social transformation.

Maoist-royalist bonhomie
The opportunism evident in the Maoist leadership seemed to allow use of any and every means to see the party to power, from using the power of money, exploiting ethnic sentiments, and turning geopolitics on its head, to maintaining 'working relationships' with all kinds 'enemies', including the royalists. It seems anything can be justified by Pushpa Kamal Dahal if it can catapult the party to the top; or, in the alternative, if it can destroy existing state-society relations and introduce chaos. Against such a backdrop, it is little surprise that even though the Maoists started their 'people's war' against a democratic system and having been in a 'working relationship' with the royal palace as per their own admission, at the opportune moment, after the June 2001 royal palace massacre, they let it be known that the war had all along been waged against the monarchy. Maoist utilitarianism allowed the underground rebels and the Narayanhiti royal palace to mouth venom in public against each other even while they were engaged in secret

collaboration. It was Maoist Vice Chairman Baburam Bhattarai who admitted in the aftermath of King Birendra's murder that there had existed a *karyagat ekata* (working relationship) withbthe slain king. Upon emerging above ground, the former rebels had no compunction about bringing the royalist in as advisors, members of the Constituent Assembly, financiers and facilitators on different fronts.

It becomes necessary to locate the ideological links, if any, between the erstwhile royal palace and the former insurgents. The strongest binding link of the radical left with the right-wing is, without doubt, ultra-nationalism. In the context of landlocked Nepal in the middle of Southasia, this means anti-Indianism and has origins in the historical animosity of the hill principalities, including the Kathmandu Valley kinglets, towards the plains rajas, nawabs and the East India Company. The Rana regime was subservient to the British colonialists in India, but they kept the anti-Mughlan fire burning amidst Nepal's isolation. By the time Nepal entered the modern era, the politicians and autocrats found that anti-plains xenophobia directed against the new post-Independence India was a tool that could be used to build political support among the Kathmandu intelligentsia.

When King Mahendra conducted his coup against the democratic government of B.P. Koirala, he used ultra-nationalism to justify and maintain his partyless Panchayat autocracy. The Maoists employed the same ideological tool to build their cadre base while underground, and, once above ground, among the larger population. Indeed, the anti-Indianism developed by Mahendra has served as the guiding philosophical matrix of the UCPN (Maoist) regardless of the fact that the rebel leadership fought the 'people's war' from safe havens in India, with the knowledge, if not the connivance, of New Delhi's intelligence agencies.

Because there do not seem to be ethical hurdles on either side, the far-left and the right-wing elements of Nepal have found it easy to collaborate on the platform of utilitarianism, beyond the matter of ultra-nationalist ideological contiguity. There are several 'pragmatic' considerations for collaboration, one of which is helping each other evade accountability, as required, for excesses committed during the armed conflict. Given that Maoists and the (Royal) Nepal Army actively participated in excesses, the former fighters and the royalists among the sitting and retired army officers will find it easy to collaborate with the ex-rebels, especially when the investigations and the truth and reconciliation process begin to kick in. This unspoken collaboration would continue the unique relationship that existed between the rebels and the army for long years into the 'people's war' – an agreement not to touch each other while the civilian government put the under-armed, unprepared Nepal Police up against the guerrillas. At that time, an army under *de facto* royal command kept soldiers from being deployed or proactive during critical episodes of the armed conflict, including at Dunai in Dolpo district, where the army watched while the district capital was attacked.

Other practicalities, as well, have also pushed the royalists and Maoists closer. Because the CPN (UML) and the Nepali Congress will have no truck with royalist diehards, the latter have had no choice but to look towards the Maoists as a large party to hitch their wagon to. Meanwhile, the Maoist party seemed to think, at least initially, that it needed the administrative, foreign policy and other expertise of the Panchayat era appratchiks. Meanwhile, Chairman Dahal's desperation for power quickly towards the royalists, whether it was to try and curry favour with the Indian political class, to raise funds, or to seek support to get back to being prime minister. Since the days of the Chunbang meeting of 2003 when the Maoist leadership's positions came to be known, it was Dahal who has emphasised the ultra-nationalist line, making it easier to cohabitate with the royal palace (and with royalists when the monarchy collapsed), while Vice-Chairman Bhattarai has sought to identify the national bourgeoisie as the primary enemy.

It must be the weak intellectual base among his party rank-and-file that allows Chairman Dahal to switch grand propaganda campaigns on and off at will, and have the party sudden about-turns without protest. Within three years, he moved from championing the republic to a position where he could accommodate revival of a 'cultural kingship'. Dahal's murky ideological line is based on a term he repeats often –'*kramabhangata*', meaning the deliberate breaking of continuity or constancy. However, there seems to be no method in the madness other than to serve himself (first) and the party (second), relegating the interests of the citizens and society at large to a distant third. If serving his own interest means reviving the kingship, which would surely destroy liberal democracy and delay Nepal's progress far into the future, he seems to say, so be it. This is the true design of 'Prachanda Path' in the post-underground era of Maobaadi evolution.

28

'The Democratic Maoist'

UML and Maoist: Who's the communist?
As the polity matures in the coming decade, we will see more differentiation among political parties, in policies and programmes that move away from the one-size-fits-all social democratic agenda mouthed by the full spectrum from right wing to radical left. Much will depend upon whether the UCPN (Maoist) abandons violence as a political tool. If the party is unwilling or unable to do so, we will be watching an outfit with a death wish, as it is likely that internal factionalism, national politics and geopolitical factors will result in the organisation's downfall.

Maoist leaders appeal to their followers with the promise that their party will not be a status-quo entity like the Nepali Congress or the CPN (UML). The suggestion is that the Maoists are somehow 'different', that they possess some ethereal formula, some transcendent ideology that makes them represent the people better, govern more efficiently. There are many in Kathmandu who insist that liberal democracy has failed in Nepal; this category has believed since the UCPN (Maoist) came above ground, and especially after its electoral win in April 2008, that Pushpa Kamal Dahal has developed a formula of governance that evaded Thomas Jefferson, Jawaharlal Nehru, B.P. Koirala and Nelson Mandela. The reality made clear once the Maoists came above ground and into government denies this wishful projection *in toto*. It is clear that the best the party can do is to try to become *like* the CPN (UML) and Nepli Congress in accepting non-violent politics and parliamentary democracy. Beyond this, what the Maoist leaders can promise the cadre and the people at large is to be better than the other parties when it comes to promoting equity and social justice, transparency, in-party democracy and governance. Even those who sincerely believed that the

UCPN (Maoist) was a visionary, revolutionary party have by now realised that it does not have a magic wand, and lately both the spirit and the flesh have been looking rather weak.

They may not be able to do it right away, but as the UCPN (Maoist) survives internal discord, challenges from other parties and geopolitical pressures, it will need to carry out some measures if it is to survive in long-term politics. Before long, the party will have to adopt a public declaration renouncing violence. In 2006, as part of the Comprehensive Peace Accord, all the party agreed to was to end the conflict. This was a first step. If it is to be anything more than a fringe party of the future, the UCPN (Maoist) will have to admit its mistake of pushing society into the armed conflict and the 'people's war'; it will have to apologise in public, openly and with conviction. All of that is in the future, however. For now, the polity would be willing to regard the UCPN (Maoist) as a 'civilian party' for a much more modest concession – if it concludes the peace process by detaching itself from its military and paramilitary wings as per the peace agreements, hands over the arms stored in the cantonments for destruction, stops the frightening calls for 'revolt' and 'state capture', and returns the property it seized from the citizenry across the country.

If the intention is to have a long innings as a unified party, the UCPN (Maoist) has no option but to become non-violent, democratic and 'civilian'. This transformation will bring with it a challenge because, as time passes, there will be little to distinguish between the UCPN (Maoist) and the parties of the mainstream left, most importantly the CPN (UML). A peaceful evolution of the Maoists, then, would leave us with two large parties to fill the mainstream left segment of the political spectrum. At that point, either the Maoists would have to be subsumed within the CPN (UML) or the other way around. The Maoist leadership has been actively seeking ways to weaken the UML, and after 2009 it concentrated on using the UML Chairman Jhala Nath Khanal himself as a pincer into the rival party. Khanal and his advisors are votaries of a left alliance which would mean a co-habitation between the UML, Maoists and some small communist parties, in contrast to the left-democratic alliance (made up of the UML, the Nepali Congress and the Madhesi parties) which many independent thinkers believe is required to challenge the Maoists to join the peace. A left alliance, on the other hand, would be a recipe for a Maoist triumph over the UML because of the former's momentum, cash in the coffers, and ability to entice away the UML faithful. But their adventurism while in government which led to resignation, the Maoist party may well have managed such an alliance in 2009. However, the effort continued right up to the secret seven point agreement that catapulted Khanal to the prime ministerial chair.

During the entire 21 months of the Madhav Kumar Nepal government, a group centered around Khanal did work to build a clandestine bridge between the CPN (UML) and the UCPN (Maoist). In this attempt to get into Singha Durbar, Khanal willingly used the 'people's republic' language of the Maoists in the secret (even from Khanal's own party leaders) seven point deal and some unwritten agreements in tandem which agreed to a turn-by-turn sharing of the prime ministership with the Maoist chairman and to letting the Maoists – still with their cantonments brimming with ex-combatants – have the home ministry and control over the police and armed constabulary. In a roundabout way, the deal also approved the idea of forming a separate force to incorporate the Maoist ex-combatants, in violation of the Comprehensive Peace Accord of 2006 (also a part of the Interim Constitution). The logical progression from the deal would have been the subsuming of the UML into the Maoist party. Besides clearing the left field of all credible competition, such a melding would have another sizable advantage for the Maoists: it would allow them to claim that a new party had emerged and thus enable them to evade responsibility for the ills they introduced into society through the 'people's war'. A mixing of the Maoist and UML parties would make the job of seeking accountability for atrocities committed during the 'peoples' war' that much harder.

In March 2011, a member of Prime Minister Khanal's kitchen cabinet suggested on a radio programme that it was entirely possible that passage of time would see the merger of his party with the Maoists. In public programmes, Dahal urged that all the parties of the left must unite under one banner. Even without succumbing to such ambitions, agreement on a left alliance would require the UML to retroactively accept the necessity of the 'people's war'. Its agreement to join a Maoist-led government without requiring Dahal's party to give up its guns, much less publicly renounce violence as part of the party ideology, would indicate abandonment of the ideology of peaceful politics propounded by the late Madan Bhandari. A left-democratic alliance, on the other hand, was logical because it would pressurise the UCPN (Maoist) to give up their arms and become a democratic civilian party. Such an alliance would have offered the Maoists the incentive of being eligible to lead government if they detached themselves from their military and quasi-military units.

It says something of the democratic consciousness of the Khanal faction of the UML that it was willing to countenance a left-only alliance. This presupposed that the public did not have a problem with the Maoists retaining their arms three years into the constitution-writing. Meanwhile, it is looking increasingly difficult for the Maoist leadership to abandon the simplistic radicalism that it was so enamoured of. Such are the schisms within the party that, as a whole, it seems willing to court disaster rather than to confront the challenge of democratic transformation. Chairman Dahal could have managed the conversion when he commanded national and international credibility in the 2008-2009 period, but, as it turned out, his leadership was devoid of vision for his party. He was guided solely by the instinct of self-preservation, feeding upon the opportunism, power-hunger and money-making on which his party followers had been groomed as it emerged from the jungle. If it publicly abandoned violence and renounced the military mindset, the UCPN (Maoist) could credibly sell itself as the 'party of change' and enter the next elections as a popular party. Without a transformation, it would have to go in with command of the government machinery, full coffers to purchase votes, and a continuing ability to intimidate the other parties and the public at large.

The future of any left alliance or left-democratic alliance would obviously depend upon the permutations and combinations within the individual parties, and particularly within the CPN (UML) and the UCPN (Maoist). Jhala Nath Khanal became prime minister in an opportunistic embrace with Dahal that also served to expose the rifts within each party. Khanal would willingly have taken the UML under the UCPN (Maoist) umbrella for the privilege of becoming prime minister, and he had the 'establishment' at his command to be able to buy support within the party through appointments and emoluments. But the disquiet among the UML rank-and-file who have to confront the Maoists on the ground found expression in the support for Madhav Kumar Nepal and K.P. Oli.

Within the Maoists, the designs of Chairman Dahal were clear, to try to implement the decision of the sixth plenum to revolt because the powerful Vaidya faction would not have it any other way. However, the growing confidence of Baburam Bhattarai in the spring of 2011 to challenge the party 'establishment' provided some relief, for its ability to question and challenge the immediate agenda as set out by the Palungtar plenum. The fact that more than 50 Bhattarai supporters dared to question on the floor of Parliament the Maoist support for Jhala Nath Khanal as prime minister indicated where Bhattarai was headed. After years of diffidence, he seemed to have sensed disquiet among the cadre about the long-term sustainability of the chairman's embrace of Vaidya's dogmatism. The cadre's growing sense that the chairman was merely manipulating them to remain on the top must have given Bhattarai the confidence to come out in open opposition, making full use of the media, for which the intra-Maoist tussle was a story which put everything else in the shade.

Some suggest that it is not an all or nothing issue, that the Maoists and the UML could survive side by side. According to this view, if the Maoist party transitions to democracy and willingly shed its radicalism, the need for ideological differentiations in a progressively sophisticated polity would make it the mainstream left and the UML, the social-democratic centre. The Nepali Congress would gradually shift towards being a conservative party. Others believe that this is an unlikely scenario, because the Maoist party, with its brittle politico-military structure and poorly schooled cadre, amidst recriminations and even violence, would break apart in its attempt to 'democratise'. In this event, except for those who joined a suddenly ascendant UML, the rest would be relegated to the fringe, albeit a violent one. None of these prognostications and possibilities can be proven right or wrong until the day the cantonments are disbanded, at which time the trend will become clear.

When a civilian party
Because the UCPN (Maoist) has discarded its 'people's war', some observers maintain that it is already in fact a 'civilian party'. This is the perspective of those who perceive Nepal as a wild and primitive place where the Maoist party's decision to abandon their 'people's war' is sufficient response to the demand for peace and that the Constituent Assembly can write the constitution even if the Maoists' fighting force does not disband. There are stages in any peace process and one does have to be patient, obviously, but it was, after all, the UCPN (Maoist) itself which signed a written commitment to demobilise the cantonments

within six months of the Constituent Assembly elections of April 2008. Only after the Maoists detach themselves from their armed force and the Young Communist League is brought out of the barrack-style organisation will the other parties feel confident about working with the Maoists – even under their leadership – in a national unity government. In fact, this change almost happened and a Maoist-led government was almost installed in late January 2011 but for Chairman Dahal's backtracking during a crucial discussion held at the Gokarna Forest Resort. There are other things that the Maoists must also do to inspire confidence, including returning property, allowing the conflict-displaced to return to their homes, and abandoning the inflammatory rhetoric of 'revolt' and 'state capture'. Instead of these confidence measures, in March 2011, the Maoists inaugurated yet another organisation to threaten the populace, the People's Volunteers' Bureau that was to be a 500,000-strong force.

The wartime need of the Maoist rank-and-file to constantly build up an 'enemy' to vent ire against will hopefully fade as the insurgency recedes to the back of the cadres' minds. Had the Maoist leaders been more committed to the Comprehensive Peace Accord and constitution-writing, the change would already have occurred. There was no need for threatening speeches to scare the populace into submission; in any case, this strategy is sure to produce diminishing returns. The Maoists should end their doublespeak, in which they promise the people and the world that they will democratise while whispering to their cadre that the peace process is but a subterfuge, a part of the grand strategy of a 'protracted people's war'. Their deception was visible to the world at the sixth plenum of the party at Palungtar in Gorkha District in late November 2010, where the three Maoist leaders – Pushpa Kamal Dahal, Baburam Bhattarai and Mohan Vaidya – presented different political documents all of which agreed on one point, that the peace agreements had been a tactical ploy for revolt and state capture.

As demanded by the people and for the sake of civility, the UCPN (Maoist) must essentially do just one thing: stand by its written commitments. Most vitally, it must formally ensure that the cantonments and their residents come under the Special Committee so that the demobilisation process begins with its integration-rehabilitation formula. In January 2011, the Maoists fooled ambassadors and the political top rung and civil society stalwarts with their make-believe transfer of the cantonments to the Special Committee at a flag-lowering ceremony and an elaborate lunch. At the very same ceremony, in full view of the dignitaries, they also announced that the chain-of-command remained with the party.

The other political parties simply want a level playing field: they demand that the UCPN (Maoist) become a civilian party, by which they mean conclude the peace process. The public wants something more. To get open support from the citizenry rather than sullen silence, the party must publicly declare that it is abandoning violence. Later, for its own growth and evolution, it will feel the need to make a formal apology to the people of Nepal for having taken a devastatingly wrong turn in 1996. When the Maoist leadership apologises for fomenting the violent conflict will be when we will have a *democratic* Maoist party amidst us. Known for innovations that surprise the rest of the world, the Nepali polity may just throw up a party known as *Ekikrit Nepal Kamyunist Party (Maobaadi Loktantrik)*, or the Unified Communist Party of Nepal (Democratic Maoist). It is only a Maoist party which respects the values and principles the population holds dear that will go in this direction, however, and not one which believes it can command by threat and force and its ability to deceive the Kathmandu intelligentsia and trusting Western diplomats.

When a Maoist is not a Maoist
When asked to become peaceful and democratic, the UCPN (Maoist) leaders remonstrate that if they did so they would no longer be Maoist. This is exactly the point. It is the abandonment of violence and the acceptance of multi-party pluralism that was the 'price' they agreed to pay, the promise they made as part of the deal that brought them above ground to a safe landing. When pressed, the Maoist leaders also retort that if they took this step, they would be no different from the Nepali Congress and the UML. Again, that is the idea. As far as the universal values of peace and pluralism are concerned, the Nepali people want the UCPN (Maoist) to fall within the existing political spectrum.

In any worldwide scale of political comparison, the UML and Nepali Congress are hardly the parties to belittle. For decades, through continuous political turbulence and autocratic attacks, Nepal's democrat-politicians have held on to the social-democratic agenda and the idea of a welfare state. With tenacity not visible in many other societies near or far, the political parties fought for pluralism for six long decades, battling right-wing regimes and the lately arrived ultra-left demagogues. Since they went underground in 1996 and after they emerged to light in 2006, the Maoists have maligned the mainstream parties, but it is the UML and the Nepali Congress that they will have to emulate before long.

There is no other path for the Maoists to take if, in fact, they respect that the Nepali population is made up of thinking, empathetic, peace-loving citizens. You can, it is true, fool certain civil society stalwarts and intellectuals in Kathmandu Valley all of the time; they demonstrate such pusillanimity that Lenin's appellation 'useful idiots' is most apt. However, you cannot fool all the people at large all of the time. If the Maoist leaders themselves are not trapped in a deception of their own making, they should learn to serve the people and not Kathmandu's civil society and intellectual stalwarts. It is one thing to endlessly claim to speak for the people and to interpret the resulting silence as acceptance of that claim but quite a different matter to actually speak for the people as a representative party elected through fair means. To accomplish the latter requires long-term service, a commitment to social revolution through mass mobilisation based on ideas and not guns. The Maoist leaders should have no difficulty in convincing their cadre to abandon violence if the high trinity of Dahal, Vaidya and Bhattarai agree to take that direction for the sake of the party's strength and longevity. The Gorkha plenum of November 2010, unfortunately, showed the three leaders going in exactly the opposite direction, with their individual propagandistic agenda all proposing revolt and capture of the state.

Because he did not take the high road when he had full command of the party, when the national polity was subdued and the internationals indulgent, in the spring of 2011 Maoist Chairman Dahal finds that he has painted himself into a corner. But if he were to be pressured in unison by the people of Nepal, speaking through civil society and the other political parties, and by the larger international community, specifically China and India, to end the peace process and agree to a democratic constitution, it is possible that Dahal would do what is right for his party faithful. If the chairman were able to wrest himself from the short-term nexus of power and money that grips the UCPN (Maoist) and give some thought to those who followed him in the genuine belief that the Maoists were the harbingers of change, he would shed all subterfuge and doublespeak and turn to his cadre with the earnestness he can switch on with such ease. He would argue thus:

> Friends, we were what they call a fringe party back in the early 1990s. We went underground to try to become the biggest political party of Nepal, and we achieved that target within a decade, a feat that now allows us to serve the people in open political competition. We took the violent road as the only way to break the logjam of politics, to ensure social justice for the people. Through the use of force and our organisational capacity, our party penetrated the rural hinterlands and is now a force to be reckoned with in urban areas as well. Our organisational strength is adequate, and we must now follow our signed commitment and disband the cantonments. Since we are the largest party in the Constituent Assembly and in a position to work towards our social and economic goals, we must disband our military organisation and abandon our military mindset.
>
> Never fear, the future of the party cadre will be secure. Some will, as promised, be integrated into the security forces while others will either be rehabilitated into society with full dignity or join our party's political organisation. The party faithful must understand that the international situation will not allow us to hold on to the PLA any longer, and, in fact, our obstinacy on this matter will destroy the base we have already built for future politics. Our strength in open society is enough to provide careers and livelihoods to each and every one of you, even without a combatant force. We got to where we are through use of force – we built a war chest through coercive means and gained a support base largely through intimidation – but we should abandon all forcible measures now, if only as a means to consolidate our gains in open society. We must act before the desire for money to promote 'the good life' completely corrupts the party. Today, we have everything that the parliamentary parties have, including international and local recognition. In fact, public opinion surveys show our leaders are more popular than theirs. Our party coffers are full, and we have youth organisations, trade unions, women's organisations. Granted, these are institutions the other political parties also have, but ours are more dynamic. We have

reached the centre space and recognition that we wanted back in 1996, and today stand at a point where we can convert all this into a long-term journey into successful politics.

Your careers in politics as members of the party are secure, but only if we attend to the demands made of us by the people of Nepal and the international community: abandon the gun, renounce violence as a tool of politics, and agree on the democratic principles that have to go into the constitution. To do this, the language and tactics we used during the armed conflict and the five years since will no longer be appropriate. To secure the goals of social justice so close to our hearts, to end the marginalisation of communities, to develop Nepal as a sovereign nation-state that bows to no one, we must now adopt changes. This is the right time to publicly disassociate ourselves from the politics of violence. We need not fear the people of Nepal if we go to them as a genuine civilian party, but we all know that if we continue to espouse revolt, violence and state capture, the deep anger of the people may boil over and swamp us. We must also consider that the next elections cannot be fought on the same plank of fear and intimidation which brought us so many seats in the Constituent Assembly in 2008. Comrades, the world will accept our decision to become democratic even as we call ourselves Maoists.

We are at a high point in our party's evolution, and if we make the right judgment, we will stay here. If we falter or lose courage to become democratic, the decline of the party will be dramatic, and the social investment and personal ambitions of the cadre and leader alike will be shattered. Why abandon our success and the political careers of our party members just because we refuse to allow the cantonments to come under the Special Committee? Why not agree to the universal values of democracy and open politics? It is under a democratic constitution that we can achieve what we seek – social transformation.

There are those in the party who do not understand the disquiet among the people of Nepal nor the international geopolitics which forces us today to reconsider the decision we made to revolt at the sixth plenum at Palungtar. These comrades who espouse the radical line will force us back to being a fringe party. A leader has to say various things at various times, you know this well. I ask you to disregard all that I may have told you in the past, in Shaktikhor or elsewhere. I tell you today that the UCPN (Maoist) has no future if it does not become a civilian party. I have to tell you that we do not have an ideological formula for governance and development any different than what the other parties have. Our armed insurgency was merely a tool to get us to this point.

I propose that we abandon all talk of revolt and state capture, stop all acts of extortion countrywide, make possible the return of all seized property, submit the cantonments to the Special Committee, disband all para-military organisations, and prepare to join the next elections peacefully. I also propose that we abandon violence as a political tool, and – the hardest of all but it has to be done – apologise for the conflict that we started in 1996.

We will henceforth be known as the *Ekikrit Nepal Kamyunist Party (Maobaadi Loktantrik)!*

29

Victims and Justice

The sense of abandonment
The peace process started in 2005 and received a fillip with the People's Movement of 2006 and the Maoists' abandonment of the 'people's war'. Since then, however, it has dragged on. The victims of the conflict, those directly affected physiologically and mentally, as well as the larger populace, which was hurt in a myriad of different ways, including the stunting of the economy and the loss of opportunities, await rehabilitation even half a decade after the fighting ended. Thankfully, there is a provision for supporting the families of those who have been 'martyred' – ten lakh rupees per victim. This step in the right direction was made possible because the former rebels came above ground with great momentum and because the benefits accrue to victims of both the state and the insurgents. However, compensation in terms of either death or maiming is often diverted to false claimants and some victimised families receive only part of what is their due. Many, particularly the wounded, have been neglected. In addition, while individual cases are addressed by the government and by international and national non-governmental agencies, there is no countrywide programme of material and psychological rehabilitation beyond the provision of *ex-gratia* compensation.

We can be happy that Nepal's unique, largely home-grown peace process has kept the state's security forces and the former rebel force from going back to war; that, barely two years after leaving the jungle, the Maoists were able to lead the government; and that the last five years of transition has given the Maoists the time to try to adjust to open society. However, the delay in the conclusion of the peace process has been cruel to victims and to society at large and new pain has been added, particularly through the ongoing violence in the mid-eastern Tarai. The neglect of the victims of violence is the saddest remaining part of the conflict saga and is directly connected to the fact that there was no real declared loser, which left the Maoists and the parliamentary parties competing amidst increasing acrimony. Nepal has not really entered a 'post-conflict phase', which would focus on reconstruction and rehabilitation as there has been no nationwide campaign to spark such a twin-pronged programme and no move by the government to launch an international fundraising effort.

As far as reparation and reconciliation are concerned, Nepalis have concentrated only on cash compensation and done little else to help victims to deal with their grief. There has been no guarantee of justice for excesses committed and no rehabilitation support. On each side, victims share a distinct sort of grief. Among 'state-side' victims, who include civil servants of all ranks, there is angst that the sacrifice of the dead and injured among the civilian police, armed police and army has not been recognised even though they went into battle on the side of the rule of law and as directed by a legitimate, constitutional government. They feel deeply neglected because the Maoists entered the Interim Government, became the largest party in the Constituent Assembly, and formed a majority government, all the while loudly proclaiming their victory over the state establishment. Among Maoist supporters, there is a burning sense of rejection by society for fighting what many believed to be a just cause. In many cases, young men and women who fought for the Maoists have found it impossible to go back to their homes and villages, where they feel ostracised. Ex-combatants and ex-cadre and their families also recount stories of neglect by their own party. At the sixth plenum of the UCPN (Maoist) held in Gorkha in November 2010, the victims and their families surrounded the party leaders and charged them with having abandoned them and letting opportunists hijack the party organisation.

In addition to the dead and disappeared who had worked for the government or were Maoist activists and fighters, a large number of unaffiliated innocents were caught up in the war. Child soldiers recruited by the Maoists to fight and provide other types of support to their insurgency were also victims. In addition to those directly impacted, the victims include the traumatised of all ages. Children who directly experienced and perceived brutality and violence number in the tens of thousands, while those traumatised by the presentation of raw news, television clips, photographs, and the never-ending torrent of violent prose and speeches number in the millions. As the conflict took its toll on the national psyche, young villagers stopped greeting strangers on the trails, families stopped talking politics, and children in school started drawing helicopters and grenades instead of flowers and mountains.

Half a decade after the end of the conflict, the living victims – orphans, widows and the elderly – have received minimal support. Except for a lump sum of cash, in typical Nepali fashion and continuing the train of history, they have been left to fend for themselves. The continuing tragedy countrywide is exemplified by the plight of the village of Jogimara in Dhading District just west of Kathmandu. This community, as documentary filmmaker Mohan Mainali recorded, lost 17 of its young men, all killed in a hail of bullets from soldiers on a combing mission while they laboured to build an airfield in Kalikot District. As Mainali discovered and *The Living of Jogimara* depicts, the pain of these abjectly poor and ethnically diverse families of victims –Chepangs, Dalits, Gurungs, Magars and Newar ethnic groups – was real and deep. Mainali despaired that they had the ability to recover the psychological trauma even with the passage of time. Fortunately, this particular community of victims did get material support from the International Committee of the Red Cross after the film was made. By providing photographic evidence of the countrywide suffering of lay civilians, insurgents, police and soldiers, the book *A People War* by Kunda Dixit also gives a sense of the scale of Nepal's mountain of pain.

Right after the People's Movement of 2006, when international recognition of the ability of Nepal's citizenry to rise up to fight for peace and democracy was at its height was the time to launch an international campaign for the funds it needed for rehabilitation and reconstruction, to address the human toll and rebuild the physical infrastructure destroyed during the rebellion. Unfortunately, the governments of the current interregnum – those led by Girija Prasad Koirala, Pushpa Kamal Dahal and Madhav Kumar Nepal – did not recognise the crying need for such a campaign and the controversially created government of Prime Minister Jhala Nath Khanal has had little time to think about reconstruction and rehabilitation while trying to merely exist.

As the Nepal conflict recedes from international memory, it will be harder to obtain support. Still, it is still critical that the Government of Nepal, encouraged by civil society, start a campaign to raise three or four billion U.S. dollars, to spend over three to four years with full transparency and efficiency. The initiative must come from within and not wait for the well-meaning donor representatives and ambassadors. The implementation of the effort to rebuild should lie in the hands of the government, but it should seek the support of Nepal's vast array of philanthropic and non-governmental organisations. Even late, support for the victims of the decade-long conflict will provide them with a large measure of comfort and security. The population as a whole, for its part, will find its hope returning as infrastructure is reconstructed and economic opportunities are revived.

Transitional justice and reconciliation
Transitional justice is a process in which in the perpetrators of human rights excesses are identified and victims confront them with truth in their hands. Unfortunately, the Nepali peace process has evolved in such a way that transitional justice has received only lip service and little commitment. The fact that both 'transitional justice' and 'truth and reconciliation' are terms imported after 2006, introduced by a donor community eager to bring its experience and wisdom from elsewhere to help Nepal return to peace, has had unfortunate consequences. 'Reconciliation' has been translated into Nepali as *melmilap*, or friendship, the political class and the intelligentsia have come to believe that the international human rights community, with all its experience, seeks to promote a 'forgive-and-forget' attitude. A grave injustice to victims and survivors who demand justice and memorialisation has been done: the parliamentary parties can be accused of lethargy and the UCPN (Maoist) has been outright obstructionist. It is easy to understand their differing attitudes: most democrat-politicians were far removed from direct action during the conflict but, as military commanders and commissars, many Maoist leaders were directly responsible and are, therefore, directly accountable. Ever since the peace process began, the Maoist party has maintained an unwritten agreement with the army, its former enemy, to obstruct court procedures. The idea is to similarly obstruct or sabotage the Truth and Reconciliation Commission so that both sides are protected; the transitional justice process must be

interminably delayed so that victims and human rights activists tire or lose heart. If he cannot block the establishment of the Commission as mandated by the Interim Constitution, the ever-wily Chairman Dahal hopes to pad it with members showing Maoist sympathies. The party has already shown how well they can throw a spanner into the works of the National Human Rights Commission and the Election Commission by sending just one commissioner of their own. It would be easy for the Maoist to make the world believe that they were enthusiastic about the Truth and Reconciliation Commission and then sabotage it at the start.

The importance of implementing transitional justice is not only to bring closure to the victims and their families and communities but also to ensure that future conflicts are free of excesses both by the state and the insurgents because they will act in the knowledge that they will be held accountable. The excesses we saw during the conflict years included extra-judicial killings, torture, disappearances, the torching and bombing of public transport, the use of 'human shields', the deployment of child soldiers, the killing of prisoners, helicopter bombings, the mining of highways, and many other extreme forms of violence. The toll of the dead surpasses 13,000, and more than 1000 were disappeared by both sides.

The burden of pain is heavy and perhaps full justice will never be done, but some of the suffering can be lessened by pursuing the guilty. The hunting down of perpetrators must happen continuously through regular police investigations and court procedures, and neither civil society nor government administrators should not be diverted with the argument that they should wait for the establishment of the Disappearances Commission and Truth and Reconciliation Commission promised in the Interim Constitution. Sadly, the Supreme Court in an interim order issued in February 2011 weakened the fight for accountability in one fell stroke when it ordered that a case against a Maoist leader accused of murder be kept pending until the Truth and Reconciliation Commission was established. The OHCHR human rights agency of the UN, in March 2011, put out a white paper which sought to refute this reading of transitional justice, saying that judicial prosecutions for atrocities was a parallel activity to that of the future commission.

The legal and judicial system has been brought low by continuing political confusion as well as by pressure from the Maoists and the national army; as a result, despite the efforts of some never-say-die rights activists, particularly in the districts, there has been no progress in the pursuit of the guilty. These activists have shown commitment and energy in investigating and documenting abuses, standing up to local-level bosses and gangs, and trying to move the police, government lawyers and the courts. Unfortunately, not one of the cases of abuse documented has made its way through the court system to judgement. Justice has not been delivered in even a single instance of excess. Understandably, the lack of action has compounded the suffering of victims and their families and deflated the morale of all in the justice system who are fighting the raging impunity.

The Accountability Watch Committee, a group of independent rights activists and organisations, suggests that to begin the process of accountability for atrocities some emblematic cases need to be pursued – right from complaint to investigation to indictment to court ruling to their logical end, punishment. The role of the justice system, including the police, prosecutors, the court and the penitentiary, must not be neglected as we wait for transitional justice institutions to be established. Even after the tortuous task of setting up disappearance and truth and reconciliation commissions, the wheels of justice must keep turning to ensure fairness and accountability and to prevent the loss of evidence. In the push for doggedly pursuing an emblematic case, there are thousands of pending cases to choose from, some of which got a fair distance in the justice system before being blocked. They include the following:

- The disappearances of 49 Maoist supporters from the army's Bhairabnath Battalion base in Kathmandu (2002-2004).
- The burning of eight-year-old Kajol Khatun from Bara District along with five other passengers in a Maoist attack on a bus in Chitwan District (February 2002).
- The murder of teacher Muktinath Adhikari of Duradanda, Lamjung District, by Maoists (January 2002).
- The killing of unarmed Maoist activists in Doramba, Ramechhap District, by an army platoon (August 2003).
- The murder of Maina Sunar in the army camp in Panchkhal, Kavre District (February 2004).
- The murder of Arjun Lama in Kavre District by a number of Maoists (April 2005), one of whom is a central party leader and a member of the Constituent Assembly.

- The bus blast in the Maadi Valley of Chitwan District carried out by Maoists (June 2005).
- The disappearance of over 150 locals in Bardia District at the hand of the security forces (2001-2003).

The Nepal Army and Maoist leadership hope that the human rights community will simply give up its pursuit of accountability and that the forgive-and-forget mantra of the 'practical' among political leaders will prevail. Indeed, many of the very democrat-politicians who were great champions of human rights in the past are willing to forego the pursuit of justice. Ministers and bureaucrats have gone through the motions towards setting up the two mandated commissions but their hearts have not been in it. Some human rights activists, too, are less than sincere: they only say what donors interested in transitional justice want to hear. The few 'Maoist' human rights groups that have recently emerged are intent only on sabotaging any activity that would block the political progression of many former commissars and commanders. The commitment of some internationals is also questionable: they want to see a truth and reconciliation commission established during their watch but care little of it will be the kind that can deliver justice. Among these internationals, there is very little appreciation of how different Nepal's situation is: here the Maoists are loud and ascendant, whereas the examples of transitional justice they provide are all of nations in which the insurgents had been defeated. Nepal's peace process is exemplary for being home-grown; its transitional justice process must be the same. Its main principles should be justice for victims and prosecution of perpetrators. Whether the position of the wily Maoist, the perfunctory politician, and the *pro forma* activist or donor representative, each demonstration of a lack of will to pursue transitional justice is an abuse of the rights of victims and of a society that seeks the rule of law and an end to impunity. In addition, to deny justice for human rights abuses and atrocities carried out during the decade of conflict weakens the foundation of an peaceful, accountable democracy.

The Maoist-Army nexus
When it comes to justice for victims, the defences of both the Maoists and the Nepal Army are untenable and must be rejected. The victims and the human rights community must muster the energy to continue

their fight, for decades if necessary, remember through the examples of El Salvador, Greece, Cambodia, and the like that it is those who do not give up the fight that ultimately set the standard for future generations.

The UCPN (Maoist) maintains that it was engaged in a 'just war' on behalf of the people against the state and, therefore, that none of its actions can be brought under the scrutiny of investigations or transitional justice. They say that their position was vindicated by their grand win in the elections to the Constituent Assembly. But the Maoist argument is like that of a divine interpreter seeking to absolve itself. The right of interpretation lies, if anything, with victims and their families and with our honourable justices, not with ex-rebel leaders or even democrat-politicians, academics and activists. The Maoists have to be told clearly that the rules of international humanitarian law under the Geneva Conventions apply equally to insurgents, and that they will be held accountable for employing child soldiers; murdering, maiming and disappearing citizens; and killing unarmed and surrendered policemen and soldiers.

Except for deaths and wounds inflicted during the heat of battle with the state security forces, all killings by the Maoists come within the ambit of investigation and prosecution, a fact that the rebels perhaps did not understand when they took and enthusiastically disseminated detailed video footage of their fighting prowess which included instances of barbarity. In addition to Maoist-produced images, the easy availability of digital photography and videography by the midpoint of the 'people's war' has produced a veritable archive of images that can help identify Maoist excess. These will slowly emerge as evidence in the era of peace.

Since the Nepal Army was first deployed in 2001, its officers have charged rights activists with bias against the military and leniency towards the insurgents. They maintain that, in the tolerance shown to abuse committed by Maoists, there has been a lack of 'balance'. This position indicates their willingness to see the army, an institution of the state meant to protect citizens under the law, as being on par with a renegade force which took pride in violating the constitution and taking justice into its own hands. No proud citizen will accept the Maoist propaganda that the insurgents were equal in status to the national army, but that is what the army officers suggest by their demand for parity. Nor is it true that the Maoists have not been held to account by human rights organisations. The Informal Sector Service Center (INSEC), which is a repository of information and data of the conflict era, and the Advocacy Forum, which specialises in prosecutions, are two notable groups that have fiercely pursued rights abusers whether Maoist or state. In the last couple of years, the families of the victims of both Maoist and state excesses have been organising and slowly making their presence felt. Society at large must be on guard to protect these intrepid souls, the sons and daughters of the victims of war, so that they are not visited by violence for their attempts to bring the perpetrators of atrocities to book.

It is tragic that there has been no final verdict on any case against the accused, whether army personnel or Maoist cadre. While little can be expected of Maoist-commanders-turned-politicians, democrat-politicians must be challenged to at least get the process started by submitting the army to the court process. The Maoists hope that the army will not be prosecuted, and the army hopes that Maoists will be let off the hook, as any inaction that lets off Maoists will help soldiers, and vice versa. Thus it is that in the last few years a curious collaboration has developed between the Maoists headquarters, now in Paris Danda, and the Nepal Army headquarters in Bhadrakali. Both realise that prosecution of the other will *ipso facto* mean action against itself, for such is the tragic 'balance' of atrocities in the public's mind.

In the latest instance, it is the Nepal Army which has played the disgraceful role of creating conditions in which, in order to order to save its own officers, it will allow Maoists who committed excesses to walk free. With the fall of the Maoist government in May 2009, the Nepal Army, after a long period of humiliation at the hands of the Maoists, gained strength and exploited the other parties' fear of the Maoist momentum to stonewall moves against soldiers accused of excess. In one brazenly defiant act, the military refused to comply with a Supreme Court directive to present an officer to the Kavre District Court for investigations related to the torture and killing of teenager Maina Sunar while she was in custody at the Panchkhal barrack. The Army brass convinced the democratic leaders, including then Defence Minister Bidya Bhandari, that the military should not be pursued in the courts because the pursuit of one case would lead to a flood of cases against the army across the country. Such recriminations, went the argument, would demoralise the military at the very time when it should be getting ready for the day the Maoists walk out of the peace process.

That Minister Bhandari and other politicians in the CPN (UML) and the Nepali Congress bought into this specious argument is clear from the lack of movement on justice during the prime ministership of the democratically-minded Madhav Kumar Nepal. Ironically, cases against the army would not proceed even if a Maoists were to become defence minister, because it would be more important for that minister to save Maoists from prosecution than to ensure justice on behalf of the Maoists supporters who were victimised. One of the reasons the Maoists insisted on getting the Home Affairs portfolio in the Jhala Nath Khanal cabinet in early 2011 was so it be in a position to cancel court cases filed against Maoists at every level, from the districts to the centre.

The army's stratagem and the recalcitrance on the part of the parliamentary parties suit the UCPN (Maoist) fine because the inability to prosecute the officer accused in the Maina Sunar case means the inability to proceed with the charge against Maoist leader Agni Sapkota on the murder of Arjun Lama. When army atrocities cannot be challenged in the courts, neither can Maoist atrocities. In October 2010, Colonel Raju Basnet, the commandant of the Bhairabnath Battallion in 2003-2004, when 49 Maoist supporters were disappeared from its precincts, was promoted with the acquiescence of the Madhav Kumar Nepal government. The UPCN (Maoist) uttered not a word in protest. The reason for its silence (and obliteration of the memory of its own rank-and-file) was obvious: raising public awareness would have seen the prosecution of Maoists for their own excesses.

The Nepal Army has an office of legal affairs which lets it be known that it has already tried and punished soldiers found guilty of excesses and that re-starting cases would violate the double-jeopardy principle. This is a farcical position on more than one count, for the punishment provided for grave offences has been tantamount to a rap on the knuckles – a momentary suspension of promotion, a few days in army incarceration. Besides, one has to take the military at its word that trials occur at all. The army's unilateral action also flouts provisions, well laid out in the law, that excesses committed by army personnel in a time of conflict are to be tried in civilian courts. On this matter, by not holding the army to a standard of civilised behaviour, the principle of the 'civilian supremacy' of elected governments over security forces, was violated by the governments of both Girija Prasad Koirala and Madhav Kumar Nepal. Naturally, little could have been expected from Dahal's government. The government's inaction on atrocities has energised the Maoist cadre everywhere and weakened the entire justice system; all sorts of public defenders – judges in the districts, prosecutors, court officials, local police, activists, journalists and others – have suffered a loss in morale.

The drawn-out transitional period which started with the end of the 'people's war' in 2006 has had the positive effect of seeing the Maoists enter open politics, but the ex-rebels have simultaneously utilised their position in the parliament and the government to stonewall moves towards transitional justice. The fear today is that the establishment of a truth and reconciliation commission will be compromised as Maoist leaders sabotage it even if it means denying those of their supporters who have been victimised by the state justice. If any one Maoist leader were convinced that the agenda of transitional justice had to be pushed for the sake of societal closure, there is little likelihood that he or she would be allowed by others to act. The desperate attempts at self-preservation among the Maoist commanders, nearly all of whom are active in politics, would prevent such an idiosyncratic move.

Interesting, even while the focus is on the army and the Maoist leadership, there is no discussion in the public sphere till date about the accountability of the royal palace and its incumbents for state-side atrocities during the conflict, especially during its latter stages when the palace was ascendant. The king was 'supreme commander in chief' of the Royal Nepal Army, but that tended to be more than a ceremonial role; military officials ensconced in Narayanhiti were known to direct affairs even to the extent, sometimes, of ordering the army chief. To prevent miscarriage of transitional justice and also ensure that the perpetrators who held behind-the-scene power are held accountable, the rights activists must follow through on any role the palace authorities, including the erstwhile royals, may have had in perpetrating abuse. To take just one example, was the decision to carry out the massacre of Maoist activists at Doramba, Ramechhap District, taken by the officer on the ground, the divisional commander, the Bhadrakali generals or the Narayanhiti authorities?

Some important *ex post facto* differences in the context of excesses committed by the Maoists and the security forces personnel need be highlighted. First, while the number of deaths escalated sharply after the army, with its superior firepower, was deployed in 2001, together with the cases of torture and killings committed by both the police and the army create a horrendous picture of large-scale state atrocity. The brutality of the targeted killings by the UCPN (Maoist), meanwhile, made a mark of their own: seeking to subdue the people in the districts, the Maoists made effective use of elaborate events of public torture, humiliation and murder. Sometimes, these horrific rituals took days to complete, as in the case of Guru Prasad Luitel, a government school teacher in Okhaldunga, who was walked around the hills even as he was abused and humiliated for days in September 2003 before he was murdered and strung up on a tree branch. The personnel of state security forces accused of abuses all need to be tried, as do the accused Maoists. What makes the Maoist accused unique is that nearly all want to remain active in politics; to do so, they will fight tooth and nail to stall the accountability process by derailing the processes of investigation, prosecution and judgement. Their fierce determination puts both rights activists and victims' families who insist on the prosecution of ex-rebels as well as the journalists who report dispassionately on the matter in danger; those who block the 'career progression' of perpetrators with political ambition must be wary of retaliatory moves.

Over the last couple of years, there has been a slow rise in activism among the victims' families and even some degree of cooperation between the victims of the state and the victims of the Maoists. The former feel relatively secure and the latter less so, but both groups feel the pain of neglect and the hurt of impunity that has allowed the perpetrators to walk free thus far. Daring to file a court case against a Maoist invites grave consequences, with the topmost Maoist leadership united against moves that would bring prosecutions at any level. Maoist leaders accused of conflict-era atrocities are active everywhere, from the UCPN (Maoist) politburo to the district and the village levels, and activists are stymied and intimidated in every direction. An example is the Supreme Court single bench order of January 2011, staying aprosecutions relating to conflict-era excess to await a truth and reconciliation commission. The UN human rights agency OHCHR and Nepal's human rights community are arrayed against that decision, as are some of the Supreme Court justices themselves. Other instances of the seeming collusion of the state superstructure are many. In Chitwan District, the individuals accused of the Maadi bus blast have been given important positions; one is head of the Chitwan National Park buffer zone. In early

April 2011, the family of murdered teacher Muktinath Adhikari finally, after nine years, mustered the strength to file a case against a Maoist leader in Lamjung District; the very next day, the accused was made coordinator of the all-party Peace Committee of the district. Ironically, the very person of causing the wounds of war was charged with healing them. The fact that all the other political parties agreed with his assignation is a reflection of Maoist intimidation.

Despite the impasse in moving the transitional justice agenda forward, victims' representatives and the human rights community must maintain their campaign for accountability; they must keep the justice system active even as they work to establish an independent truth and reconciliation commission. There can be no acceptance of a general amnesty; excesses have to be investigated and taken through to their judicial conclusion, meaning the assignation of guilt or the declaration of innocence. To those found guilty, no one other than the victims and their families have the right to grant pardon. It is important to keep memories alive, for as long as necessary, and not forget to pursue those who have taken innocent lives, harmed innocent citizens, and transgressed the laws of war. Instead of 'forgive and forget', the guiding principle of transitional justice in Nepal should be 'forgive perhaps, but investigate, prosecute – and never forget'.

30

The Right Federalism

Who's afraid of federal Nepal?
The members of the Interim Parliament created a unique situation on 28 December 2007 by declaring Nepal a federal democratic republican state while leaving it up to the forthcoming Constituent Assembly to define the nature of the federalism. That federalism was a *fait accompli* was due to the momentum of the Madhes Movement, the backing of the leadership of the ethnic identity movement, and the Maoist leadership's exploitation of the situation to garner support by promising federalism based on ethnicity, a promise it would find hard to fulfil. A more logical process would have been to go enter the Constituent Assembly with a federalist agenda and emerge with a declaration in the new constitution. As it was, the buggy was placed firmly in front of the horse and marginalised communities embraced federalism as a matter of faith. A populist wave has been created suggesting that the mainstream parties are against federalism, when, in fact, the main worry of the democrat-politicians is not federalism *per se*, but federal formats which would spark communal tension and ultimately retard social and economic growth.

There is no need to fear federalism, or what some nations call a union. Properly defined, federalism is the ideal state structure for a country like Nepal with a fractured geography and heterogenous population. In fact, Nepal has been a Kathmandu-centred country for much too long and could do with a dedicated attempt at devolution through federal re-structuring. The devolution of fiscal, representational and political power to the provinces will place governance closer to the ground and to the people and make state administration more responsive and accountable. Nepal's experience with local government in the late 1990s and early 2000s indicates that a crafted federal structure will be a step forward because the public already have enough awareness to be able to hold provincial authorities accountable, but there still have to be constitutional provisions in place to enable the public to demand that accountability.

For all its possibilities, if federal units are not defined appropriately for Nepal's unique situation, federalism could devastate the nation. In the present state of populist politics, where emotionalism rather than scientific inquiry prevails and the UCPN (Maoist), in particular, exhibit little sense of societal accountability, federalism poses the danger of creating deep cleavages in society. Federal units must be defined in such a way that the central-provincial-local division of power is practical and efficient, the delineation of the federal units stands up to economic scrutiny, and the cost of maintaining the provinces does not bleed the exchequer. The naming of provinces after designated communities must be handled with care and the demand for political 'prior rights' (*agradhikar*) rejected so that the inter-community discord has already surfaced does not grow.

It is a given that an economically viable province will be a boon to the communities and identities that live within it. Because Nepal's demography is characterised by concentrated pockets of particular population groups, people will benefit most if federal provinces are defined in a 'secular' manner that maximises opportunities for economic growth and political clout. Majority groups will find a representational advantage at the provincial level that will enable them to vie effectively for greater visibility and opportunity at the national level. because of the economic viability of the province, the members of all its communities – especially the dominant one – will also feel fulfilled in seeking positions of power within the province. Creating a small, economically unviable ceremonial province to satisfy the lust for power of a few would-be local satraps would cheat the larger population of the possibilities for both economic growth and representational power. Federalism should not be a formula for relegating Nepal's various marginalised communities to economically unsound *bantustans* and depriving them of power at the centre.

Without economic viability as its main criteria, the federal structure will fulfil the desires of a few elites of particular communities but leave everyone else, including other members of those communities, feeling cheated. Because they fail to consider class, provinces that privilege identity over economics are bound to collapse as public frustration mounts. The federal unit must be defined on the basis of economic efficiency and linked to geography; power and authority must be delegated among the central, provincial and local spheres in a way that supports economic growth and efficient state administration. The spatial concentration of specific marginalised groups in various parts of Nepal's hills and plains means that, even if provinces are not defined by community, these communities stand to benefit.

The weakening of scholarship in terms of anthropology, sociology, history, political science and economics can be seen in the weak debates on federalism thus far. Additionally, the press, radio and television have tended to favour those scholar-activists who speak in extreme language, giving a false sense of the academic median when it comes to the study of ethnic federalism. Indeed, it becomes increasingly clear that elite scholar-activists are speaking for the elites rather than for the lay members of the designated communities when they push for ethnically defined federalism, including 'political prior rights' for two electoral terms. Interestingly, the size of the largest ethnic group (say, Limbu) in each of the proposed ethnically-defined provinces is such that it could easily be sidelined when two other smaller but nevertheless sizeable groups (say, Rai and Bahun) form an alliance to keep it (the Limbu) from power. In this sense, ethnic federalism may be mis-designed to destroy the socio-political advance of the very communities the proponents seek to support.

Federalism in the Assembly

Nepal was declared a secular, federal democratic republic by the Interim Parliament in December 2007; this declaration was repeated by the Constituent Assembly at its first sitting on 28 May 2008. While other critical matters relating to the separation of powers, electoral systems, affirmative action, and governmental structure are also pending in the spring of 2011, the most critical and volatile is, without a doubt, the definition of federalism. Three pending questions concern the demarcation of the boundaries, the naming of the provincial units, and the right to equality of the population within them. In its almost three years of existence, the Constituent Assembly's state restructuring committee did not once conduct a transparent debate on federalism and outside the Parliament the populist tide that pushed ethnically defined federalism affected the ability of the public to discuss the matter with ease. With the predominant worries centred on *seemankan* and *naamankan* (the definition of the boundaries and the naming of the federal units), little thought was given to either the division of powers between the centre and the provinces or the protection of local governance.

Not only were constitutional debates conducted in a questionable manner, but the Assembly was affected by the effervescent identity politics that bubbled in the society at large. Outside, activists continued to assail the state for historic marginalisation, and, inside, the Assembly was unable to nurture give-and-take between communities that lead to consensus. Because various thematic committees in the Assembly passed reports through majority vote rather than consensus – a strategy merely postponing real negotiations for debate in the plenary – the members sought to grandstand on the matter of provincial definition rather than to reduce the rhetoric and seek the common ground among various positions. No genuine debate was to be found in the general society either. Given that the Bahun were considered, *ab initio*, biased against ethnic federalism, many Bahuns in the intelligentsia – and they form a majority of that group – decided to keep their own counsel during the nearly three years of debate. With little crosscutting discussion within the Assembly or outside, the polity was hardly ready to take a decision on something as monumental as how to define federalism.

The UCPN (Maoist) exploited the Assembly sessions to build its party base by vociferously demanding ethnic federalism and using faulty procedure to railroad the sub-committee on state restructuring into defining 14 provinces, nine of them along ethnic lines. The party even included a provision for 'political prior rights' for the designated community in each of the ethnically defined units, an incendiary provision that is sure to create divisions on the ground, but then the party seemed intent on inviting conflagration. The few Maoists leaders who now concede in private that a mistake was made in seeking federalism on the basis of exclusivist identities are unable to publicly confront the vehemence of the diehard ethnic federalists within the party fold. The UCPN (Maoist)'s opportunism has come close to irreparably harming communal harmony in Nepal, though maybe the foundational resilience of inter-community relationships will ward off further dissension.

The Constituent Assembly was thus unable to evolve into a place in which the 'vertical' demands placed before the state by various population groups could be adjusted with the need for agreement among the various communities inhabiting the same space to allow a federal structure that responds to identity demands through the prism of economic geography. While the ethnicity-focussed identity movement roused one section of the population, it was the Madhesi cultural identity which roiled the Tarai. The newborn and competing political parties seeking to build their base among the populace adopted the slogan *'ek Madhes, ek pradesh'*, seeking a single federal unit that was 500 long miles by 20 miles wide. Everyone knew that a province of this scale was unworkable, but for two long years after the Madhes Movement of 2007 – until the Madhesi citizenry in Birgunj, Janakpur and Rajbiraj itself began to question the construct – Kathmandu commentators and editorial writers were unwilling to challenge the idea for fear of the verbal backlash from the plains.

The Maoist party leadership, having used the ethnic card to amass support during the 2008 elections, found itself unable to back out even as, at long last, it began to perceive the risks of ethnically defined federalism. It even contemplated proposing six provinces that would have been more geographically sound but then got cold feet and reverted to its original plan for 14 provinces.

The exclusivist activist
In large parts of the hills as well as the western Tarai, activists demand federal units defined along ethnic lines. This demand is problematic because Nepal is a country of micro-communities with a heterogeneous mix of communities right to the village level. There are regions of ethnic origin and there are areas of ethnic concentration, but in no proposed region not in any of Nepal's 75 existing districts does any single ethnic group has even a simple majority. The ethnic communities for whom federal provinces have been proposed constitute, on average, one third of the total population. Just as it did with the single Madhes province, the cautionary note on ethnic federalism has come from the districts, where locals perceived the dangers of inter-community conflagration close-up. The Kathmandu-based elite scholar-activists, as well as some Nepali and non-Nepali scholars in overseas universities, in contrast, seemed not at all worried in promoting a formula that had the potential to spark communal discord. For them, ethnic federalism is a tantalising experiment and a risk worth taking.

Even as the complexities of exclusivist federalism came to the fore and cautionary noises began to be heard from the districts, those in the national intelligentsia who believe in the importance of economic-geographic criteria – particularly the Bahun – felt intimidated enough by the scholar-activists that they maintained a steady silence. To build a robust future through something as useful and promising as federalism, there should have been the open space and atmosphere needed for a genuine debate in which even opponents were heard. Those who felt that the success of decentralisation of the late 1990s was being abandoned were not heard and neither were the federations of municipalities, DDCs and VDCs which sought to defend the record of local government. The vehemence of the ethnic federalists, who included the Maoist leadership, rendered sober discussion within and outside the Constituent Assembly impossible. The same was true with the Madhesi politicians' agenda to create a single plains province. Courage was required even to utter the word 'local government', much less 'decentralisation', both concepts regarded as anti-federal taboo subjects. It was incredible to watch ethnic elite activists as well as Madhesi activists both hitting out at the decidedly Bahun-dominated state, but rarely feeling the need to talk to each other and to compare notes in order to help fashion a proper federalism that incorporated elements of what each sought.

It was left to the citizen-thinkers in the districts of hill and plain, far away from the opinion-making media, to send a cautionary message to Kathmandu. The years from 2006 to 2010 were a time when Kathmandu's academia, civil society, development community and think-tanks, by and large, remained silent on the federalism debate. Scholars knew, even though they kept their own counsel, that ethnic federalism was dangerous for communal harmony – not just between caste and ethnicity, but between ethnicity and ethnicity – and, further, that it would not be economically viable and would harm the very ethnic communities that the formula sought to uplift.

While the intelligentsia sat mum as the Constitution Assembly set sail towards potential disaster, the international community tended to see Nepal at just two levels: state and community. It was not able to discern the third layer, hidden behind the veil of populism and represented by the deep disquiet in rural Nepal about what elite scholar-activists and opportunist politicians of the Maoist and Madhesi parties were up to. Nor were many Western donors able to comprehend their own role in propping up apolitical, rigid and non-conciliatory positions dangerous for the safe evolution of Nepal into federalism through their funding of some misguided projects which created a technocratic terrain which ignored the reality of socio-cultural inter-linkages and created a harsh environment of polar opposites. The fact that the discourse tended to be controlled by urban scholar-activists and non-governmental organisations rather than by the rural intelligentsia which would feel the hurt if the prescription of ethnic federalism went awry made it distanced and exclusivist.

Economic advancement is the primary human urge everywhere, and the people of the hills and plains of Nepal are no different. For a few years, however, 'class' was sidelined by 'identity' with the only-partly valid assumption, proffered by the Maoists and propped up by patterns of donor funding prioritising 'the disadvantaged', that poverty in Nepal was synonymous with ethnicity or marginality. The (marginally Marxist) Maoist party's promotion of ethnic exclusivity in order to expand its cadre strength was not challenged adequately because this line complemented the advocacy of scholar-activists, themselves influenced by ethnographies of communities in isolation.

It is a measure of the failure of the Constituent Assembly that identity politics are still developing and that many communities, large and small, have yet to find their voice. In this state of incomplete evolution, it is unwarranted to define federal units by ethnicity or community. We have not even begun to identify and understand the existing primary identities, much less the secondary and tertiary identities of the modern-day Nepali citizen, or the multiple horizontal linkages between and within ethnic communities and between castes and ethnicities. It was irresponsible to close the debate and place the country in a community-based federal straitjacket based on a linear reading of history and a willingness to equate identity entirely with class.

Carried away by the extant populism, some ethnographers who studied individual communities in their 'verticality' have now tilted towards presenting the entire conglomeration of ethnicities as a united front opposing the Kathmandu-centric Bahun-Chhetri establishment. This perspective is useful in terms of forcing recognition of ethnic marginalisation but will not help in defining federal provinces. When communities are seen as free-standing entities, without linkages to other communities, it is easy to be attracted to the idea of ethnic federalism.

Only if one believes – erroneously – that there are regions of exclusive ethnic habitation in present-day Nepal, as there are in Afghanistan among the Hazara, Uzbek, and Pashtun, and in Burma among the Karen, Shan, Kachin and Bamar can one justify federal units based on ethnicity. Nepal's villages and districts, however, are characterised by dynamic interaction among communities and would suffer badly under any ethnic model.

There is great danger built into the fact that no ethnicity constitutes a majority in any of the ethnically-defined federal units proposed by the Maoists or other parties. The designated ethnicities (including Rai, Limbu, Magar, Tharu or Tamang) which would have their 'own' provinces are not so much larger than the next largest ethnic group in the same are, which, naturally, would feel short-changed. Straightforward logic suggests that rewarding nine communities with provinces in their name when they are not much larger than other groups will not work. Scholar-activists console the leaders of smaller ethnic groups with the promise of autonomous sub-provinces to cater to them. When new identity claimants come forward, as they are bound to, their logic would lead to the establishment of autonomous sub-sub-provinces and then autonomous sub-sub-sub-provinces. There would be no end to divisions. Clearly, the proponents of ethnic federalism have not thought deeply of the Pandora's box they are opening, even among groups that seem united today.

One huge problem with dividing up the country along ethnic and communitarian lines, a problem that has been deliberately pushed under the carpet by scholar-activists, is the issue of Dalit rights. Historically denigrated by the 'upper' castes and ethnicities alike, the Dalit of the hills and plains together make up the most deprived community of Nepal. Indeed, the one instance in which community identity is indeed synonymous with class marginalisation is the case of the Dalit, yet the proponents of ethnic federalism are quiet on this count as it is impossible for them to locate an exclusive region for the Dalit to rule as they, like the Bahun-Chettri, are sprinkled all over the country. When pressed, the activists lamely propose a 'non-territorial council' for Dalits, not even believing themselves that the idea will be taken seriously. Nor does the ethnic federalist like to talk of the very poor among the Bahun-Chhetri/Thakuri (Parbate) castes, who make up one of the largest groups living under the poverty line. The Dalit and the poor Bahun-Chhetri are likely to reject any attempt to railroad them into an ethnic federal model. For now, the Bahun-Chhetri is quiet in the face of strident populism and the Dalit leadership seems lost in the maze of seminars and workshops – but both groups will make their voices heard when the worry that ethnic federalism will indeed be implemented starts to set in.

There are some who believe that a broad-based pan-ethnic Janajati (ethnic) identity will consolidate over time to challenge the Parbate (Bahun-Chettri) establishment that today has such a grip on the country's political, educational, bureaucratic and judicial systems. Others believe that this pan-ethnic identity will not be able to coalesce beyond a point, especially as more, smaller communities find themselves sufficiently empowered to enter the arena close to state power. At some point, there may be friction between the more advanced and the more marginalised ethnicities. The hope, therefore, is that Nepal's movement towards an egalitarian society will continue without the diversion towards ethnic-exclusivist provinces that will create local power brokers while impoverishing the ethnic and other masses. Such a step, surely, would take Nepal back to the pre-unification days of two-and-half centuries ago, with scores of principalities each with its own princelings. The economies of scale that the unifier Prithvi Narayan Shah sought to develop back in the 18th century would be lost in a tide of vainglorious politics in the 21st. The Nepali state would be weakened, within itself and in relation to neighbouring countries and regions, at the very moment that it was getting ready to shed the discriminatory shackles of the past and to mount an economic advancement in an inclusive democracy.

The greatest danger of the ethnic model of federalism is the possibility of inter-community anger within the Janajati fold triggered by the provision of provinces to some ethnicities and not to others. The fact that protest has been muted till now does not mean that it will not detonate in the future. In the confusing and competitive sphere of activism, groups and sub-groups are still trying to understand and to organise. What is seen for now as merely a Parbate vs. Janajati battle could easily, and unexpectedly, change into a conflict among Janajati groups. While scholar-activists seem to recognise only the likelihood of Parbate-Janajati friction, there is also a possibility of Janajati-Janajati rifts, especially between the designated ethnic group in a province and another large group which perceives itself as having been relegated to secondary status by the prior-rights provision, the naming of the province, or some other factor.

Those who defend political prior rights for the designated ethnicity within a province offer unconvincing logic that a Magar living in the 'Limbuwan' province in the east, for example, would be satisfied that the members of his community receive prior rights in a province named 'Magarat' in the mid-west. Who knows for sure? Some suggest that this scenario of possible friction among the Janajati is exaggerated, in this instance by a Bahun writer who is biased against ethnic federalism. But the question is whether we have such a good handle on the psycho-social aspects of provincialism to be secure in our certitudes. Why would we want to risk a situation in which the provision of prior political rights to only nine or so ethnic groups ignited social tension with other groups, both caste and ethnic? The possibility that caste-ethnic and ethnic-ethnic strains will be the result of this 'social engineering project' is so great that it is a path best not taken.

Signs of possible dissonance already exist. In March 2009 the Tharu rose up in a movement against the 'Madhesi domination' of the Tarai and in the Far-West, the mid-hill ethnic and Tharu factions within the Maoist fold have clashed. In the east, there is disagreement between the Rai and Limbu regarding the demarcation of the projected 'Khambuwan' and 'Limbuwan' provinces, and the latter has been challenged by the Koch of the plains and the Lepcha (Rong) of the hills. More divisions are likely to crop up among other groups and sub-groups if and when it becomes certain that ethnic federalism will be imposed. Till such time, amidst the populist tsunami propelled by the Maoists, some donors, and scholar-activists, these groups and sub-groups keep their own counsel.

It is the spring of 2011. We could proceed with implementing the ethnic federal units proposed by the Maoists and elite scholar-activists in the fervent hope that everything will be all right. Or, as makes more sense, we could first study the international experience regarding boundary demarcations within mixed societies. The last few years of discourse presents the marginalised Janajati and the Madhesi as arrayed against the Parbate-dominated state establishment, but things are somewhat more complex than that. The very diversity which provides such a beautiful texture to Nepali society may also provide various planes for quarrel, in various permutations of dozens of groups, including the

Parbate, Madhesi, Pahade Janajati (mid-hill ethnic), plains Janajati, hill Dalit, plains Dalit, Muslim, Himali (Bhotiya), ultra-marginalised Janajati, sub-groups of main Janajati communities, and so on. We may just need to understand our society better and to respect individual freedoms amidst the demand for community rights we offer adventurous formulae for federalism.

The Madhes strip-province
The concept of an exclusive single province for the stretch of the Tarai (*ek Madhes radesh*) was proposed in the first flush of post-2006 identity politics which emerged to reject Kathmandu-centric governance. Propelled by an identity movement of the culturally diverse Madhesi community, the concept ignored the fact that an exclusively plains-based federal unit would short-change the citizens of the plains. 'Madhes' is a socio-cultural construct rather than a geographical region and 'Madhesi' in the main refers to the non-ethnic, non-Muslim people of plains origin, particularly of the eastern half. In broader (but not yet set) usage, the term also denotes all communities residing in the plains other than those of mid-hill origin. The inclusion of the term 'Madhes' in state documentation and in the media and academic discourse is in response to the power of the Madhes Movement of 2007. The fear of angry reaction kept many members of the predominantly mid-hill intelligentsia of Kathmandu from challenging the proposal to create one province encompassing the entire Tarai. That such an impractical suggestion was allowed to rule the national discourse for more than two years without strong resistance indicates both the power of populism as well as the weaknesses of the intelligentsia.

Without help from the scholar-activists of Kathmandu or from their own political representatives, over time opinion-makers in the plains themselves concluded that a single Madhes province was not practical. Such a 'strip province' would be administratively unwieldy for its length and socio-politically unfeasible given its linguistic diversity (its residents speak Awadhi, Bhojpuri, Maithili, Tharu, Hindi, and, of course, Nepali) and demographic spread (its peoples include the Tharu, Muslim, Pahade ethnicities and castes, and social divisions within the Madhesi). The geography and settlement patterns in the Tarai must give the one-Madhes proponents pause, because they reveal that such a province can work only in the mind, not on the ground. Besides, some districts, such as Jhapa in the east or Chitwan in the centre, are dominated by mid-hill groups while others have large populations of the Tharu or Muslims. Still other Tarai districts are dangerously divided between plains people in the south and mid-hill people in the north, with the East-West Highway serving as a dividing line.

The Tarai contains more than half of Nepal's total population and is important for this reason alone, but it would be wrong to think or claim that the population of the plains is united in the nature of its opposition to Kathmandu. The unsettled politics of the moment results from an evolving demography, which is made up of ethnic groups and caste communities settled in jungles and farmlands since historical time; settlers who moved in from the hills or from India to clear forests in the last century; and 'new arrivals' *(naba agantuk)*, large numbers who took untoward advantage of the 2006 decision to provide citizenship papers to all who had been 'domiciled permanently' in Nepal since April 1990.

As the impracticality of the one-Madhes province idea became clearer, almost as a fallback, many plains politicians and civil society stalwarts proposed dividing the Tarai into three separate units, between the Maithili, Bhojpuri and Awadhi populations. The Maoists got into the act by proposing four Tarai provinces, one each for the Koch and Tharu ethnicities in the east and west respectively, and one each for the Maithili and Bhojpuri-Awadhi in the central regions. The Maoists' parcelling out of the Tarai was nothing more than an attempt to appeal to identity as a basis for political support without the slightest concern for the wellbeing of the citizens of the plains.

Deep down, the Madhesi politician, as well as the scholar-activist of the mid-hills, know that a secular egalitarian federal state is best achieved when there is a north-south definition of federal provinces based on economic geography. Such a province links the Tarai through the mid-hills to the High Himalaya and enables Nepal's numerous communities to take advantage of their demographic concentration for political clout and the geographical synergy for economic growth. As time passes and the dust settles, the Madhesi intelligentsia will hopefully come around to accepting the suggestion that the densely populated plains areas be linked to the north in order to share in the wealth generated in the highlands, including hydropower, service industries, agro-forestry and tourism. Likewise, the hills would benefit from the irrigated agriculture and industrialisation of the plains, as well as from easy access to adjacent and distant Indian markets and beyond.

Those who insist on single or multiple plains-exclusive provinces will have to explain to the public why they would want to limit the economic advancement of the people of the Tarai – both Madhesi and non-Madhesi – by cutting them off from the hills. Why, for example, would Upendra Yadav, the main flag-bearer of the Madhes Movement and head of the Madhesi Janadhikar Forum, be keen to create conditions in which farmers from Sarlahi District are kept at arm's length from the hydropower wealth of Dolakha District or those from Rupandehi do not profit from the tourism dollars of Kaski? If agriculture and industry are to remain the primary economic activity of the plains, simple logic dictates the need for Tarai-dwellers to be part of a north-south province whose mid-hill flow of the rivers they can claim as their own, for the sake of irrigation and water supply, rather than have to negotiate prices with an upstream province that might be unwilling to share. As with is the case with ethnically defined provincialism, a one-Madhes province can only deliver ceremonial federalism that will benefit existing provincial elites, not the average citizen in the province. It is past time for the ethnic federalist and the Madhesi politicians to come out of their parochial cocoons and exchange notes on the definition of federalism. When they do so, it is more than likely that they will opt for the north-south geographical province as making the most sense in terms of political empowerment and economic growth.

Activism in the time of populism
Even under present circumstances of 'un-knowability', we must try to locate the most feasible – and the least potentially dangerous – format for federalism rather than float along on the basis of hunches and intentions. The search must be based on an acceptance of the reality of the degrading, dehumanising Kathmandu-centricism of the past, which prevented whole communities from feeling and taking advantage of state ownership. At the same time, the polity must resist the push of those scholar-activists who harbour an antediluvian desire to take society back to the pre-unification 'state structure', when what was to become modern-day Nepal was made up of about three score principalities. As Nepal seeks to progress from the pluralism it achieved in 1990 towards making a more egalitarian and inclusive democracy, it would

be regressive to divide up the country by ethnic and Madhesi identities and lose economies of scale, geopolitical clout and political stability. Why would anyone seek to fracture and destroy the economy just as the nation is on the cusp of political evolution towards a prosperous and egalitarian state?

Just when the population is hoping to take advantage of the benefits democracy, decentralisation and federalism is hardly the time to risk all in a state-restructuring exercise with the potential of inviting inter-community and inter-regional conflict even if it might – just might – make up for centuries of marginalisation. What Nepali citizens require is a state structure which delivers administrative efficiency and opens up the possibilities for markets to grow while at the same time ensuring the goals of equity, social justice and secularism. A future conflict based on identity rather than class would derail society even more than the 'people's war' did, pushing back hopes for a prosperous, stable democracy by at least another decade. For a population that has already lost 15 years of progress to the Maoist insurgency and its chaotic aftermath, there would be a debilitating loss of hope and, in time, uncontrollable rage. Nepal's citizens and communities must be able to utilise the fruits of a landscape and a history which have given us a country rich in its geography, strategic location and social 'unity in diversity'. We must insist on a model of federal restructuring that recognises identity as important but that insists on economic viability as its foundational criterion.

From their silence, the Kathmandu-based civil society stalwarts seemed to acquiesce to the push for ethnic federalism. They do harbour misgivings but prefer to leave it to others to protest and take the rap for being 'anti-federal'. At the village and district levels, the breadth of opinion on the matter is larger, and there is concern among many that the federalist structure pushed by the scholar-activists and Maoists in remote Kathmandu will have a negative impact on the lives of citizens and communities on the ground. The Maoist party lives and breathes centralism and would, if given half the chance, control society through commissars rather than elected representatives. It is impossible to believe that such a party is serious about federalism; quite the opposite, it exploits the concept to gain supporters. The demand for ethnic as well as Madhesi federalism comes from the elite among the hills and plains communities, people angered by the Bahuns' dominance over the national polity in the democratic era after 1990. These elites must utilise the possibilities of a shaken-up polity to seize for themselves political power at the centre as well as in the provinces and districts; to do so, they will need a state structure with federal provinces that are economically and politically viable, not simply ceremonial.

In discussing the attempt to revive our ethnically exclusive past, one must consider whether the pre-unification principalities were economically viable. They probably weren't. In fact, the unification of Nepal by Prithvi Narayan Shah had an economic imperative; besides political unification, he sought to develop economies of scale as Subcontinental commerce and governance was being turned on its head by the East India Company. In fact, it was the construction of a viable economic model that has helped Nepal remain the oldest continuous nation-state on the Subcontinent.

The problem with Prithvi Narayan's Nepal lay not in unification but in the fact that, despite the economic rationale for the Nepali state, the resultant polity denied most people equity and inclusion and concentrated power in the nobility of Kathmandu Valley. The genius of the Nepali people was compromised and the economy shattered by imperial ambitions that over-reached, spanning more than half a century of court intrigue, 104 years of rapacious rule by a single clan, and three decades of royal autocracy, right up to 1990. If the state's problem was its unrepresentative nature and marginalisation of whole communities, then the first step toward inclusion and equity was taken when democratic and representative governance arrived in 1990. It was this democratic transformation that finally gave the people in the districts representative power over the national government. Social activism surged as the people rediscovered their ability to organise and bring about transformations, and, albeit very late in the modern era, we finally saw what we had always hoped for – genuine participatory development

The agenda of federalism is now to overlay this representative polity with a federal structure that will lead to more dynamic state administration, from the central to the provincial, district, and village levels. The introduction of a proper federalist structure can, therefore, be seen as Nepal's natural coming of age. It will provide conditions for social and economic growth to a people that have waited much too long. Ethnic or one-Madhes federalism, on the other hand, would be a regressive trip back in time, bereft of political vision and economic logic.

Village, district, zone

It is an interesting exercise to consider which administrative divisions have been dissolved, which can be expected to last, and which must be created. During the Rana era, the regions were defined by their distance from Kathmandu, with the mid-hill districts termed East 1-2-3-4-5-6 and West 1-2-3-4-5 and beyond. *Anchals* were the 14 administrative zones established by the Panchayat regime, primarily to maintain the centre's control over the hinterland. Most were narrow strips that ran from the northern to the southern border. In the era of autocracy, when most parts of the country were not connected by roads, the *anchaladhis*, or zonal commissioners, were appointed by the royal palace to rule with an iron hand. The *anchals* were divided into 75 districts *(jillas)*, most defined with some thought to geography and cultural history. These districts continue to run to this day, administered by the chief district office, while the zones were abandoned with the advent of democracy in 1990. Today the *anchal* is a vestige of the past, recognisable only in the odd place, such as in the number plates of vehicles and the working divisions of political parties.

The 'development region' *(bikas chhetra)* was a concept developed under King Birendra when he became king in 1971. It was a response to modern times when, due to roads and communications, it became necessary to develop administrative units that were larger and more symbiotic than the zones. Each development region was a conglomeration of zones and districts and had there been a proper devolution of power, they would have developed as effective federal units. However, Birendra was a man wanting change but without the political will see through his reforms, so he pulled back from devolving representative, administrative and budgetary power to the development regions. They became, and remain, ceremonial non-starters.

Given that the development regions have remained mere shells, more or less inoperative since their establishment in 1975, and that zones were abandoned in 1990, it is the district which has emerged as the definitive unit of governance. With the development of the road and highway network and the energising of local government and participatory development through the Local Self-Governance Act and other initiatives, the *jilla* attained additional relevance even as the power of the chief district office was curtailed due to the introduction of elected local government representatives and the overall weakening of the state during and after the conflict period.

An interesting evolution since 1990 is that, even as the identity movement (whether by ethnicity, region, language, religion) has gained momentum, there has been a parallel energising of the district as a repository of the public's 'secular' identity. The rise of the district has allowed people of all communities, including those caste groups who feel excluded by the ethnic definitions of their home regions, to seek togetherness on the basis of their district of origin. Thus, one of the most active of civil society and political groups has been the *'jilla samparka manch'*, self-help groups and lobbying units defined with reference to the home district of their members. Even within the future federal provinces, however they are defined, the districts, more or less without change, are expected to remain the primary unit of governance. The number and boundaries of the village development committees within each district are also likely to remain largely intact even though there will be attempts at gerrymandering. For all the political turbulence that has overtaken society and the insecurities related to the definition of federalism, one of the reasons that society remains relatively robust is the deep-down conviction that the structural foundation of the country – the village and district units – will remain as it is. In order to provide stability at the base of the national political pyramid, it is important to organise elections at the village and district levels as soon as possible.

Opportunities and dangers
Nepal's federal provinces must exhibit economies of scale, a criterion which precludes tiny units. Wealth and opportunity should be distributed so that there is no stark differentiation between resource-rich and resource-poor regions. Both geographical and economic asymmetry must be avoided, and one region and its inhabitants should not be allowed to benefit at the expense of others. There must be geographical proximity as well as a historical and psycho-social affinity between the various parts of proposed provinces and concentrations of ethnicities and communities must provide the possibility that representational power will work in favour of the historically marginalised.

The federal units should be defined for development and economic growth rather than be a regressive social engineering experiment to fracture the land and send people back two-and-a-half centuries. The various parts of each province must be able to cooperate for overall advancement, and the province as a whole must be able to reach out to neighbouring provinces as well as across international borders. The historical experience of vigorous trade with India must not blind us to the possibilities to the north, made stronger with the arrival of a railway line from interior Chinese to Lhasa. The extension of the railway westward along the Changtang plateau of Tibet will benefit all provinces along Nepal's northern border and enable them to serve as the link between the high plateau and the Ganga plains. Sheer economic good sense, therefore, suggests that the federal units of Nepal must stretch north-south, taking advantage of traditional trade routes, the hills and the river valleys, the possibilities of synergies between the various ecological and economic zones, as well as the new prospect for longitudinal north-south trade between Tibet/China and the Indian states of Bihar, Uttar Pradesh, and West Bengal, as well as farther afield, all the way to Bangladesh.

Seen in this light, the federal provinces could be defined by river basin, in which case we would have the large Kosi, Gandaki and Karnali provinces, and the capital region nicely incorporated into the smaller Bagmati river basin. The provinces could also be overlaid on the five existing development regions, the Eastern, Central, Western, Mid-Western and Far-Western, developed in the Panchayat era by King Birendra with the expertise of Dr Harka Gurung, Nepal's pioneering geographer and development planner.

In planning federalism, one must recognise and plan for potential pitfalls. A federal structure meant to make good governance a reality must not impose an unaffordable political and administrative infrastructure on the inhabitants of any province, and it would be a travesty if funds allocated for local government were siphoned off to support the provincial structure. The establishment of provinces should at the least not weaken, but better strengthen the thrust towards decentralisation and local governance, as guaranteed through elected DDCs and VDCs. We must guard against the curtailment of human rights in the provinces, the sparking of communal fires due to conflict among communities, the absence of an equity-based approach to governance, and destruction of in-province democracy by the rise of a warlord, in whatever guise. Dangers include conflict between adjacent provinces or a centre which either so unreasonably applies 'Presidential rule' it retards the democratic growth of a province or is so weak that it cannot extend its authority over a province to protect the populace against human rights abuses, mal-governance and communal disharmony. National democracy cannot survive amidst provincial autocracy.

Province = development region
In the spring of 2011, there are numerous hurdles in the way of defining federalism in Nepal, from the 'federalism rejectionists', who have been gaining ground due to the poor level of discourse, to the ethnic federalists and Maoists, who insist on a parochial mapping and naming scheme. Polarisation and rigidities have led to deadlock and even the successful end of the peace process will not now be enough to see a smooth conclusion to the constitution-writing. The best way to support the aspirations of ethnicities and communities while establishing a devolved state structure that spreads authority and responsibility is to convert into federal provinces the dead-letter development regions introduced three and half decades ago. This is an idea nurtured by many but, amidst the prevailing demagoguery, uttered by few.

Many scoff at the idea of development regions becoming viable units, claiming that they represent a failed experiment of the Panchayat era. The last part is true, but that was because King Birendra did not have the courage to devolve political and representational power to them. If he had carried the exercise through to its proper conclusion through devolution, Nepal would have had federalism a long time ago, though it would probably have been called 'decentralisation'. By now, nearly four decades later, there would have been a stable structure of representative government at the provincial level and a decentralised state, and the inclusive politics nurtured in the provinces would have strengthened national democracy.

The regressive view that decentralisation and federalism are antithetical has driven those who defend the success of local government to the periphery. We should not be tied too rigidly to terms and terminology as we seek to federalise and decentralise the Nepali state, which is an exercise to bring governance closer to the people. Federalism, when all is said and done, is a kind of decentralisation, a taking away of political power from Kathmandu Valley by creating provincial entities that will enjoy their own political power. Built with the support of the various social science streams, secular federalism will make the government more accountable, take it closer to the people, and unite the citizens of each province by creating inter-dependence within an economically powerful unit. Pride in being the resident of any given province will be added to the existing pride in national citizenship. Built improperly, however, with communal exclusivity rather than individual freedoms in mind, federalism will create hurdles at every turn.

Federal provinces based on development regions would include districts of diverse physiography, from those in the High Himalaya in the southern Tarai and the mid-hills between. In short, each would encapsulate a microcosm of Nepal. The units would be economically syncretic and efficient. They would be mutually supportive, engaging in healthy competition and taking advantage of economic possibilities with regions across the international borders. The montane, mid-hill and plains communities would come together in each province to build a common future in a manner that would make Nepal an example for Southasia, much more impressive than even community forestry, local government and the FM radio revolution. In contrast with the promise of 'secular federalism', the ethnicity-first agenda will divide communities and an exclusive Madhes province(s) would wreck the future of the plains people by distancing them from the economic wealth of the highlands.

Some are wary of a secular federalism which incorporates the development region or some other criteria of economic geography, maintaining that it would allow the Bahun-Chhetri combine to rule the roost. This view undervalues the great transformation which has overtaken Nepalis society. Today, people of all communities are primed and ready to seek political power through representation. The governance of the development regions as federal units will be representative of the population groups within, giving each real power according to its proportion while allowing meritorious individuals of any community to shine. Bahuns with the privilege of learning, in particular, took advantage of their socio-cultural station after 1990 but the opportunities and possibilities now beckon to all communities. As far as the controversy over *naamankan* is concerned, the future development regions could be named anything the inhabitants desire, to be decided by a provincial referendum if necessary.

Looking east
With the stridency of scholar-activists and Madhesi politicians on the wane as the complexities of ethnic and or one-Madhes federalism, it

is now possible to consider 'north-south federalism' without fear of violating an unspoken taboo. In fact, a north-south federal unit has already been proposed although it goes under the name of an exclusivist federal unit and was the brainchild of the local ethnic leadership. East of the Arun River, some of the proponents of the 'Limbuwan' province have been developing their thinking along the lines of a viable secular federal blueprint. The province as projected is naturally north-south because the Limbu region, before it was subsumed into the Gorkhali state, did stretch that far.

As their idea has developed, these proponents claim that though they want to preserve the name 'Limbuwan' for the sake of historical association, the Limbu will have no political prior rights and that all inhabitants will be equal inhabitants. The abandonment of prior rights is critical, for it immediately defuses the alarm of all the other groups of the east, including the non-Limbu hill and plains ethnicities; the Parbate castes, including the hill Dalit; the Bhotiya (Himali); and the Madhesi. For now, the two challenges in relation to the 'Limbuwan' proposal are a) the demarcation of the province vis-à-vis overlapping claims made by the Rai (Khambu) community immediately to the west; and b) whether the name 'Limbuwan' is acceptable to all who would live within the territory. The matter of the second issue could be left to the people of the province to decide democratically upon demarcation.

The proposed 'Limbuwan' (or, if the inhabitants agree, the 'Kosi Pradesh' or 'Purbanchal') province would encompass much of what is currently the Eastern Development Region. It would provide a unique platform in which the local inhabitants could aspire for positions of great representational power. The Limbu, because of their preponderance, would likely see the most political benefits, but they as well as the Rai, Rong (Lepcha), Sherpa, Bhotiya (Himali), Rajbanshi (Koch), Meche, Tharu, Dalit, Maithili, Newar, Chhetri, Bahun, Newar, Marwari and other communities would discover that the province had immense economic prospects. Without prior political rights to create insecurity, all would inject their energy into creating a dynamic provincial polity that would plan for its own growth in a manner that Kathmandu could never envision or impose. This eastern province alone would have economic prowess rivalling that of Sikkim-Darjeeling or Bhutan, and its chief minister would be treated as an equal by his or her counterparts in India in the nearby states of Assam, Bihar, Sikkim or West Bengal and by the Tibet Autonomous Region leadership in Lhasa. Aspiring for and taking leadership of such a vibrant entity would be more fulfilling than leading a ceremonial province or sub-province or an autonomous region based on a communal identity, be it that of the Limbu, Rai, Koch or Madhesi.

The pioneering federalists of the east are in a position to convert a historical aspiration into a modern-day provincial unit that respects the humanitarian aspirations behind economic-geography. Because the Limbu as a group are, as a result of their unique history vis-à-vis the Gorkhali state – their sublimation was through treaty rather than through conquest – much more forceful than other ethnicities, their development of a secular federal model will serve as a path-breaker. This 'formula of the East' may help other ethnic federalists west of it, including the Rai, Tamang, Gurung (Tamu), Magar and Tharu, to consider the advantages of a north-south federal definition to their communities.

There is no reason to be afraid of federalism if it is seen and developed as a sub-national layer of administration and governance that recognises our fractured geography and diverse demography. But there is reason to fear it if the concept is hijacked by political demagogues and academic opportunists, and if the Valley civil society lacks steadfastness and a stout heart. Because of polemic and invective inside and outside the House, the Constituent Assembly spent three years without getting into a single genuine debate on the practical aspects of federalism, but that debate will start once the peace process is successfully completed and unhindered discussion becomes possible. When the discourse on federalism gets serious, ideas that have not been floated before by diffident community leaders, scholars, activists and politicians will suddenly create a new landscape of possibilities. The negotiations on Nepal's definition of federalism may happen in an extended Constituent Assembly, a high-level state restructuring commission or some other entity. Resisting the pressures of the extremes represented by the anti-federalists and the exclusivist federalists, it should be possible to re-structure Nepal in a way that will ensure the growth of all parts of the country, geographic and demographic.

31

India, Nepal

The bigger brother
To call India Nepal's 'big brother' is a Kathmandu cliché, revealing a fatalism that simultaneously exaggerates New Delhi's influence over the polity and the lack of agency and resolve among the national intelligentsia when it comes resisting New Delhi. As a flourishing and immense economic power which stretches across the Nepali horizon beyond the open border, India certainly is 'big' and certainly is a 'brother'. While we could turn that vast market to our advantage, India has served only as a safety valve rescuing us from the economic failures of our state rather than an opportunity adding value to our lives. Kathmandu's attitude towards New Delhi is characterised by a near-total absence of self-confidence: the anti-Indian bluster on the surface covers a deep-set subservience, lately exemplified *in extremis* by Maoist Chairman Dahal.

In trying to understand India as an influential power vis-à-vis the Nepali polity, rather than stating *ab initio* with ultra-nationalism, one should start with a reality check on the people-to-people links and dependencies. The Kathmandu political class, deeply influenced by surface antipathies nurtured since historical times and polished to a shine by the more recent autocracies, has tended to use the relationship with India as a convenient tool to generate popular support and to lash out at political opponents. India, which lies south of the plains and across the hills of the east and west, is an overwhelming presence in our economy because the relative impenetrability of the Himalayan chain has made landlocked Nepal essentially India-locked. The economic opening to the Tibet Autonomous Region is only now just beginning to show possibilities but the open border to the south goes back to before the

East India Company's consolidation in India. The open border allows the traditional family and clan relationships of the plains communities on both sides to continue unhindered and supports Nepal's poorest by allowing for unencumbered labour migration. It also gives our economy the possibility of benefiting from India's runaway growth; even Bihar, India's 'basket case' has undergone a sudden, unexpected and welcome rise. There is no reason why Nepal cannot do the same, and for this the open border is an opportunity.

If you think of Nepal-India relations as a people-to-people more than a state-to-state affair, then it is the matter of labour migration that is the central, overarching concern. For more than two centuries, the Indus-Ganga plains have provided recourse for Nepal's poor, serving as a place of refuge and economic survival while the rulers in Kathmandu revelled in national insularity. This poignant exodus continues till the present. In fact, it escalated during the decade's conflict and its aftermath because of rural insecurity, the collapse of local markets and the absence of employment expansion. Estimates vary, but it is said that India hosts four to six million permanent labour migrants from Nepal's hills and plains. Impermanent and seasonal migration swell that number considerably. In addition, there are three million or so Indian citizens of Nepali origin. The migrants from Nepal are the country's most destitute. They travel to the far corners of India to fill unskilled positions such as household help, *chowkidars*, agricultural and horticultural workers, *dhaba* and teashop employees, and workshop assistants. These days, villagers with more resources venture to Malaysia and the Persian Gulf, but the poorest still cross the open border into India. Unfortunately, oversupply and competition from Bangladeshis, and various depressed demographic groups in India, including the Adivasi and the Dalit, have pushed down salaries and wage rates.

As with the case of labour migration, some of the other most significant aspects of the Nepal-India relationship are those least discussed in Kathmandu, or interpreted most tendentiously. Among the former is the pegging of the Nepali rupee to the Indian rupee, which has been a vital crutch for the Nepali economy through times of conflict and economic decline. This pegging would be disadvantageous if the economy were to progress and the currency to rise in value, but it has been a boon during the never-ending political upheaval. One could say that this arrangement gives New Delhi the ultimate political tool against the Government of

Nepal, should it choose to use it. However, as far as one can make out, New Delhi has never exploited this path to fulfil its diplomatic objectives. Indeed, the 'handlers' of Nepal in New Delhi have developed an indulgent attitude towards the Kathmandu politicos and civil society, who mouth passionate ultra-nationalist sentiment, such as demanding the abrogation of the 1950 Indo-Nepal Treaty of Peace and Friendship or restricting the open border, but without follow-through.

Another notable aspect of the bilateral relationship not confronted squarely by the opinion-makers is a tradition that dates back to the early colonial era – Nepali citizens' joining the Indian military and paramilitary forces. Even though the tradition existed before the arrival of the East India Company, it gathered steam when Company Bahadur started raising Gurkha regiments in the early 1800s. Today, Nepali citizens are found in India's Gorkha regiments, the Assam Rifles, the CRPF armed constabulary, industrial security and other forces, as well as in the British Army (as 'Gurkhas'), the French Legion, the Singapore Police and elsewhere. Despite the laudable goals of Southasian solidarity that the South Asian Association for Regional Cooperation espouses, there is no hiding the fact that Gorkhas fought Pakistan in the various India-Pakistan conflicts, including the latest one in Kargil, or that Nepali passport-holders were part of the Indian Peace Keeping Force in Sri Lanka in the 1980s. The fact that Nepali citizens fight in India's security forces rarely finds mention in the anti-India discourse, though this anomaly clearly weakens Nepal's status as a sovereign country. In the past, those very far from the seat of power used to raise this issue as a political tool against the Kathmandu establishment, but even their voices have trailed off recently.

Recruitment into foreign armies, through official agreement, is a historical tradition attributable to the extreme poverty in Nepal's villages, itself a centuries-long, continuous tragedy when one considers the countryside is so rich in resources. A rush to abandon recruitment is certainly not the way to go, even though some unthinking diehards such as the Maoists suggested it was (believing, incidentally, that it would never happen). The only solution is to develop the national economy, improve livelihoods and employment, making Nepal so prosperous that its citizens do not need to serve in a foreign military. Certainly, no citizen would willingly serve and even sacrifice his life for another country if there were opportunities at home. For now, the incongruity of Gurkha/Gorkha recruitment must be confronted and accepted head on, so that there is no move to dismantle the tradition impetuously and put tens of thousands of livelihoods at risk. The national focus should be to promote democratic peace in order to spur on the economy, raise employment levels, and obviate the need for future recruitment into foreign armies. (Incidentally, the decade-long activism by retired British Gurkhas for equal benefits with their British counterparts may bear fruit for retirees, but it endangers the recruitment of the next generation as our relationship with the UK establishment sours. This activism may prove short-sighted if Nepal continues to flounder and fails to create economic opportunities for the young of the 'martial races'.)

While currency pegging, labour migration and military recruitment rarely make the news, the Nepali media takes delight in highlighting border disputes and monsoon inundation. The matter of the disappearance of border pillars assumes great importance, as if there were a conspiracy afoot to redraw the frontier. The border disputes between Nepal and India are relatively minor compared to, say, those between India and Bangladesh (and the latter were largely settled through bilateral talks in 2010 and 2011), but they are sensationalised. The craze to build embankments in Indian districts just south of the border is a major concern for the Nepalis side because of the lay of the land invariably leads to flooding on our side, but this need not be seen as a conspiracy by the Indian state. Resolving the problem simply requires more coordination between the local administrators on the two sides.

The security of Nepali citizens working in India and the challenges they face in Indian road and rail transport to and fro is a major concern that, in contrast, is not given due importance by the editors or politicians alike. Another considerable concern is finally taking centre stage. For decades, the trafficking of Nepali women to Indian metropolis for sex work was a matter that remained in the realm of hazily outlined myth till the early 1990s, but today there is a regular flow of public information.

Aid and economy
Besides the fact that two-thirds of Nepal's trade is with India, Nepal's links to the international market are almost exclusively through Indian territory and are regulated by separate trade and transit treaties. All of Nepal's petroleum needs are provided by the Indian refinery at Barauni

in Bihar. Though figures are hard to come by, India is also one of the largest development contributors in Nepal even while, unusually, the Government of Nepal allows the Indian Embassy to distribute aid directly without going through the Ministry of Finance as all other donor governments do. Indian ambassadors thus have more scope to pick and choose and influence the Nepali polity more directly than other donors and diplomats. Indian Embassy officials like to point out that no overhead or administrative costs are subtracted from the amount allocated for Nepal as they are from many other bilateral assistance programmes. India's involvement in the development of Nepal has been extensive: from the first highway to Kathmandu completed in 1956 to a decades-long goitre control programme that has contributed to the control of goitres and cretinism, it has underwritten both physical and social development efforts.

The influence of the Indian Government in Nepal has been multiplied because, over the decades, many of Nepal's topmost politicians and bureaucrats have received educational scholarships from the Indian Embassy for their offspring and relatives. There are plenty of critics of Indian assistance, many of whom maintain that funds are provided selectively to buy support and stifle opposition, but no challenge has ever developed a critical mass, indicating once again a lack of commitment for follow-through among India's detractors. While Kathmandu's excitable middle class rises in cycles of anti-Indianism that dissipate almost as soon as they spark, the Indian Embassy seems secure in the knowledge that a populace which is so dependent upon India – for labour migration, military recruitment, development assistance, economic stability and investment – knows the limits of ultra-nationalism.

India is the potential buyer of Nepal's hydropower and the potential user of stored water from future reservoirs built in Nepali valleys. The tourist destinations and various shrines of Nepal are future attractions for travellers from the densely populated adjacent plains, which are beginning to see the sort of economic growth that will lead to a rise in leisure activity. While temples in the mid-hills and plains long attracted pilgrims and modern times have seen the advent of casino trippers and shoppers in Kathmandu, it is the highlands of the Central Himalaya that are set to see an exponential rise in visitors from India. Interestingly, Indian tourists will see the allure of the mid-hill trails, lakes and forests that have been neglected by Western tourists whose aim is the high Himalayan valleys; their interest will help spread the benefit of tourism across the country. Not only *shaktipeeths* (power places) such as Swargadwari in Pyuthan District and Pathibhara of Taplejung District, but also Janaki Temple in Janakpur; Lumbini, the birthplace of Siddhartha Gautam; and scenic destinations such as Rara Lake, the Khaptad highlands and the numerous waterfalls that dot the Mahabharat range will come into their own once Indians and other Southasians discover what a peaceful Nepal has to offer in their search for leisure destinations. Their arrival will spread the benefits of tourism more broadly than trekking and mountaineering have managed to do thus far. To attract Indians other than the casino tripper, the pilgrim and the occasional honeymooner, Nepal must develop banking, medical, hospitality and other services that the growing Indian middle and upper classes seek.

Realistically, Nepal cannot benefit when an ideology of ultra-nationalism guides our powerful political parties. For the people of Nepal to benefit economically from all that the country can deliver, the key hurdle to surmount is the knee-jerk anti-Indianism that is ignited at regular intervals. Nepal's spiteful ultra-nationalism has been based not on national pride or the search for sovereign equality with New Delhi but on the self-serving personal agenda of individuals such as King Mahendra and his descendants. This selfish attitude has been replicated by Pushpa Kamal Dahal and his acolytes, who care little that anti-Indian ultra-nationalism destroys prospects for investment, market openings and tourism, and undermines the security and livelihood of Nepali citizens working in their millions in India. The more ultra-nationalist Nepali society becomes, the more we will miss the investment of above-board businesses and multinationals and fall into the stranglehold of carpetbagger businessmen from India.

Episodes such as the 'Hritik Roshan episode' of December 2000, in which an innocuous remark made by the Bollywood actor was seen as being anti-Nepal and spawned a violent movement that started in Chitwan District and spread across the mid-hills, exemplify the knee-jerk anti-Indianism harboured by the middle class. Such an attitude not only hurts the economy in numerous ways, from forgone investment to the loss of market for Nepali products, but also puts all Nepali speakers in India at risk, however remote they are from Nepal in mind, geography or citizenship. Nepal's economy will not prosper and the people will not benefit unless this programmed anti-Indian xenophobia is replaced by a bold, non-chauvinistic nationalism which allows politicians to talk to New Delhi confidently on an equal platform.

Xenophobia in Nepal is almost exclusively anti-Indian in nature: it has not touched the Chinese at all and is only just lapping against Western shores. As long as the politicians of Nepal rely on retrograde anti-Indianism to build their populist base, Nepal will not be a place where Indians will want to travel to or invest in. Nepal will remain a playground for opportunists from India, while investors with long-term interest who could help boost employment through transparent, competitive business will stay away. The fact that India is the only buyer of Nepali hydropower and the major market of the future in every sphere means that Kathmandu must be more circumspect in how it deals with India and Indians. Since the Panchayat era, the development of water resources and hydropower has been enmeshed with ultra-nationalism, and exaggerated suspicions India are pervasive, so much so that Nepali politicians and technocrats tend to shy away from the negotiating table.

It must be said, though, that the Indian side has not always been fair and transparent. For a long time, it attempted to negotiate with Nepal on the basis of hydropower value alone, keeping silent on the value of the water stored in Nepal's reservoirs for downstream irrigation, urban use and river transport. When political stability arrives at long last in Nepal, we will hopefully get a state administration able not only to stand up to New Delhi but also able to quash in-country ultra-nationalist populism. A robust state would allow Nepal at long last to benefit from selling clean hydropower power to India, taking advantage of the great and expanding economy of the south and arriving at a negotiated, optimum price.

South Block diplomacy
The cumulative weight of India's influence, which is greater than the combined influence of the Western diplomatic or developmental presence in Nepal, overwhelms Kathmandu. In the political arena, India's concerns are seen in the deep interest that the Indian Embassy, the 'South Block' foreign office in New Delhi, and the Indian intelligence agencies take in Nepal. These concerns include the political stability

of a neighbour across an open border, the possibilities for involvement in economic and infrastructural activities, including hydropower and irrigation, and the perceived dangers of third-country militant infiltration. The Indian Embassy in Kathmandu is said to be the second largest of India's legations worldwide and the challenge of being ambassador to Nepal makes it a high-profile assignment for those seeking career progression in the South Block.

Indian influence in the modern area, amidst the chaotic politics of Nepal, was clear enough as the Rana regime wound down. The Indian government decided to activate its ambassador, the DC-3 flying pilot C.P.N. Sinha, to play political mentor and Machiavelli. For decades, the Nepali intelligentsia believed that the presence of the Ranas in the interim government after their fall was based on a tripartite understanding among King Tribhuvan, Prime Minister Jawaharlal Nehru, and the Nepali Congress leaders, until B.P. Koirala wrote in his late-life memoirs, published posthumously, that there had been no such understanding; instead, everything had been more or less decided by Nehru in coordination with Tribhuvan and in exclusion of the young Nepali democrats.

Indian interest in Nepal can be deep and is often intrusive. The intensity depends, of course, upon the personality of the individual ambassador, but often the Nepali players themselves invite New Delhi's involvement. Kathmandu's opinion-makers welcomed proactivism when Indian politicians such as the late Chandra Shekhar, later prime minister of India, came to Kathmandu and spoke up for democracy against the Panchayat regime in 1990 or when and India helped facilitate the negotiations in New Delhi between the seven party alliance and the Maoists in New Delhi in 2005. The period between 2005 and 2009 was a period of smooth sailing, but then the Maoists got disenchanted and put their anti-India propaganda machine into high gear. At first it was President Ram Baran Yadav who was propped up as the enemy, but when that campaign faced diminishing returns, Chairman Dahal fell upon India. Some of the Indian Embassy's actions in relation to the Nepali media may have added unnecessary facets and the abrupt style of the serving ambassador may not have helped, but it was silly to blame Indian diplomats for the sudden run of anti-Indianism in Nepal as some commentaors sought to do both in Kathmandu and New Delhi. The attempt to spark ultra-nationalist anti-Indianism was part of the campaign of cynical manipulation by the UCPN (Maoist) chairman to buttress his populist base.

India is a vast polity made up of different interest groups and its government is made up of many wings, the right sometimes not knowing what the left does. It is impossible that Indian intelligence agencies were unaware that Maoist leaders took refuge and organised from Indian territory during the 'people's war' or that they ran training camps in West Bengal, Punjab and elsewhere. However, a despatch from the US embassy in Kathmandu towards the end of the conflict years, which was released by WikiLeaks in March 2011, makes the case that the South Block may not always have known all that happened vis-à-vis Nepal in India's name. The Indian Research and Analysis Wing and the Intelligence Bureau probably colluded, but it is hard to believe that the Indian state had a policy to foment instability in Nepal by supporting the Maoist 'people's war'. Nevertheless, many Kathmandu opinion-makers will not be rocked from their belief that the Maoist party is an example of Indian handiwork designed to penetrate, destabilise and ultimately destroy the Nepali state and that New Delhi turned against the insurgency only when its unexpected growth threatened to affect its own internal security.

As far as day-to-day diplomacy is concerned, many Kathmandu commentators would like to believe that the Ministry of External Affairs in New Delhi has little better to do than constantly conspire against Nepal. Take the matter of government formation in the last couple of years. If the UCPN (Maoist) were to be believed, the formation of the Madhav Kumar Nepal government in May 2009 was the handiwork of New Delhi, and the elevation of Jhala Nath Khanal in February 2011 with Maoist support was a victory against Indian interference. When Khanal found it difficult to expand his cabinet, which was the fallout of his secretive seven point deal with Dahal, that failure was blamed on mischief by India. Nepali opinion-makers wholeheartedly join the excitement of government formation, following the permutations and combinations among the political parties, yet fatalistically announce that all matters are decided in New Delhi.

Indian officialdom has, of course, over the years tried to influence Nepali affairs, sometimes through Madhesi politicians at other times through anyone handy. At times, individuals in the Indian embassy do get a big head because Nepali players abjectly approach them pleading for intervention. There is even some disdain for the Nepali political class that comes from seeing a politician who spouts anti-India venom at mass meetings slink into the Indian Embassy grounds in Lainchaur for a confessional heart-to-heart. On the whole, though, New Delhi is not able to influence the flow of events as much as the Maoists would self-servingly have the willing intelligentsia believe.

Indeed, the arrogance sometimes exhibited by Indian diplomats, academics and analysts when meeting their Nepali counterparts is directly proportional to the subservience exhibited by the latter. Nepali submission to the Indian will was nurtured during the Panchayat regime, which professed anti-Indianism but secretly sought to appease New Delhi on key matters. This Panchayat-era attitude has now been taken to a new height by the UCPN (Maoist), whose leaders are not even embarrassed to openly meet Indian intelligence operatives. Chairman Dahal has begged the *'prabhu'* to allow him to form the government or at least be allowed a face-saving visit to New Delhi while simultaneously promoting virulent anti-Indianism. He is is indifferent to the fact that fostering such xenophobic and chauvinistic sentiment harms the economy as well as all kinds of national interests in relation to India. At the sixth plenum of the Maoist party in November 2010, the main topic of contention among the three main factions was deciding whether the party's 'principal enemy' was to be India alone (the Vaidya line), 'domestic reactionaries protected and directed by Indian expansionism' (the Bhattarai line) or 'the fusion of domestic reactionaries and Indian expansionism' (the Dahal line).

Since there is no question that India will continue to look after its interests in Nepal, it is up to Kathmandu to protect its own space and manoeuvrability and to prevent the South Block from feeling comfortable micro-managing Nepal affairs. Unfortunately, the Nepali players are so schizophrenic in their simultaneous desire for and rejection of Indian involvement that Indian diplomats and operatives have a strong incentive to remain active. In the days ahead, as the era of Maoists demagoguery makes way for a time of peace and stability, responsible Nepali politicians must not continue to entertain exaggerated notions of Indian activism in our national affairs. At the same time, they should understand that New Delhi will throw all decorum to the wind if threats to its national security emerge from the direction of Nepal. The Kathmandu political class should desist from creating situations in which a fearful

India contemplates intervention in Nepali politics. In short, they should not take their cue from Dahal.

The history of anti-Indianism

With knee-jerk anti-Indianism so strong, the Kathmandu polity has failed to adjust to modern times, to change tack and use agile diplomacy. A country which seeks to benefit from the expanding Indian market across the open border and from economic globalisation generally must be cognisant of Indian concerns. An example in the Southasian neighbourhood can be seen in how the Indian establishment reacted with overwhelming goodwill in January 2010 when the government of Bangladesh showed its willingness to consider New Delhi's security concerns in relation to its Northeast insurgencies. Kathmandu's political class should likewise show the courage to respond to India's concerns without jeopardising Nepal's national interest. For example, at a time when it is common practice to allow sky marshals to enter one's country on foreign airlines, Kathmandu politicians should have had no difficulty in allowing India this facility when it came asking. However, the politicians said no when they were requested because opinion-makers were not there to support them or prepare the ground.

The Indian establishment expresses deep concern that the open border with Nepal will be misused by third-country militants. As one Indian editor told me, 'The open border is meant for the benefit of Nepal's citizens and not third-country operatives.' Kathmandu's opinion-makers need not succumb to the fear-mongering characteristic of news leaks from Indian intelligence agencies, which paint a picture of the dangerous, large-scale infiltration of India by Islamic militants who exploit first Nepal's open visa regime to fly into Kathmandu and then the open border to penetrate India through its 'soft underbelly' – the states of Bihar and Uttar Pradesh. At the same time, the opinion-makers must acknowledge that there will have been untoward use of the open border, including by militant organisations active in India. Since the unfettered frontier benefits Nepal in its present state of under-development more than it does India, it is for Kathmandu to be proactive in keeping the border open, including taking initiatives to prevent its misuse. If it lets matters take their own course, Nepal may find itself in a difficult situation, given the growing concern about the open border among the national security establishment in New Delhi.

Anti-Indianism, which forms the bedrock of ultra-nationalism in Nepal, has its origins in the fears nurtured by the hill principalities and Kathmandu Valley rulers towards the plains rajas, nawabs and badshahs. Mughlan, the land of the Mughals in the Indus-Ganga river basin, was appeased just as much as required but always kept at arm's length. The same was the case with the British Crown, to which the Rana regime swore fealty while maintaining an isolationist policy. In the 1960s, King Mahendra revived the latent anti-Indianism present in Kathmandu to generate support for his autocracy, and, for decades, the Panchayat propaganda against the Nepali Congress leaders in jail or exile centred on their status as *arastriya tatwa,* pro-Indian anti-national elements. In the democratic era after 1990, the left opposition used anti-Indian rhetoric to hit at the incumbent Nepali Congress government but went silent when it entered Singha Durbar itself.

For decades, the Nepali polity was able to take advantage of the personal rapport which existed between democratic leaders such as B.P. Koirala, Krishna Prasad Bhattarai and Man Mohan Adhikari and India's top-rung political class. Their affinity helped make up for the absence of confidence in contacts between the bureaucracies, academics, media and civil societies but evaporated when Girija Prasad Koirala, the last of the stalwart of the 1940s still in active politics, died in 2010. Krishna Prasad Bhattarai, who in any case had been out of active politics for a decade, died in March 2011. Now that the personal linkages are gone there is all the more reason to develop professionalism and process in Nepal-India relations. Nepal's political class must develop a relationship its Indian counterparts so that bilateral relations are not left to diplomats – or to intelligence operatives. A sad reminder of the reduced level of political engagement is seen in the regular bilateral meetings organised in Indian cities by the public affairs division of the Indian Ministry of External Affairs in various Indian cities like Benaras, Lucknow and Patna. These meetings are attended by the senior-most Kathmandu politicians but not their Indian counterparts.

The ideal for a proud Nepali citizen would be to see Kathmandu stand shoulder to shoulder with New Delhi, making demands and granting concessions as two sovereign entities should. Instead, what exists is a severe lack of confidence in bilateral dialogues on the Nepali side and exasperation and haughtiness on the Indian. The hope that the People's Movement of April 2006 would give the political establishment the confidence to speak on par with New Delhi has, unfortunately, been belied by the continuing political chaos.

When politics is conducted in a society new to transparency and freedom, with civil society and media relatively weak, politicians seem to require straw figures to serve as an enemy. This requirement was even more urgent for the Maoists, who had built their party and groomed their combatant cadre to fight an enemy. After signing the Comprehensive Peace Accord in November 2006, the party had difficulty locating a convenient villain, and it rapidly used up their possible stock. First they concentrated on demonising the defanged kingship, then Girija Prasad Koirala. By the fall of 2009 they had used up the mileage they got from President Ram Baran Yadav and were looking for a new enemy. When Chairman Dahal found that the game of parliamentary numbers did not allow him to become prime minister, and that his grip on his own party was slipping, he had no hesitation in bashing India in front of the propaganda-prone cadre.

A sovereign people capable of bringing down a royal autocracy and restructuring the state can certainly change a government on its own. And yet, the UCPN (Maoist) would have us believe, and the Kathmandu intelligentsia buys the line, that practically everything in our politics happens under New Delhi's dictates. In fact, the South Block's preferences do not necessarily carry the day even when it does decide to intercede. For example, King Gyanendra's first concessional speech in April 2006 was acceptable to India, but Nepali politicians rejected it. In Also in response to the Nepali political process, New Delhi was forced to backtrack on other matters, including the deployment UNMIN and the 'two-pillar policy' which tied democracy to constitutional monarchy. Good or bad, Nepalis are makers of their own destiny.

'Greater Nepal'
The tendency in Kathmandu's parlours is to, *ab initio*, consider any Indian position to be inimical to Nepali interests, even when New Delhi supports constitutionalism as it did by supporting the government of Madhav Kumar Nepal that came in with a majority in Parliament, however distasteful that might have been to the UCPN (Maoist). When it came time to consider disbanding UNMIN in January 2011 because its continuation would block the peace process, many analysts were against the idea simply because New Delhi, for its own reasons, was

for it. 'If India wants it, it must be against Nepal's interest,' was how many newspaper columnists came to their conclusions about UNMIN's departure. There was no consideration that something that India desired could possibly, and independently, be in the interests of Nepali society.

While New Delhi should be asked to make reparations for the damage it has done to Nepal – the border pillars it has destroyed, the embankments it has constructed without consultation, and the inundation its raised roadways have caused – every action India takes cannot be read as part of a deep-seated conspiracy to weaken Nepal. Many of the border disputes between Nepal and India have been caused by meandering rivers, and most have been sorted out in a mapping exercise over the last decade, yet the party cadre are ever ready to raise the alarm and rush with flag in hand to the disputed stretches. Curiously, the fire-breathing politicians have gone silent on the most important border issue pending between Nepal and India, that relating to the Kalapani area in the northwestern tri-junction between the Indian state of Uttarakhand, Tibet and Nepal's Mahakali catchment. It is likely that King Mahendra secretly provided India with this strategic valley leading up to the Tibet frontier after the 1962 India-China war. As a sovereign country, Kathmandu should be able to muster up the courage to seek open discussion on the history of the ownership of this valley, and the two countries must amicably submit the matter for international arbitration if so required. First of all, though, Kathmandu's intelligentsia must brush up on its reading, gain some confidence, and make its arguments.

For decades, Nepali patriotism has been fed with fervent songs and write-ups that recall and revive the grandeur of a 'greater Nepal' – whose territory briefly extended from the Sutlej to the Teesta rivers in the West and East respectively. While there is no real move to get back the lands lost to the East India Company under the terms of the Sugauli treaty which concluded the Anglo-Nepal War of 1814-1816, an undercurrent of narcissistic ultra-nationalism continues to titillate both the ultra-left and the royalist right. That this extra-territorial jingoism is not a serious challenge is perhaps why Indian diplomats do not seem concerned although occasional intelligence leaks do rake up the matter. As far as Nepali ultra-nationalists are concerned, before making plans for renewed imperial expansion, they had best ask the inhabitants of Sikkim, Darjeeling, Kumaon, Garhwal – and even Himachal – how they would take to the proposal.

Save the open border

Unlike the India-Pakistan and India-Bangladesh land frontiers, which are the legacy of British-defined Partition, Nepal's 1125-mile border with India evolved historically and, in consequence, is unbound. This unrestricted frontier stands today as the ideal demarcation between Southasian countries, allowing for the free passage of citizens while retaining sovereign space and flexibility for the much smaller neighbour, Nepal. For a long time, ever since the Panchayat era, Kathmandu's opinion-makers have been calling for the regulation or closure of the open border. This call was made more to exploit anti-Indian feeling and challenge the sitting regime or government than with the expectation that it might actually happen. It showed no understanding that any system more stringent than benign monitoring would devastate the daily lives of the plains communities along the border and harm the millions of migrant labourers and travellers who travel to India every year. The demand for border closure has traditionally been made by leftist parties and, expectedly, the Maoists picked up the call more raucously than others when they started their underground movement in 1996.

Over the last few years, the tables have turned, with the Kathmandu cognoscenti toying with the idea of frontier closure and the Indian establishment, particularly its national security apparatus, demanding regulation, if not outright closure. There is even talk of building a border fence much like the ones India put up along its frontiers with Bangladesh and Pakistan. Whether true or exaggerated, the reason given by the New Delhi offcials for restricting the open border is its use by militants of all hues, including Islamic extremists, Kashmiri separatists and insurgents from the Indian Northeast. They are also concerned by the transfer of fake Indian currency into India via Nepal, and, lately, by the possible export of Nepali instability into India. The occasional reports sourced to Indian intelligence claiming that there are militant training camps north of the border are not credible – as administrative units Nepal's districts are too small for chief district offices not to be aware of such activity. On the other hand, there can be no doubt that militants, exploiting the ability of a 'Southasian face' to easily take the overland route into India, have made use of the open border over the years.

Nepal's open regime – its liberal visa system and its open border – is precious and something to be protected, almost at all costs. Besides benefiting the Nepali population and economy, the regime also points to the ideal frontier status for the other countries of the Subcontinent. The unbound frontier gives Nepali production centres and industries access to the much vaster economy to the south. It is a historical legacy to be proud of, a system that can serve not merely as a survival crutch but as an economic prize unique in Southasia. The average Kathmandu well-to-do flying over the open border to destinations in India tends to forget how difficult it is for citizens of neighbouring Pakistan and Bangladesh to visit India and vice versa.

Because the Nepal-India frontier holds hope for the evolution of more open border regimes for the rest of Southasia, keeping it unrestricted should be of interest to the broader Southasian civil society, including Pakistani and Bangladeshi. Simultaneously, the activists and thinkers in the neighbouring countries must also be alert to the possibility of third-country agencies and organisations misusing this open border so that they can help stop such abuse. The reaction of Nepali opinion-makers to suggestions of cross-border infiltration tends to be head-in-sand rejection; a more constructive starting position is that the open frontier is meant for the benefit of the citizens of Nepal rather than those from elsewhere. Remaining within the strict bounds of national sovereignty, Kathmandu should seek to create conditions, like extradition agreements which are clear and transparent and do not unduly penalise any Southasian or Asian neighbour, in which the open border cannot be exploited by others.

From the Nepali perspective, the argument for changing the border regime will have merit only when the country upgrades its economic status enough to want to protect that prosperity through a restricted border. Until then, it is the poor of Nepal more than any other category that needs the frontier to remain unencumbered. Other arguments against a closed border are that it would be impossible to implement and that we must exploit the openness to envision the triangular growth of Bihar, eastern Uttar Pradesh (Purvanchal) and Nepal. That Bihar is seeing an economic spurt which will soon touch Purvanchal and that Nepal has an abundance of natural resources at its command plus the potential dynamism of sovereignty means that a three-way symbiosis would be of advantage to all who live in this 'growth triangle'.

It is possible that with the advent of a 'smart' national identity card authorities will be able to monitor even massive numbers of daily border crossings with minimal intrusion. The collection of data using a means which offers little possibility of harassment at the hands of border authorities or security personnel but which can collect data for various purposes will be a welcome step when the technology is able to kick in. Although few believe this now, there may come a time that the people of the Tarai will themselves want monitoring in order to control cross-border crime as well as migration, for it is they who will bear the brunt of Indian inundation when the Nepali economy begins to rise to its potential. All of this is a matter for the future, however. For now, while starting free and frank debate on the status of the frontier Kathmandu's political class and civil society must a) resist talk of restriction, closure and fencing, for the sake of the poorest citizens who use the open border; and b) be alert to the abuse of the border crossing by third-country people and speak up against it. The unfettered frontier is advantageous for Nepal and we must go the extra mile to keep it so.

It used to be, barely a decade ago, that the people of Bihar were appreciative of the relative peace in Nepal. Today it is Nepal's Tarai that is seen as the 'badlands' of the Ganga plains. Bihari families used to seek grooms from the relatively prosperous Nepal side of the border; today, within less than a decade, the situation has been reversed. Bihari industrial labourers in the Biratnagar corridor of the east and Bihari barbers in Kathmandu Valley have begun to return in order to take advantage of prosperity at home. An undeclared restriction of the border is already in place, with India's Sashastra Seema Bal paramilitary deployed every few kilometres across the length of the frontier, and already the people are feeling the pinch. Before the movement for closure or restriction gathers steam in the Indian bureaucracy and before some militant-related incident in India directs fearful eyes in this direction, it behooves Kathmandu's intelligentsia to start discussions on the nature and future of the Nepal-India border.

Treaty of peace, friendship

Three India-Nepal treaties have defined Nepal's sovereign space: the 1816 Sugauli Treaty following the 1814-16 Anglo-Nepal War, the 1923 treaty between Great Britain and Rana Prime Minister Chandra Shumshere, and the 1950 treaty between independent India and Mohan Shumshere. While the 1923 treaty suffers from benign neglect in the present-day discourse, the other two documents have been presented to the public as constricting Nepal's independence. If all three documents are analysed in the context of the overarching power of the East India Company, British imperialism and the newborn Indian nation-state respectively, they could also be read as having prevented Nepal from being converted into a province, colony or dominion.

The 1816 treaty represented the denouement of the Kathmandu court's imperial ambitions. While cutting Nepal down to its present size, the Sugauli treaty nonetheless recognised the Nepali state as sovereign at a time when the East India Company was 'picking cherries', quashing sovereign rajas and nawabs all over the Subcontinent. The 1923 'treaty of perpetual peace' confirmed the sovereign status of Nepal, a coup for Prime Minister Chandra Shumshere given that no other aspirant for sovereignty in the Subcontinental mainland was left standing as the British Empire swept across the land. The 1950 Treaty of Peace and Friendship saw the newly created nation-state of India, with Jawaharlal Nehru as prime minister, acknowledging Nepal as a sovereign country with equal status, not as a protectorate or a dominion.

As with the matter of the open border, the discourse on the 1950 Treaty is tied up in a lot of angst and suspicion. The real problem is not the treaty or its so-called 'accompanying letter' but fears of Nepali incapacities relative to its larger neighbour. The 1950 document, signed between newborn India and Nepal's dying Rana regime, has long been lambasted by the Kathmandu intelligentsia as an unequal document which forced Nepal into subservient status. The signatories were hardly of equal status – the document having been signed on 31 July 1950 by the Indian ambassador to Nepal and Nepal's prime minister. However, it is important to study the 10 articles of the treaty to try to understand who really won and who lost, so to speak. What is curious about those who demand a revision – and the treaty may well need to be revised – is that many have not perused the individual articles of the treaty or the accompanying letter. Rejection of the treaty is repeated as a matter of faith, unmindful of what a revision or abrogation could do to Nepal's bilateral and geopolitical position or what would replace it.

Only two articles in the treaty are substantive; one promises equal treatment to the citizens of each country by the other and the other requires each country to inform the other when importing arms. The second article was never honoured by India, and over time it has been ignored on the Nepal side as well, with Kathmandu importing arms from third countries without notification. A 1968 exchange of letters which is said to have bound Nepal to seeking New Delhi's agreement while sourcing arms and ammunition from third countries – sought by India in connection to the withdrawal of the Indian military mission-posts which used to be stationed in Nepal earlier – has similarly gone into limbo. In relation to the first article in the 1950 document, the accompanying letter of the same date releases Nepal for an indefinite period from its obligation to reciprocate. This is obviously a concession given to protect the Nepal's smaller economy from being swamped by Indian citizens, particularly those from the neighbouring states of Uttar Pradesh and Bihar. In the meantime, Nepali citizens are free to roam the far corners of India in search of jobs, though they do tend to be blocked on the way to the Indian Northeast and of late India has begun to restrict the access of Nepali citizens to government jobs. At the same time, Nepal is becoming wide open to business conducted by Indian citizens. Given the changes that have overtaken the politico-economic landscape in the last six decades, there is surely a need to discuss the 1950 treaty. And the most important question is whether to let the treaty and accompanying letter stand as they are in all their vagueness or to risk either a revision or a brand new treaty.

The longevity of the 1950 Treaty despite the unrelenting bad press it gets in Kathmandu perhaps indicates that it inflicts no harm on Nepal. In the post-1990 democratic era, it has been a political ritual that Nepali delegations in bilateral talks – starting with the one Nepali Prime Minister Man Mohan Adhikari held with Indian Prime Minister V.P. Singh in 1995 – bring up the matter of revision. And yet, when the Indian government acquiesced to discussing a possible revision at the Adhikari-Singh summit, the Nepali side was unprepared. In the latest instance, Maoist Chairman Dahal, when he assumed prime ministership in 2008, was quick to demand the rewriting of the 'unequal treaty'. Such shrill demands for equal treatment, spoken obviously from an uncalled-for perception of weakness by insecure leaders, can be contrasted with Krishna Prasad Bhattarai during his visit to New Delhi as prime minister of the interim government in 1990 – when, in response to insistent queries, he was able to in no uncertain terms reassure New Delhi's journalist brigade about Nepal's sovereign status.

If one interprets the 1950 document in a certain way, Nepal could well be demanding not its abrogation but its implementation: specifically, that the Nepalis who are not treated on par with Indians be so treated. On the other hand, perhaps the treaty could simply be allowed to lapse unremarked. After all, there are many other bilateral treaties and agreements between India and Nepal, including those on trade and transit, and one overarching document to define a relationship that is historic and symbiotic may not be necessary. Rewriting the treaty seems fraught with risks for Nepal. It is quite possible that India, with its heightened national security concerns will, once the Pandora's box is opened, seek onerous terms in a future treaty. It might, for example, want to place restrictions on the open border. Most likely, it would annul the letter exempting Nepal providing equal treatment to Indians.

One could even suggest that the 1950 Treaty was a parting gift from the Rana regime to the people of Nepal, in that Prime Minister Mohan Shumshere managed to negotiate equal status with the powerful new nation-state of the Subcontinent, one that had inherited the imperial mantle from the departed British. The treaty may have buttressed Nepal's independent status, leaving the terms of the 1923 treaty untouched, because of Prime Minister Jawaharlal Nehru's close rapport with Nepali Congress leaders who had fought alongside him for India's freedom. There were other Indian leaders, such as Sardar Ballabhbhai Patel, the home minister, who were not as inclined to be magnanimous.

Kathmandu's well-known reliance on polemic rather than homework is seen in the fact that Nepal has made no haste to activate the committee set up at the foreign secretary level between the two governments in 1995 in order to discuss the 1950 treaty. In fact, that committee has met only twice in 15 years. That the political activists who demand that the treaty be revised do not demand that the committee be revived gives rise to the suspicion that the treaty is nothing more than a political football. The best thing for Kathmandu to do about it during the present time of societal transition and till such time as the country gains political stability and geopolitical strength may be to 'let sleeping treaties lie'. There will come a time when Nepal's geographical placement and sovereign status will allow it to negotiate a treaty and a relationship that strengthens the country without compromising the survival needs of its people. Now is not it.

In the not-very-distant future, the citizens of a prosperous Nepal will not have to fight in foreign armies or migrate in search of menial jobs. Nepal will be able to protect its economy and population while showing off its unencumbered international frontier as an example worthy of emulation by the rest of Southasia. Looking forward to such a day, the political gatekeepers of Kathmandu should perhaps take a long and hard look at the 1950 Treaty of Peace and Friendship, beginning by reading the 10 articles that make up the document.

New Delhi and Maobaadi
Nepal's Maobaadi insurgents maintained training camps in India in the initial years of the 'people's war' and made full use of the open border to supply their operations in Nepal as well as to seek refuge in India. During the insurgency, Indian diplomats in Kathmandu were on the defensive, providing a stock answer when challenged: 'India is a large country. We cannot track our own militants, how can you expect us to look for your Maoists?' While supporting Nepali Maoists could not have been the state policy of India, it is impossible to believe that New Delhi's intelligence agencies were not aware of the violence being wreaked in Nepal from safe houses south of the border. It was only when the Nepali rebel force became large enough to pose an internal security threat to India that the politicians and diplomats in New Delhi intervened and brought their muscle to bear in bringing the 'people's war' to an end and facilitating the 12-Point Agreement between the Maoists and the seven party alliance in New Delhi in 2005. Even while they were meeting Indian authorities in New Delhi, back in Nepal, rebel leaders were propagandising and preparing their cadre and general villagers for an 'Indian invasion', creating bunkers and trenches in schoolyards and public spaces. The ability of the Maoists to simultaneously condemn and appease New Delhi is cause for wonder.

The Maoist leadership made little attempt to hide while in India, and Chairman Dahal openly admits he spent eight out of the ten years of the 'people's war' in Noida, Shimla and other Indian towns and villagers. Photographs in a biography of Dahal released by an Indian publisher show Dahal and his family at various vacation spots in India. His penchant for visiting resorts near Kathmandu during times of stress in the years above ground seems to hark back to those days of comfort he enjoyed even as war raged in the Nepali countryside. Indian operatives were fully in the know, and are said to have helped with the logistics, when Nepali politicians met the Maoists at the height of the 'people's war' in Siliguri, Lucknow, and elsewhere. Indian agents played a crucial role in saving Baburam Bhattarai when he was placed under house arrest under orders of Chairman Dahal in January 2005, whisking him off to New Delhi. At the same time, it is important to remember that some Maoist leaders and activists were also nabbed in India – C.P. Gajurel in Chennai in August 2003, Matrika Yadav and Suresh Ale Magar in Lucknow in February 2004, Mohan Vaidya in Siliguri in March of that year, and, in June the same year, a large group in Patna – indicating a certain selectivity in how Indian authorities responded to different Maoist factions.

There is evidence that contact between Indian intelligence and the Maoist leadership has continued since the latter emerged above ground; indeed, some contacts have been quite brazenly open. At the same time, the position of the Indian state vis-à-vis the Nepali Maoists has grown progressively negative, especially since 2009, when Chairman Dahal and other leaders began exhibiting anti-Indian hostility. In the context of the escalating conflict between New Delhi and the Indian Maoists, it is likely that operatives of India will continue to watch the UCPN (Maoist) as a party closely but also to actively consult some of its factions.

The Indian government is now engaged in a pitched conflict with its own Naxalite insurgents, who are known locally as 'Maoists' since two main groups were consolidated under the Communist Party of India (Maoist) in 2004. Nepali Maoist leaders say that they now share nothing more than ideological affinity with their comrades in India, but few Indians believe them. It is unfortunate for the Nepali Maoists that the lay public in India sees the Maoists of the two countries as alike even though the UPCN (Maoist) has come into open politics while the Communist Party of India (Maoist) is still in its revolutionary arc. The developing political dynamics within India have definitely hurt the prospects of the Nepali Maoists, for rigid public opinion gives Indian decision-makers less room to manoeuvre.

The romance of the transforming revolutionary Nepali Maoist party caught the imagination of many opinion-makers in New Delhi. The initial position of the Indian establishment and New Delhi's civil society was also to glamorise the foreign insurgency's change-of-course. They sought to show to the brewing Indian insurgency that it was possible to come above ground, abandon their 'people's war', and land on both feet with power and recognition. This internal message, more than love for Pushpa Kamal Dahal, was what explained the exuberant welcome accorded the Nepali 'revolutionary' at the Hindustan Times Leadership Summit in New Delhi in November 2006. Sitaram Yechury, leader of the Communist Party of India (Marxist), was much lauded by Kathmandu's intelligentsia for supposedly helping broker peace in Nepal. However, more than his devotion to Nepali citizens, Yechury was helping defuse the Maoist 'revolution' in Nepal as part of a strategy of his CPI (M) aimed at the Indian Maoists. Apparently, all long, Yechury had also been fronting in Nepal for an Indian infrastructural mega-company with an eye on Nepal's hydropower resources.

The India-Nepali Maoist relationship has changed dramatically since 2006. Things did not go quite as New Delhi had expected when the Maoists ran away with the ball during the 2008 elections. New Delhi could, however, very well have lived with the outcome had the Maoists not become adventurists in their nine months at the helm of government, with ministers secretly crossing the border into Tibet as guests of the Chinese military, stoking anti-Indianism by trying to oust the Karnataka abbots of the Pashupatinath temple, and engaging in brinkmanship with the Nepal Army. Their actions raised fears in New Delhi about its own national security and also fired up Indian public opinion against the UCPN (Maoist). In terms of the peace process, the Maoist party also broke its promise to India and to the larger international community (and to the Nepali people themselves) by refusing to abide by the agreement to disband the cantonments through the formula of integration and rehabilitation. Such actions convinced New Delhi that its national interests would be compromised by a Maoist regime in Kathmandu. Further proof was provided by the anti-Indian ultra-nationalism exhibited by Chairman Dahal and others after he resigned from the government in May 2009. It must be repeated, however, that, Dahal's propaganda notwithstanding, New Delhi's distaste for a Maoist government does not mean that it has the wherewithal to define government formation in Nepal.

The political configuration in India has transformed since the time the Maoists were in government in 2008 and 2009, and the new United Progressive Alliance (UPA) government which rose in New Delhi after the April 2009 elections has not been in the Maoists' interests. Yechuri's CPI (M) is no longer in the UPA coalition and therefore unable to hold the hand of the UCPN (Maoist), for which it has a soft spot, and smooth its relationship with Indian authorities. Moreover, as it is faltering even in its own three-decade old bastion of West Bengal, the CPI (M) has been weakened nationally. Thus unencumbered by the presence of the CPI (M) and bent on escalating the battle against Indian Maoists in states like Jharkhand, Chattisgarh and Madhya Pradesh, the Congress-led government has hardened its stance on Nepal's Maoists. The sudden weakening of the Manmohan Singh government as a result of assorted scams and allegations over the winter of 2010 and 2011 has emboldened the Bharatiya Janata Party, whose stance on the Maoists is even more negative than that of the Congress. Against such transformed and transforming Indian national politics, the Chairman Dahal's projection of himself as rabidly anti-Indian in a last-ditch effort to garner support can only work to the detriment of his party.

32

China, Nepal

Beijing in the radarscope
Nepal's geographical and historical links to the north are, of course, with Tibet, both when it was sovereign and when now, when it is under Chinese suzerainty. Nepal also had historical links with the Chinese mainland, but that contact was mostly through Tibet. Modern-day Nepalis believe that this relationship was cemented by the young architect Arnico, who travelled to the court of Kublai Khan in Beijing at the same time that the more famous adventurer Marco Polo did. Arnico carried architectural concepts like the tiered pagoda temple and the votive stupa developed in the valley of Kathmandu and helped propagate them in Beijing and beyond. Kathmandu fought two wars with the Tibetans and Chinese, the last of which was concluded in 1792 with a treaty requiring Nepal to send five-yearly tribute missions to the emperor in Beijing, a practice that continued till the first decade of 20th century, when the custom ended with the fall of the Qing Dynasty in Beijing.

The cross-border links of communities in Nepal and Tibet are important, and the city states of Kathmandu Valley had significant artistic, cultural and trade links with Lhasa. However, in relative terms, the relationships with the Indian plains were, of course, more encompassing. This was primarily because of geography, the Himalayan ramparts and the lay of the land linking the populous mid-hills and plains more easily across the southern border. Coming into modern times, the dominance of New Delhi in the Nepali scheme of things has required the Kathmandu intelligentsia to bolster, and exaggerate, its relationship with China in an effort to present some sense of equidistance. The unquestioning appreciation of Beijing found in the Nepali polity reflects its desire to counterbalance the overwhelming presence of India. Beyond that, there is the fact that the two foreign states are quite different in nature: India is a democracy quite flexible about criticism while the Chinese demand continuous shows of fealty. For instance, Nepali officials must reiterate on every bilateral occasion that they support a one-China policy and do not allow pro-Tibet activities.

The importance of China/Tibet in the Nepali firmament it is bound to increase in the days to come as the development of transport infrastructure reduces the ability of the Himalayan range to serve as a formidable barrier to commerce and human movement. In the modern era, Beijing's influence was limited to the distribution of Maoist badges and literature in the 1960s and the construction of some high-profile highways and other projects, including, in 2002, the Birendra International Convention Centre, which is now the chamber of the Constituent Assembly. The future will doubtless build on the tentative out-reachings of the past, fostering a much deeper relationship which will incorporate not only trade and connectivity but also a new height in geopolitics.

As economic growth, the exploitation of natural resources and the growing rail network begins to change the face of the Tibet Autonomous Region, the future Nepal-China relationship is bound to become deeper. This is already beginning to happen, with the Beijing-Golmud-Lhasa train link, which opened in July 2006, bringing goods, passengers and tourists to Tibet in large volumes. Some of this influx, including cheap Chinese goods to compete with Indian products, has already spilled over into Nepal, and the trend is bound to escalate. Not only is Nepal going to be a destination for Chinese products and services, the next decade will see commerce between the Tibetan plateau and the Ganga plains through Nepal, facilitated by the railway snaking westward across Tibet and the development of north-south roads.

Beijing and the Subcontinent
Since the time that Mao Zedong and Chou En-Lai met successive Nepali leaders in the 1960s, China has suggested that Nepal falls within the Indian sphere of influence. Beijing's interests have been limited to preventing any kind of 'free-Tibet' movement from taking root in Nepal. Kathmandu has been attendant to that concern and there has been no repetition of the kind of CIA-supported Khampa rebellion that used Nepal's Himalayan valleys as a base for infiltration in the early 1970s.

There are indications that this limited policy on Nepal is beginning to change in tandem with the meteoric rise of China's economic status. King Gyanendra and Chairman Dahal believed that Beijing wished to flex its geopolitical muscle in Southasia. During their rules in 2005-2006 and 2008-2009, respectively, they flaunted what they thought was the 'China card', seeking to play New Delhi against Beijing. To their chagrin, both discovered that China's presence in Nepal and its ambitions in Southasia had not matured enough for their gambles to pay off. However, this bilateral relationship is bound to evolve in the days ahead, at least in the eyes of Beijing, as a 'strategic friendship'.

To bolster both its economic security and its geopolitical clout, China is investing in ports from Burma to Balochistan, pursuing a 'string-of-pearls' policy designed to encircle India. Nepal may or may not be one of the beads on the string, but there definitely has been a sudden spurt in Chinese economic and strategic interest in Nepal, as evidenced in the successive visits by Chinese officials over the last couple of years, support for the study of Chinese language in small towns, radio broadcasts, the promotion of cultural exchange, and private investment in Kathmandu, Lumbini and elsewhere. China has made known its interest in supporting large road projects and in developing Nepal as a destination for Chinese tourists.

In the past, one would have said that India and China are cooperating and competing at such a stratospheric height that it would be foolish for Nepali leaders to think they can play one off against the other. However, recent signals have been conflicting. Amidst the ambivalent gestures emanating from Beijing, it is becoming increasingly clear that China is jettisoning its hands-off policy on Nepal. It is not above trying to make New Delhi jittery as part of its 'great game' in Southasia and the Indian Ocean. The year 2010 was marked by heightened tension between the two Asian powers: they sparred over travel papers for Kashmiris going to China and the Arunachal Pradesh frontier, which is an old bugbear. Whatever the larger interests of Beijing and New Delhi, it would be unfortunate if Nepal were caught up in the geopolitical tussle between the two giants – and there are indications that this is happening.

While the UCPN (Maoist) was in government, three of its ministers made a secret visit to Tibet at the invitation of the Chinese military, leaving even their closest aides on the Nepali side of the border. In the autumn of 2010, at a time when the Maoists were making much in Kathmandu of their connections with Beijing, ten senior Maoist military commanders made a 'private' visit to the People's Republic of China. Shortly thereafter, Chairman Dahal made a trip to Shanghai and Beijing; upon his return, he said that the Chinese leadership had asked him to mend fences with India.

With the end of the monarchy, Beijing seeks a partner in Nepal which it can trust to loyally uphold its security concerns in Tibet. Not wanting to take any risk on this count, Beijing seems to have decided to support the collaboration between the moderate and radical left in Nepal, which is why it encouraged the Dahal-led UCPN (Maoist) to come together with Chairman Khanal's faction within the CPN (UML) to form a coalition government. In the long term, knowing that any Maoist-led combine will naturally be pro-Beijing, the Chinese seem to want a consolidated, politically strong left party in Nepal. The argument of Nepali democrats, that the cohabitation of the democratic left CPN (UML) – the legacy of the late Madan Bhandari – and the radical left is incongruous, is obviously academic for Chinese strategists. Chairman Dahal and King Gyanendra lost their bet in playing the 'China card', but as Beijing upgrades its friendship with Nepal to a 'strategic friendship' things could change in the future for some other player.

The pilgrim-refugees of Tibet
It would be foolhardy for any Kathmandu government to ignore Chinese sensitivity regarding Tibet. When great Western powers shudder every time the Chinese dragon breathes fire and mute their receptions when the Dalai Lama visits, it would be too much to expect Kathmandu to stand up taller than a Copenhagen or a Washington DC. And yet, Nepal ought to have enough diplomatic clout to be able to invite Tenzin Gyatso, the 14th Dalai Lama and the winner of the Nobel Prize for Peace, to visit Lumbini, the birthplace of Siddhartha Gautam, the Prince of Peace. When Nepal entered the democratic era in 1990, it seemed that a private, non-political visit might be possible, but no longer. Beijing's concerns about the high-profile protests organised in Kathmandu during the Beijing Olympics of 2008 combined with continuing protests within Tibet have led to intense pressures Kathmandu is unable to withstand. With the changing political dynamics within Nepal, which includes the rise of the UCPN (Maoist), a party less than democratic and not just

sensitive to but enthusiastic about Beijing's worldview, a sojourn by the aging Dalai Lama to Lumbini has become impossible.

The Tibetan refugee families of Nepal, most of them arriving in the late 1950s and the 1960s, were settled in camps in Kathmandu and in various parts of the hinterland. They are considered one of the most successful refugee communities of the world and have served as a catalyst in several sectors of the Nepali economy. The Tibetan refugees started the carpet industry which, for a long time in the 1980s, was a mainstay of the economy. Various sects of Tibetan Buddhism established their seat of exile in Kathmandu, and their presence has brought economic vitality and cosmopolitanism to the Valley. Nepal has also become a staging ground for tourists to visit Lhasa and for pilgrims from India and overseas to climb Mount Kailas in western Tibet. Overall, the level of economic interaction between China and Nepal is low but the prospects for more linkages are high. As Tibet has been the historical partner of Nepal more than the faraway Middle Kingdom, one hopes that the inhabitants of the Tibetan Autonomous Region as well as the diaspora of refugees can be part of the growing economic interdependence over the Himalayan divide, which is less and less a divide. As China develops political freedoms that necessarily will follow its shooting economic growth, it may develop a more benign gaze on Tibet, which can only help in cementing an exemplary friendship across the Himalaya.

The Tibetans who today make the arduous trek over the Himalayan passes into Nepal are overwhelmingly pilgrim-refugees. Evading Chinese border guards and risking capture by the Nepali police, their destination is Dharamsala, Himachal Pradesh, the seat of the Dalai Lama and his government-in-exile. For decades, there has been an informal understanding between Chinese and Nepali authorities to allow a refugee reception centre in Kathmandu to process these pilgrim-refugees and facilitate their movement to Dharamsala, with the assistance of the refugee agency UNHCR and the Dalai Lama's representative.

It is in the interest of the well-settled Tibetan refugees in Nepal that their lives and livelihoods not be jostled by raucous activism that embarrasses Beijing. Such agitation weakens the hand of the Kathmandu government when engaging with Beijing and affects the refugees' standing in Nepal. Most importantly, Tibetan activists have to consider how their protests affect the Nepali authorities' ability to facilitate the transfer of the pilgrim-refugees that continue to emerge from Tibet. Already, the Chinese embassy in Kathmandu is actively monitoring the work of the Nepali police along the Himalayan districts, and its diplomatic activism is expected to accelerate in the days ahead. No one would deny the Tibetans' right to peaceful protest, and Nepal did allow it for a long time. But at a time when the Western powers are bowing to Chinese pressure and the Indian government forbids protests when Chinese dignitaries visit New Delhi, it would be unrealistic – and inexpedient – to expect Kathmandu to stand tall and defend human rights to the hilt.

There has been no anti-China-free-Tibet activity in Nepal of any import since the Khampa rebels were crushed by Nepali soldiers in 1974. Nor are the Tibetan-Buddhist communities along the northern edge – the Bhotiya, or Himali – politicised in such a way that would affect the cross-border relationship. And the Chinese Embassy is not really fearful of Tibetan activism in Kathmandu evolving into an insurgency. It is the bad publicity that it abhors. When Nepali policemen confront monks and other activists and news photographs and video feeds go out to the world; that is when the Chinese, literally, see red.

The state of Nepal, which espouses democratic values that authorities in Beijing do not, used to allow peaceful demonstrations by Tibetan refugees near the Chinese Embassy and United Nations offices in Kathmandu Valley. Matters came to a head during the run-up to the 2008 Beijing Olympics, when, on a daily basis, photojournalists presented to the world scenes of protesting monks being accosted and manhandled by Nepali police. To the authorities in Bejing, it must have looked as if the world of anti-Chinese sentiment was concentrated on the streets of Kathmandu. Stung by the bad press, which occurred just as it was presenting its best face to the world in its management of the Games, Beijing decided that it would not be humiliated again.

The Chinese Embassy in Kathmandu is now in overdrive to browbeat the Kathmandu authorities into cracking down on demonstrations; indeed, it is so gung ho that refugees find it difficult even to mark the Dalai Lama's birthday in the Baudha 'Tibetan quarter'. Weak transitional governments, and one prime minister in particular who wanted to develop ties to the extent of making Beijing uncomfortable, have essentially succumbed to the Chinese demand that Nepal prohibit peaceful protests. While respecting Beijing's security interests and seeking to develop a strong economic relationship with the north, the Nepali polity should remain alert against compromising fundamental democratic values, for that will ultimately rebound against our own people and their sense of self-worth. An open society, after all, is the foundation for Nepal's progress and international standing – and a politically liberal and tolerant neighbour is good for Nepal's political advance and economic growth.

Reports that Chinese embassy officials are actively involved in accosting and sending back pilgrim-refugees caught in Nepal's Himalayan districts should have created disquiet among commentators in Kathmandu, but it did not. Its automatic support for Beijing became evident when human rights activist Liu Xiaobo was announced the recipient of the 2010 Nobel Peace Prize: Nepali commentators were either silence or made an immediate, knee-jerk claim that Liu's selection was nothing but part of a Western conspiracy to isolate China and prevent its rise as a world power. A study of the reaction to the explosive Maharagate scandal of September 2010 is also instructive. Why didn't the intelligentsia raise a ruckus when Chairman Dahal's seniormost aide, Krishna Bahadur Mahara, was caught on tape speaking to a Chinese-sounding voice seeking Rs. 500 million to buy the prime ministerial elections? Why did they say nothing when he was later made deputy prime minister? First, opinion-makers were scared of being hounded by aggressive Maoists; second, the fact that the Indian Embassy was proactive in distributing the audiotape soured the pitch; and, third, even the remote possibility of Chinese involvement in promoting the Dahal candidacy for prime minister was enough to make many commentators want to leave the matter alone. The link to Beijing, even if it was only a voice with a Mandarin accent, was enough to stifle coverage of a scandal beyond compare.

As a democratic country, Nepal must try to keep the window open for anyone, including Tibetan refugees, to conduct peaceful protests on the streets of Kathmandu. At the same time, the refugee community surely understands that the Government of Nepal, as its economic and political ties with Beijing grow, has increasingly less space to speak up about affairs in Tibet. It is in the interests of the refugee community within Nepal to be left alone to carry on with their lives in conditions which are better than they are for most refugees in the world, including for Tibetans elsewhere in Southasia. Long-time refugees in Nepal should discourage firebrand activists from Dharamshala and elsewhere from travelling to Kathmandu to trigger fiery demonstrations that could only harm the refugees. As far as the government-in-exile is concerned, its primary interest is not to jeopardise the long-standing protocol that allows pilgrim-refugees from Tibet to proceed to Dharamshala via Kathmandu. Free passage has been allowed for decades, and the policy should continue. Against this backdrop, no one wins by creating conditions in which where the frail Kathmandu government is cornered by an enraged Chinese dragon.

33

Hail, the New Constitution!

Hopes for a democratic constitution
The peace process in Nepal made a rapid start after the People's Movement of April 2006, as the parliamentary parties made a deal with the Maoists to abolish the monarchy, adopt federalism, and hold elections to a constituent assembly. The peace negotiators developed the euphemism 'arms management' to refer to the demobilisation of rebel combatants and willingly held an election even though the Maoist fighting force was still intact (though nominally sequestered in cantonments). Most independent analysts agree that the interim government of Girija Prasad Koirala was too lenient in the face of continuing Maoist excesses; it is not clear why he gave the Maoists such liberty. He may have feared jeopardising the peace process, but more likely his poor health had made Koirala lose the sure touch he had maintained throughout his political career till that point. The Maoist leaders moved the goalposts after they came above ground, hoodwinking the romantic intelligentsia in the capital and reneging on their promise to let go of the tools and rhetoric of aggression.

The expectation was that, with ever-increasing maturity forced on them by the dictates of an open society, the Maoists would, sooner rather than later, submit to the realities of national politics and geopolitics and agree to the closure of its cantonments, the 'management' of the ex-combatants, the disbanding of the barrack system of the Young Communist League, and the return of seized property. These steps would lead *ipso facto* to the writing of a democratic constitution, for a Maoist move towards concluding the peace process would mean that the party leadership had been able, at long last, to convince the cadre to abandon their hopes of state capture and a one-party state. But it is not enough to want this outcome. Democrat-politicians and members of civil society had to work towards it by challenging the UCPN (Maoist). Meanwhile, by the spring of 2011, Chairman Dahal had lost so much control over his party that he was willing to experiment with any kind of radical pronouncement, constitution-writing be damned. How could any party, let alone the largest in the Constituent Assembly, that decides in a plenum to adopt an official line of 'revolt' and discusses whether or not to nominate a neighbouring country or some other entity as its 'principal enemy', be considered serious about writing a constitution?

It is urgently required that all who believe in pluralism and democracy work in concert to confront the UCPN (Maoist) leadership and insist that violent invective and chameleon-like transformation have no credibility. The Maoists must submit to the universally accepted principles of peaceful politics and constitutional democracy. There is a sense of frustration among democrat-politicians and democratically minded intelligentsia as they battle with the Maoists over principles everyone had thought were secured way back in 1990 – pluralism, the separation of powers, fundamental freedoms, and the supremacy of judiciary. If the Maoists are not challenged there is a danger the nation will regress from the liberal democracy it achieved through the Constitution of 1990 and that its movement towards an inclusive democracy will be obstructed at the very start.

We have to be clear – the UCPN (Maoist) will probably transform into a civilian party if confronted by the intelligentsia, the international community and the civil society acting in concert. If we rely solely on the goodwill of the UCPN (Maoist) leadership to change, however, a one-party state or something close to it will be a political *fait accompli*. Such a state would bring long-term economic ruin to Nepal, much worse than the three decades of doldrums that the Communist Party of India (Marxist) wreaked on West Bengal. There is no possibility that the Maoist will transform voluntarily; they must be challenged relentlessly so that the peace process concludes as specified in the Comprehensive Peace Accord and the constitution that is written is democratic. It is better not to have a new constitution at all if the draft fails to rise to the standard of modern-day pluralistic values. Instead, the text of the existing Interim Constitution should be adjusted retaining, of course, the guarantees of a republic, secularism, federalism and affirmative action, and the nation should move on.

To see a new constitution written, the parliamentary parties are asking the Maoists to uphold the terms of their written agreement and to abandon their control of the cantonments, allowing for the integration or the rehabilitation of ex-combatants. The prevarication of Maoist leaders, who do not seem to have the courage to deal honestly with their cadre, is proving costly for society as a whole. Some internationals with an inadequate understanding of the Nepali democratic experience think that an incomplete peace process and a half-democratic constitution that is high on polemic but low on fundamental freedoms would be adequate but, fortunately, the good people of Nepal know better. The polity will not allow the drafting exercise to be conducted under the shadow of the gun, and any attempt to push through an undemocratic constitution will end in a people's movement sooner rather than later.

Drafting the constitution
Will the new constitution be written? This is a fair question and it is easy to be a sceptic in answering it. The constitution will be written if, to use the phrase on everyone's lips since the 2008 formation of the Constituent Assembly, a 'logical conclusion of the peace process' is achieved. The Constitution will be written if the Maoists come down from their high horse and agree to the foundational democratic principles that should guide constitution-writing. How can a constitution be written if the Maoists continue to maintain their cantonments? How can a constitution be written if the Maoists push for a 'people's republic' draft in which the parliament dominates the judiciary, fundamental freedoms are not guaranteed, and the freedom to organise political parties is compromised in the name of 'national interest'? No one who believes that our country must have an unhindered, unabridged path to a democratic future promising inclusive growth can accept these conditions. The addition of the word 'people's' to the constitutionally established 'Federal Democratic Republic of Nepal' will result in a situation far worse than the three decades of Panchayat rule created.

Holding nearly 40% of the 601 seats, the UCPN (Maoist) is the largest party in the Constituent Assembly. Still, it does not form a majority and thus must win the trust of the other political parties, in particular the CPN (UML), the Nepali Congress and the Madhesi parties, in order to constitute the two-thirds majority required to adopt a new constitution. The Assembly will not be able to write a constitution if the Maoists insist on their version, a dangerous document released by Vice-Chairman Baburam Bhattarai in May 2010. The other political parties will not agree to the key ideas of the 'people's republic' draft, for they are run by experienced politicians who developed or honed their values during the democratic era from 1990 to 2002 after having fought for decades against the Panchayat. If it turns out that there is a deadlock between those Maoists who want an undemocratic constitution which perverts fundamental rights and those who want a democratic one based on universal values, there can be no 'mid-way compromise'.

A peaceful 'logical end'
It is hardly unreasonable of the parliamentary parties to ask that the cantonments be disbanded and the process of 'managing' ex-combatants be started as agreed. In response to blustering Maoist pronouncements, like that uttered by Chairman Dahal in the Shaktikhor videotape (that each and every ex-combatant, all 19,602, should be integrated into the national army) some leaders of the parliamentary parties have insisted that not even one ex-combatant should be integrated, as the army would be soiled by any level of their inclusion. Some civil society stalwarts present an alternative that the Maoists welcome: setting up a parallel state security force. But that 'solution' will be tantamount to allowing the so-called 'PLA' to continue acting as a psychological burden on the populace just under a different name. There are some democrat-politicians who claim it is better to keep the Maoists within the state security forces rather than allow ideologically brainwashed, trigger-happy cadre to roam the villages in the current environment of statelessness. On balance, the right formula still seems to be the original gentleman's agreement based on the Comprehensive Peace Accord: a modest number of ex-combatants who fufill the recruitment criteria to be integrated non-unit wise into the security forces and the rest to be rehabilitated. Society needs the psychological release that will come from the demobilisation of the Maoist fighting force.

To wind down the peace process sufficiently to allow the new constitution to be drafted in earnest requires a timetable and process that convinces the parliamentary parties, civil society and the international community that progress is irreversible. In addition, the political parties insist – logically – on the disbandment of the quasi-military structures of the Young Communist League, most importantly of the barracks where the cadre are kept as on-call units to enforce the Maoists' will. Finally, The CPN (UML) and Nepali Congress require that the Maoists agree to a credible procedure for the return or compensation of the property they confiscated, much of which belongs to the activists of the two parties. None of these three steps have been adopted, and to give a sense of the recalcitrant Maoist mindset, it is enough to note that in March 2011 the party made a frightening announcement of the establishment of a People's Volunteer Bureau with military-style structuring, with plans for a membership of 500,000 countrywide.

None of the decisions regarding the peace process are really difficult for the Maoists to take if they feel for the people, and the leadership could make up for its past prevarications even at this very late hour. Nothing is preventing the triumvirate of Chairman Dahal, Baburam Bhattarai and Mohan Vaidya from agreeing to disband the cantonments under an agreed upon formula, starting with the basics – the total number of the soldiers and officers to be integrated and at what level. There is no doubt that, while there will be some murmurs of dissent, the three leaders can get decisions passed to conclude the peace, and also for the writing of a constitutional draft that is democratic. On the other hand, the people of Nepal should not be asked to commit hara-kiri, to knowingly destroy their future just because some ideologically rigid and opportunist leaders of one party do not get along with each other.

There was great hope for the peace process when Chairman Dahal was riding the wave of popularity in Nepal and internationally, when he alone could have driven his party towards a conclusion. Whether due to ideological blinders or an absence of accountability towards his own party's democratic future, Dahal failed to educate his followers about the promises he had made and lately has focussed on consolidating his own place in the party by spouting ultra-nationalism and mouthing false promises of 'full integration'. He almost made an about turn in February 2011: in negotiations at the Gokarna Forest Resort, belying his public calls for revolt, Dahal agreed upon a number for integration, the precondition being that he be allowed to become prime minister again. After the lunch break, however, he returned to reject the deal. Once again, it seemed that the peace process was stuck due to nothing else but the divide within the Maoist party; in fact, the very fate of the new constitution hangs in balance because of internal dissension within the Maoist party. If this is true, none of the debates and discussions outside of the

Maoist fold on what might happen with the peace process and what is to be done with regard to constitution-making makes any sense.

The UCPN (Maoist) leadership plays a dangerous game with its delays in managing the ex-combatants because before long the public will decide that it cannot live with the uncertainty any more, and there will be no outrage when the commitment to integration and rehabilitation is abrogated by the other parties. For now, the Nepal Army can be made to accept a limited number of Maoist combatants into its ranks. The Maoists may also have failed to appreciate fully that India sees its own national security tied to the peace process in Nepal, especially in the context of the growing battle between the New Delhi government and the Indian Maoists. While one hopes that India is able to distinguish between its internal Maoist issue and the demands of the peace process in Nepal, the Nepali Maoists need to move quickly if it is to secure its aims of rehabilitation and integration.

With the selection of the experienced former general Balananda Sharma as the coordinator of the Special Committee Secretariat and the withdrawal of the UNMIN security blanket after January 2010, the situation suddenly looked conducive for ending the peace process at long last, and, in consequence, for advancing the constitution-writing process. The handover of the cantonments to the Special Committee was carried out amidst great pomp on 22 January 2011, but it turned out to be a damp squib, or, rather, a flagrant fraud. 'Nepali Maoists sever ties with their army,' read one headline, and all over there was applause for the handover of cantonment management to the Special Committee. Nothing of the sort happened. After feeding the august international gathering an elaborate lunch and going through the charade of flag lowering, the UCPN (Maoist) refused to transfer the chain-of-command to the Special Committee. This deception did not receive adequate attention from the commentators, but it did make all the other groups, other than the pro-Maoist faction of the UML headed by Prime Minister Jhala Nath Khanal, more wary than ever about Maoist intentions and designs.

Threats to constitution-writing
To begin with, constitution-writing is threatened because the UCPN (Maoist) is not yet a democratic force. Its speeches, pronouncements and official documents leave no doubt that the party would like to convert Nepal into a one-party state, a People's Republic of Nepal.

Some say such fears are exaggerated and that the Maoists will ultimately submit to a democratic constitution, but it is clear that this transformation will not happen without pressure. The biggest challenge to constitution-writing is to heed the fact that social justice cannot be delivered in the absence of complete democracy and that there is no path ahead but to divert the UCPN (Maoist) from its autocratic – or, more accurately, feudal – ambitions.

The rules of procedure in the Constituent Assembly were drafted in such a way that they allow for the passage of draft articles in individual committees through majority vote rather than through consensus. This has led members from parties large and small –especially the Maoist party and the newborn Madhesi parties – to grandstand and take obstinate positions rather than to compromise. Such posturing increases polarisation among the constituent parties and will make it very difficult for them to secure the two-thirds majority vote required to pass each and every article. Though the committees have completed their relatively easy job of sending draft provisions to the Constitutional Committee, the tough battle ahead of trying to reach a consensus has not even begun. The only positive thing that happened in the spring of 2011 was that a sub-committee was formed within the Constitutional Committee with Chairman Dahal as coordinator, which did informally manage to narrow down differences on some contentious issues. However, there were questions: one of them being whether this was being done by Dahal only to show only the amount of momentum required to extend the life of the Constituent Assembly a second time. The fact that the ultra-radicals within the UCPN (Maoist) tried to keep Dahal from serving as coordinator, as well as the possibility that the Maoist can easily reject every point that they have informally agreed to in the sub-committee, makes constitution-drafting an exercise conducted with no certainties.

There are other dangers with respect to constitution-writing that do not have to do specifically with the Maoists or any other party, but with the fact that Nepal is undergoing a phase of first-run identity politics rather late in the modern era. The dust has not settled enough to allow cool heads to concentrate on constitution-writing: the identity movement among the ethnicities and the Madhesi communities is still effervescent and there is, amidst many uncertainties, a deep lack of trust in the political parties. The hope that the Constituent Assembly would be the venue in which all the crosscutting issues of identity politics, whether those of the Janajati, the Dalit, the Madhesi or any other group, could be discussed and resolved has been shattered. Sadly, the House has failed to serve as an arbiter and polarisation, both among communities and between communities and political parties, has increased. Nepal's democratically minded citizenry will ultimately reject a constitution which negates the values it holds dearest – pluralism and non-violence. There are other issues not as critical, but which could nonetheless derail the new constitution even as it is being drafted. To take one example, we really do not know how the constitutional delineation of provinces (when it is finally decided) will be accepted by various ethnic and Madhesi activists. Forces that we have not even contemplated could rise and foment a movement to reject what is offered. Other imponderables relate to whether we should adopt a Presidential system, as the Maoists want, a directly-elected prime minister as some in the CPN (UML) argue for, or the traditional prime minister-in-parliament that the Nepali Congress is comfortable with. The idea that has not been brought into discussion enough is that a society such as Nepal's cannot allow overwhelming power to be concentrated in one office – a directly-elected President or prime minister. Nepal's experience, however, has demonstrated that a system in which the prime minister is elected from within the Parliament provides protection from a takeover by a demagogue.

Another matter that will need to be decided on the basis of practicality is the electoral system, whether Nepal should retain the traditional system of direct representation, embrace fully proportional representation, or adopt a 50-50 formula as it did during the Constituent Assembly elections. An Assembly largely devoid of jurists and social scientists, unwilling to take advice, and pulled by the nose-ring of populism, is being asked to make the correct choice when a mistake would mire society for a long time to come. An example of the imponderables will serve to illustrate: it was the UCPN (Maoist) which sought a fully proportional system for the Constituent Assembly polls, but, as it turned out, the party would have done much better, even won a simple majority, through direct elections. The advantage of a mixed system, which is likely to be selected, is that under-represented communities can make it into Parliament through the proportional list. To avoid making a travesty of the principle, a caveat is in order: party leaders should not be allowed to cherry pick from a proportional list provided earlier to the Election Commission as they did in the 2008 election. Hopefully, as confidence in the political parties increases after a few general elections are successfully held, the polity will go back to the direct election system. It is when people vote directly for their individual representatives that the latter become most accountable to their constituents.

'Scholarship' has been at a premium in a constituent assembly flush with donor funding and many members have travelled aboard to study the systems of governance and constitutionalism in faraway Switzerland, Scandinavia and South Africa. Few, however, have observed successful models and experiences much closer to home: those of Bangladesh, India, Pakistan and Sri Lanka. Little has been learnt about constitution-writing and constitutionalism from Nepal's Southasian neighbours, even though it is next door that one would expect to find the most relevant expertise. That B.R. Ambedkar, the main framer of India's Constitution of 1949, has received almost total neglect from Nepal's Constituent Assembly memberships itself speaks volumes.

There is a grave danger that, in an attempt to mollify every constituency across the nation, Nepal will get an overly detailed and unwieldy document rather than the more preferable option – a brief, politically liberal constitution that sets broad guidelines for establishing an open society and accountable government and that leaves implementation to laws later enacted. We may, however, be headed for a constitution which will seek to address the specific concerns of each community, promising and declaring as justifiable a whole spectrum of economic and social rights which the state will be unable to provide. Establishing a careful balance between promise and practicality may not be possible under the existing circumstances. It does not help that guidance comes largely from Western rather than Southasian advisors and experts. Even the few that are from the Subcontinent are influenced by the 'donor agenda', much of which sees Nepal in caricature. Amidst the smoke and mirrors in the Constituent Assembly, some novel and welcome provisions are bound to pass, for example, provisions relating to social justice and positive discrimination. But the danger remains of including as substantive provisions elements and ideals that would more appropriately be mentioned in the directive principles of state policy.

The constitution-drafting exercise has been a hit-and-miss exercise because of the extreme polarisation between and within political parties and the lack of coordination among the various committees in the

Assembly. More significantly, the exercise was begun without agreement on the basic principles to guide the drafting or on the kind of state structure envisaged. By contrast, the writing of the 1990 Constitution, which was the product of three radically divergent forces (the Congress, the left and the royalists), proceeded efficiently because all forces agreed ahead of time on the basic principles and the state structure. In the absence of a strong intellectual tradition among the constitution framers and jurists in society generally, and its reluctance to seek help from constitutional experts within the country and the Southasian neighbourhood, the Constituent Assembly could well prepare a document that will be difficult to implement.

One hopes that, amidst the confusion and unrequited, multiple, and contradictory demands, when the Assembly's 601 members are faced with a deadlock, they will agree to adopt a relatively brief constitution, one which defines state-society relations; guarantees the rights of citizens and define their duties; confirms secularism, republicanism and federalism; and creates constitutional bodies – but leaves it to successive parliaments to write the laws to run the country. Such a constitution would not have to see many amendments, and the writing and amending of laws could be done efficiently and lead to a smooth and stable polity. If there is such an insurmountable impasse that even a 'framework constitution' cannot be written, at the very least the major political forces must agree on the structure of the state and electoral system so that these could guide the polity despite complete disarray.

So, will the new constitution be written?
The flaw that has dogged the Constituent Assembly throughout its nearly three years of existence is that its work was begun and continued as a part of the peace process, whereas we should have stipulated that constitution-writing should not start until the peace process was successfully concluded. During this period, the parliamentary and other, newer political parties kept their own counsel on many matters of constitutionalism, just as they had done regarding Maoist election-related malfeasance, because peace was not yet at hand. As time passed and the UCPN (Maoist) shifted the goalposts, it began to look as if the constitution would not be completed at all – primarily because no one other than the Maoists wants a constitution written while the cantonments are still in existence. In the meantime, the delay provided the opportunity for

royalists to organise and anti-federalists to agitate, helping build an undercurrent of disquiet not visible in newspaper reports and commentator columns.

The greatest weakness of the constitution-writing process was the lack of an initial agreement on its founding principles, its basic platform. It was this shortcoming that allowed the drafting exercise to go astray from day one as the need to keep the peace process on track made the parliamentary parties diffident in demanding that the UCPN (Maoist) agree on the founding principles. As 42 concerned citizens from around the country suggested in a declaration made public in April 2010, the following eight basic principles of a democratic constitution should be included as the founding principles of the new Nepali constitution whenever the Constituent Assembly, or any other entity formed to draft it, decides to seriously consider the matter:

- Separation of powers
- Secularism
- Pluralism
- Civilian supremacy
- Nationalism
- Supremacy of the judiciary
- Social justice
- Inclusion

The Constitutional Committee

Democracy is not new to Nepal, nor is constitution-drafting. Our best experience was with the Constitution of 1990, promulgated in November of that year and written by a committee representing three forces: the democrats, the left and the royalists. The 1990 Constitution was a ground-breaking document in that it defined sovereignty as residing in the people and guaranteed fundamental freedoms, judicial supremacy and democratic governance. The 1990 Constitution made possible all the advances that Nepal achieved thereafter, from participatory development to socio-economic progress.

The parliamentary system adopted by the 1990 Constitution was suited to the fact that Nepal is a pluralistic society on many different planes – ethnic, caste and geographic among them. The few weaknesses in the 1990 Constitution could have been erased through amendment.

What is perceived as the biggest fault of the Constitution – its inability to promote egalitarianism – was not the fault of the document itself but its implementation, which was stymied by the great turbulence of the decade-long 'people's war'. It was unfortunate that there was no farewell salute to the 1990 Constitution when it was annulled in 2006 and the Interim Constitution took its stead. Nevertheless, all the values of democracy and pluralism that were part of that document must be transferred into the new constitution of the Republic of Nepal. The new constitution should be an advance on the 1990 Constitution not a regression from it.

Over the course of nearly three years of make-believe work, words upon words were added in each of the ten thematic committees of Constituent Assembly, but the main differences among the parties have remained unaddressed. The drafting exercise came close to becoming a farce as the Maoist members insisted on provisions that were far from the democratic ideal; they even refused to accept the term 'pluralism' and demanded a laudatory reference to the 'people's war'. A critical decision relating to the definition of federalism in the state-restructuring committee was pushed through using questionable procedures, which is also how a false agreement was reached on 14 provinces with the majority defined using an 'ethnic' and 'Madhesi' formula. From demanding weaponry training for the citizenry to challenging the concept of judicial supremacy, the provisions of the new constitution had observers worried that the country was going back to the drawing board, as if the fight for liberty from the Ranas had not happened, as if the three decades of battling the Panchayat had been in vain, as if the 1990 Constitution had not been written, and as if the People's Movement of 2006 had not demanded non-violent politics and an end to autocracy of all kinds.

With his finely calibrated sense of timing, Maoist Chairman Dahal was careful to relent occasionally on some draft provisions in order to give the public a sense of momentum. Once, it was his dramatic announcement that the Maoists had agreed to retain the unique double-triangled national flag – as if there had ever been a question about that. The image that was projected was of Maoist flexibility, as opposed to the demands for a rigid, top-down, non-participatory, undemocratic constitution which was demanded at other times.

Not only was the work of the thematic committees done without crosschecking and the procedure of majority vote in the thematic committees a travesty of consensus, the entire constitution-writing exercise was done back to front as there was no initial agreement on state structuring or fundamental principles. Thus, it was only at the fag end of the third year of the Assembly that the Constitutional Committee was asked to take up the matter of state structure, the very first concept that should have been agreed upon.

Over the winter of 2010-2011, the Constituent Assembly decided to give the Constitutional Committee the task of collating the reports of the thematic committees. The committee is chaired by Nilamber Acharya, who was the minister-in-attendance when the 1990 Constitution was drafted, and is, fortunately, one of the few individuals in Nepal who can be called a jurist right and proper. As the deadline of the Assembly's extended term drew nearer, the Constitutional Committee was given tasks to sort out differences as well, and a sub-committee formed for the purpose.

The hope of deriving a constitution – a democratic one – through the Constituent Assembly is entirely dependent upon the UCPN (Maoist). And only a dramatic turnaround by the Maoists, incorporating their concession to the demands of democratic forces across the board, could see that possibility materialise. After all, it is the position of the UCPN (Maoist) on key matters that are holding up a democratic constitution and, additionally, only the Maoists have the ability to convince the most antsy among the community groups (other than Madhesi groups) not to reject the document that is promulgated. There could be one motivation for the Maoists to suddenly agree to a democratic constitution: knowing that his party would be able to make a good showing in the next general elections, Chairman Dahal may want to wrap up the constitution-writing and set about organising for the polls in a year's time. If the Maoists could hold the prime minister's position as well as the Ministry of Home Affairs, the party would be even keener to adopt a constitution even if it were a democratic one.

Ironically, therefore, for all its prevarication, the UCPN (Maoist) could agree to a democratic constitution as a means to get international applause while guaranteeing long innings in power by manipulating elections to get a two-thirds majority. The Maoists could do very well indeed in the first general election after the promulgation of the Constitution of the Republic of Nepal 2011 for the following reasons:

the party's war chest is full and in control of the chairman; the party has built up momentum despite the factionalism within its leadership; the public remains subdued in the face of the Maoist threat of violence, the presence of the YCL, the cantonments and the newborn People's Volunteer Bureau; the CPN (UML) as the mainstream left has been compromised by Jhala Nath Khanal's cohabitation with Pushpa Kamal Dahal; and the other parties have not gained impetus in most rural areas. Besides, the party has the experience of the elections of April 2008, of browbeating the electorate, compromising the state institutions including the Election Commission, and hoodwinking national and international election observers. On top of this is the unwritten part of the seven point deal with Prime Minister Khanal, according to which Chairman Dahal will become prime minister when the constitution is passed.

Not-so-worst-case scenario
What if no Constitution emerges? What if the process of drafting and promulgation, burdened by the weight of contradictions and polarisations in the polity, collapses? There is still the Interim Constitution to keep us going at that point. The Nepali public knows full well that the Maoists are not about to go back to the jungle voluntarily and that the other mainstream political forces are not about to force them back there. The citizenry knows that it has a society and a geography that can deliver peace and prosperity; its perspective allows it to locate order and peace of mind where outsiders see a 'failed state'. The public at large has not been as frustrated as either the Kathmandu Valley commentator brigade or members of the international community, because they knew that writing a constitution was not going to be cakewalk to begin with.

The people of Nepal may not know comparative history but they do understand and understand well that their country, while it is indeed the oldest nation-state of Southasia, is engaged in nation-building at long last and that, in the scale of historical time, these few years of disquiet are but a brief interlude to struggle through and to overcome. Knowing that Nepal is a country gifted by history, demography, climate, geography and natural resources to become the model state of Southasia, the people are not willing to derail the constitution-writing process.

If we can make democracy and pluralism work for the people through equity and social justice, this country can set an example for the rest of Southasia, a region home to nearly a fourth of the world's population.

While all Nepalis may not articulate their feelings in the same way, it is our understanding of the grandeur of what we are trying to achieve, especially given what history has left us with, which will keep us from panicking if the new constitution is not written on time. If the deadline for promulgation comes and goes with no final draft produced, the people will first ascertain whether enough progress has been made that there is hope for completing it. If this is the case, they will be agreeable to any credible course that the parliamentary parties and the UCPN (Maoist) decide.

If completion of the drafting work looks impossible and there is an impassable deadlock, the parties can at least try to seek agreement on the state structure – Presidential, prime ministerial or Westminster – which would presuppose a meeting of minds on its electoral system (direct, proportional or mixed). With agreement on just this much, there would be enough guidance for any credible entity to lead society forward towards elections. If even this looks impossible, in order to avert a constitutional vacuum, the public would be agreeable to the next-best option –to regularise the Interim Constitution and adopt it as the basic law which guarantees republicanism, secularism, federalism and inclusion. The door would be left open for later amendments to cover the details that are not included, including the definition and delineation of federalism, affirmative action, the structure of the state and the election systems.

34

Loktantra Jindabad!

The pitfalls of certitude
Given the myriad variables that come into play in times of extreme instability and political transition, prediction and prognosis can be dramatically incorrect. Indeed, the writing of opinion is a challenge in a society in volatile transition, with class- and identity-based issues extant and the extreme left and the germinating right both poised to take advantage of lawlessness.

That said, I believe that it does not do to keep one's opinions to oneself, that it is best to air them clearly and without hand-wringing. There is no contribution to be made from equivocation or after-the-fact claims to prior knowledge. Like any journalist, I have the obligation to use reportage, research and logic, and to try to avoid bias. Yet when it comes to two fundamental values – pluralism and non-violence in public life – it is not possible to maintain neutrality. On the matter of non-violent politics and democracy, one has to be a citizen, and I have offered this book as a citizen's submission.

We went into the Constituent Assembly elections seeing it as part of the peace process, but the writing of a constitution that is meant to carry us into the future cannot be part of that same process. A consitution must be written in a situation of peace. Nearly the entire three years of the Constituent Assembly may be written off as a cooling-off period for the Maoist party, but the constitution-drafting itself must break free of the shackles. The framers of the new constitution must respect the desires of the citizenry, as spoken through the People's Movement of 2006. The Constitution of the Republic of Nepal 2011 must be built on the ground-breaking Constitution of Nepal 1990.

The Maoists have shown their ability to adjust their tactics and strategies according to the writing on the wall. The tragedy is that no one has been penning the message. Even if a democratic constitution goes against the perceived self-interest of the un-democratised Maoists, if Nepal's democrat-politicians, civil society and the international community were to stand as one in demanding that the UCPN (Maoist) abandon violence, complete the peace process, and wholeheartedly embrace the idea of a pluralist democracy, the party would come through. Besides, despite their having created numerous hurdles, the Maoists may very well agree to a democratic constitution in the rush to organise for the next elections If that is the case, it will be up to the other parties, which are fractured internally and weak in spirit, to generate the willpower to go to the districts and villages and energise the masses for democracy and growth. That first election must be organised by a neutral, technocratic government. In the very worst case that the peace process is not concluded, a democratic constitution is not written, and the radical left or a reactionary right comes to power, sooner rather than later the citizens will rise up again in a people's movement to bring back democracy and peace.

The extreme right and the radical left – the latter of which includes the UCPN (Maoist) as the largest party in the Constituent Assembly, from whom the people expected so much more – hope for the sort of chaos from which they can benefit. But even if chaos overtakes the land, and our hopes for development and economic growth are postponed for a few more years, we, the people of Nepal, will rise and ensure a full democracy and a full peace. The people of Nepal know well that for growth to be equitable and for representation to be inclusive, society has to be unfettered from the village to district, province and nation. It is only under a liberal democracy, simply understood and ably implemented, that all the people of Nepal will benefit. This is why, the people of Nepal know only one cry for the sake of peace, constitutional governance and equitable growth, a cry they shouted loud and clear during the People's Movement of 2006: *Loktantra Jindabad!*

Suggested readings

Bista, Dor Bahadur. 1987. *The People of Nepal.* Kathmandu: Ratna Pustak Bhandar.
_____. 1991. *Fatalism and Development: Nepal's Struggle for Modernization.* Hyderabad. Orient Longman.
Caplan, Lionel. 2000 (1970). *Land and Social Change in East Nepal: A Study of Hindu-Tribal Relations.* Lalitpur: Himal Books.
Dixit, Kanak and Shastri Ramachandran (eds). 2002. *State of Nepal.* Lalitpur: Himal Books.
Gaige, Frederick H. 2009. *Regionalism and National Unity in Nepal.* Lalitpur: Himal Books.
Gunaratne, Arjun, 2002. *Many Tongues, One People: The Making of Tharu Identity in Nepal.* Ithaca: Cornell University Press.
Gupta, Anirudha. 1993. *Politics in Nepal 1950-1960.* Delhi: Kalinga Publications.
Gurung, Harka. 1998. *Nepal: Social Demography and Expressions.* Kathmandu: New ERA.
Höfer, András. 2004 (1979). *The Caste Hierarchy and the State in Nepal: A Study of the Muluki Ain of 1854.* Lalitpur: Himal Books.
Joshi, Bhuwan Lal and Leo E. Rose. 1966. *Democratic Innovations in Nepal: A Case Study of Political Acculturation.* Berkeley: University of California Press.
Koirala, B.P. 2001. *Atmabrittanta: Late Life Recollections.* Lalitpur: Himal Books.
Koirala, Girija Prasad. 2007. *Simple Convictions: My Fight for Peace and Democracy.* Kathmandu: Mandala Book Point.
Koirala, M.P. 2008. *A Role in a Revolution.* Lalitpur: Jagadamba Prakashan.

Kumar, Dhruba (ed). 2000. *Domestic Conflict and the Crisis of Governability in Nepal.* Kathmandu: CNAS.

Ogura, Kiyoko. 2001. *Kathmandu Spring: The People's Movement of 1990.* Lalitpur: Himal Books.

Sharma, Prayag Raj. 2004. *The State and Society of Nepal: Historical Foundations and Contemporary Trends.* Lalitpur: Himal Books.

Stiller, Ludwig. 1968. *Rise of the House of Gorkha.* Ranchi: Patna Jesuit Society.

_____. 1973. *The Silent Cry: The People of Nepal 1816-1839.* Kathmandu: Sahayogi.

Regmi, Mahesh Chandra. 1988. *An Economic History of Nepal 1846-1901.* Varanasi: Nath Publishing House

Rose, Leo E. 1971. *Nepal: Strategy for Survival.* Berkeley: University of California Press.

Thapa, Deepak with Bandita Sijapati. 2004. *A Kingdom under Siege: Nepal's Maoist Insurgency, 1996-2004.* London: Zed Books; and Kathmandu: The Printhouse.

Whelpton, John. 2005. *A History of Nepal.* Noida: Cambridge University Press.

About the author

Kanak Mani Dixit, 55, is the publisher of *Himal Khabarpatrika* and the editor of *Himal Southasian*. He has been a journalist since finishing high school in Lalitpur in 1971. He went to college in Kathmandu, studied law in Delhi, and got a Master's degrees in both international affairs and journalism in New York City. Dixit taught law briefly at Tribhuvan University before working at the United Nations Secretariat in New York between 1982 and 1990. After that, back in Kathmandu, he pioneered the field of Southasian journalism and immersed himself in Nepali-language media. In the late 1990s and early 2000s, he became involved in the civil rights movement, i.e. during the Maoist insurgency and King Gyanendra's autocracy and was also active in the People's Movement of 2006. Since then, Dixit has been involved in activism to roll back violence and ensure the promulgation of a democratic constitution. He also works in the areas of disability, public transport, archiving, and architectural and environmental preservation. His most popular work for children is the much-translated *Adventures of a Nepali Frog*. He also translated Bisweshwor Prasad Koirala's *Atmabrittanta: Late Life Recollections* and, in the fall of 2009, brought out *Dekheko Muluk* (*The Country Witnessed*), a personalised review on the violence and political upheavals of the previous 15 years.